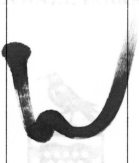

CORT

CORNWALL
COUNTY COUNCIL

The Book of
MAWNAN

Celebrating a South Cornwall Parish

MAWNAN LOCAL HISTORY GROUP

HALSGROVE

This book is dedicated to the people of Mawnan past, present and future.

First published in Great Britain in 2002

Copyright © 2002 Mawnan Local History Group.

Frontispiece photograph: *'Seining' on the Helford River.*

British Library Cataloguing-in-Publication Data
A CIP record for this title is available from the British Library

ISBN 1 84114 148 8

HALSGROVE
PUBLISHING, MEDIA AND DISTRIBUTION

Halsgrove House
Lower Moor Way
Tiverton, Devon EX16 6SS
Tel: 01884 243242
Fax: 01884 243325
email: sales@halsgrove.com
website: www.halsgrove.com

Printed and bound by
Bookcraft Ltd., Midsomer Norton

Whilst every care has been taken to ensure the accuracy of the information contained in this book, the author disclaims responsibility for any mistakes which may have inadvertently been included.

FOREWORD

The village of Mawnan Smith was once destined to become the dormitory of Falmouth. I wonder if this has happened? Its situation is perfect – to the south runs the Helford River, to the east lies Falmouth Bay, and to the north are the rolling hills of Cornwall. My family have lived here since the early 1790s and have been developing the Carwinion Valley since then. This runs parallel to the valleys of Glendurgan and Trebah. My great grandfather, William Rogers, was the local vicar for many years during the nineteenth century.

The village has changed greatly over the years. Many old shops and businesses have disappeared; their places now taken by new and thriving activities, while long-established landmarks such as The Red Lion still survey village life as they have always done.

Tourism plays a big part in the prosperity of the locality, helped by the fact that Mawnan Smith boasts more important gardens in its immediate vicinity than any other village in Cornwall. It also stands adjacent to the beauty and amenities of the Helford River.

I wonder what our ancestors would think of today's Mawnan Smith? I think they would thoroughly approve. Congratulations are due to all those who have worked so hard to produce this wonderful history.

Anthony Rogers
2002

Thomas Pascoe and his mother outside the Old School House, Mawnan Smith.

ACKNOWLEDGEMENTS

This project would not have been possible without the help, enthusiasm and support given by so many people, near and far, who remember how things were years ago. Their contributions are gratefully recognised. The assistance offered by Mawnan Women's Institute and its archivist, Heather Garland is appreciated.

Aerial photograph of Mawnan Smith, c.1970.

CONTENTS

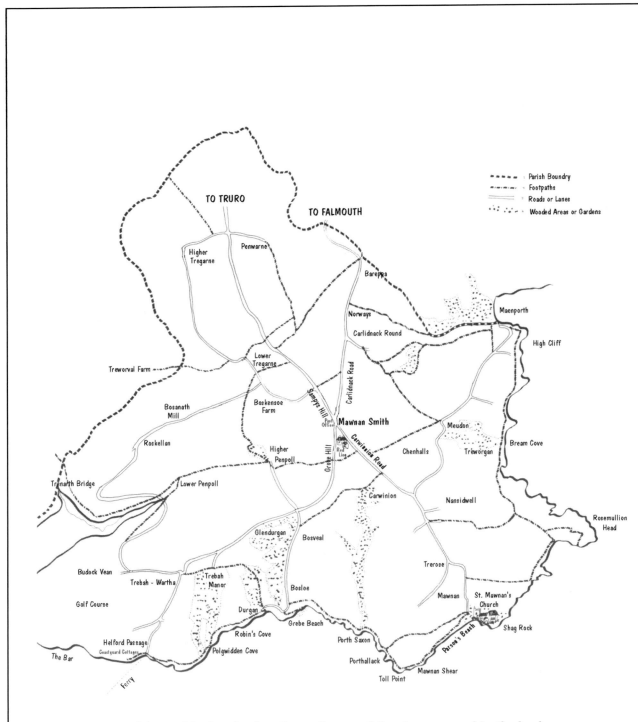

Map of the parish showing locations of some of the places named in the book.

Chapter 1

MAWNAN: THE EARLY DAYS

In 1085, the Domesday Book listed 34 holdings and estates in the hundred of Winnianton, now the district of Kerrier. The parish of Mawnan and the old manors were not listed. The closest named estate was Treliever, which was under the Bishop of Exeter. Among his possessions were five wild mares, two cows and thirty sheep.

According to *Govers Cornish Place Names*, in 1281 Ecclesia Sancti Mawnani was recorded, and by 1535 Mawnan was first used. The history of the name is unknown, but it is doubtful that it was a personal name. The Penwarne family of Mawnan was listed as Penwern in 1327 and Penwarne in 1657. The suggested origin of the name is Pen-an-gwern, which means Alder Grove. The Penwarne family were Justices of the Peace, Members of Parliament and dispensed the law. There was a Free Chapel and burial-ground on the estate. Queen Elizabeth I reduced the powers of the manorial system and the Penwarnes, like so many of their kind, found their powers

ebbing away. By 1834 the last Penwarne had left Cornwall forever.

The manor of Trerose, listed as Treros in 1284, lay along the coast from Trebah to Maenporth. Durgan, Bosveal, Nansidwell, Rosemullion, Chynalls, Treworgan and Meudon were all within its lordship. Amongst its owners was John Whalesborough (or Whalesbrew), to whom the Bishop of Exeter granted a licence in 1374 to celebrate divine service in his chapels or oratories within the manor of Trerose. The Killigrew family of Falmouth later took over Trerose and Sir William Killigrew, Knight, Groom of the Privy Chamber to James I, sold the estate to Sir Nicholas Slanning, Governor of Pendennis Castle. He later became leader of the Cornish Army, and was killed at Bristol during the Civil War, a Royalist to the death.

It is on the foundations of the two manors, Penwarne and Trerose, that the Mawnan we know today was created.

Aerial view of Mawnan Smith, 1951.

Left: *A cottage on Penwarne Estate, c.1930s.*

Below: *and as it is in 2001.*

Left: *Another cottage on Penwarne Estate, c.1890s.*

Below: *And as it is in 2001.*

Chapter 2

THE MANORS OF PENWARNE & TREROSE

Penwarne

The manor and barton of Penwarne is situated on the highest ground in the area (350 feet). The celtic name can be taken to mean 'the homestead on the high ground (pen) near an alder grove (gwarne)'. Its spring water and advantageous position close to Maenporth suggests it was settled in ancient times and in 1313, when it was mentioned in the Mawnan Assize Roll, it was the principal place in the parish.

In the Middle Ages the possessor of the manor of Penwarne was Lord of the Bailiwick, of the hundred of Kerrier, responsible for all administration. Every month the bailiff held a manor court where land disputes were settled and minor offenders brought to trial. He was also responsible for impounding stray animals. The fields at Penwarne, called Higher and Lower Pound and Stray Parc, were still used for this purpose until early in the twentieth century. This area was the home of the Penwarne family who it is said were descended from the Bloyou family who died out in the thirteenth century. The Penwarnes prospered by acquiring extensive land and considerable influence until their decline in the eighteenth century. In 1729 Peter Penwarne sold all his properties, except the manor and barton, for £1100 to John Russell of Falmouth, before moving to Penryn. The family's fortunes continued to decline and following the death of Thomas, his son, in 1742, he was without an heir.

An aerial view of Penwarne House and Farm, 1944.

Peter's brother John sold off most of the remaining estate and the family settled in Penryn. In the late 1770s the Penwarnes befriended the Cornish artist John Opie and remained friends with him throughout his successful years in London until his early death in 1807.

Michael Nowell, a wealthy Falmouth merchant and Sheriff of the county, bought the estate in 1786 – the year in which he was also knighted by King George III for presenting an address to the same on his escape from an assassination attempt by Margaret Nicholson. Sir Michael and Lady Nowell, daughter of General MacCormick the Governor of Pendennis Castle, took up residence at Penwarne and the estate prospered once more. A new Georgian-style mansion was built to the north of the old Penwarne House, and the adjoining land at Penjerrick, Boskenso and Tregarne was again acquired. However, the Nowells had no heir; there is said to have been a curse placed on the barton by the impoverished Penwarnes that disallowed any son to succeed to the property. Even up to the present day, no son has ever inherited the land.

The estate subsequently passed via two nephews, Stephen and Revd Robert Usticke of Botallack in St Just (neither of whom left heirs), to another nephew in 1858, Revd Michael Nowell Peters, Vicar of Madron. He was responsible for laying out and planting the Penwarne gardens during the 1860s and '70s and gave a stained-glass window at the west end of the north aisle in Mawnan church. When he died in 1907 the eldest of his five daughters, Mrs Mary Tonkin, inherited the estate. She married late in life and had no children, so when she died in 1924 at the age of 91, Penwarne passed to her nieces Lydia Mary and Catherine Borlase, daughters of her sister Lydia. An elaborate tombstone in Mawnan churchyard marks the grave of Mrs Tonkin and her sister Mrs Borlase.

In 1927 the Misses Borlase sold Penwarne to Mr and Mrs Ayerst Ingram, in 1939 Mr and Mrs Church were the owners and in 1945 it became the home of the Holmans for 23 years until their daughter and son-in-law Mr and Mrs Williams, along with their young family, moved from Buckinghamshire to live there. In 1983 Dr Beister of Essen bought the house and garden, although the Williams family continued to live at the old Penwarne estate of Estray Park, or Stray Parc and Hundred Pound, as it was once known. The house and garden are opened occasionally for charity in the spring when the camellias, magnolias and rhododendrons are in bloom.

The Penwarne chapel is thought to have stood west of the old manor house in what was known as Chapel Garden. A small plantation still known as the graveyard is where interments were found many years ago.

In addition to the owners of the manor, Penwarne was also home to those who worked on the estate. A hind or bailiff managed Penwarne Farm until the late 1850s and around 25 workers were employed at the time of the 1851 census. In the 1890s the farm was first leased and then sold to Humphrey Mann from West Cornwall, whose family continue to farm there in the year 2001.

The old mansion of the Penwarne family, which seems to have been built during the sixteenth century, was sited where the stables and farm now stand. One wing still stands and is now a workman's cottage. The jamb-stones of what was evidently the main entrance form a kerb in the stable yard. Besides these there are numerous pieces of cut stone, some of which may have come from 'an old unendowed and free chapel and burying place in public use before the church of Mawnan was erected.' (*William Hals Parochial History of Cornwall*, 1690).

Entrance to the well on Penwarne Farm, which goes back for several feet.

Right: *Granite entrance to what is believed to be an old chapel or monastery at Penwarne Farm. It is now used as a cottage.*

Left: *Part of the Barton on Penwarne Farm.*

Below: *Geoffrey Thomas, Master of Cury Hunt outside Penwarne Estate, 1990.*

The Gardener of Penwarne

Peter Hart, together with his wife Jean, arrived at the Penwarne estate in 1959 from their home in Devon. They took up residence in one of the Penwarne cottages where they brought up their five daughters and still reside at the time of writing. Peter firstly took up employment as a farmworker at Higher Tregarne Farm, then owned by Percy Holman. After some 12 months he was employed as under-gardener on the Penwarne estate which was also owned and lived in by Mr Holman. At this time there were seven full-time gardeners on the estate, one of whom had the additional task of milking the cows on the farm twice a day. Some of these gardeners were Wesley Christophers, Garfield Curtis and his daughters Anne and Delia, Bill Rashleigh and Dennis Yendle. In 1936 the outdoor staff consisted of Joe Chinn, Fred Pitts and Harold Benny. In 1968 John and Jennifer Williams bought and came to live at Penwarne and Peter continued to work for them. By this time only Wesley Christophers and Peter remained as gardeners. On Wesley's retirement Peter remained as the sole gardener. Dr Beister, the owner in 2001, bought the property in 1983 and Peter continues to work as the only full-time gardener. However, over the last year he has had one other person helping him for three days each week.

In 1999 Peter was awarded a Long Service Badge by the Trustees and Council of the National Gardens Scheme Charitable Trust. This came in recognition of his 38 years of gardening at Penwarne in support of the Scheme. The gardens are opened to the public three or four times a year in support of the Trust.

Inset: *Peter Hart in the orangery on Penwarne Estate where he is the gardener.*

PENWARNE: AN ACCOUNT BY STELLA THORNE (NÉE MANN).

Penwarne Estate was owned by Mrs Tonkin. A little land and the house was later sold to Mrs Ingram and son Martyn. The Mann family came to Penwarne in 1886 from St Buryan. Before the war, on Easter Sunday mornings, the children from Estray Park Farm, the cottages and farm (us) were invited to hunt for Easter eggs around the gardens. We were given little baskets and always found lots of lovely eggs. Later we were taken into the sitting room to see Mrs Ingram where she arranged for us to have home-made lemonade and biscuits.

During the war, troops were stationed in Penwarne House. Many carved their names and number in the house, and I understand they have only been removed within the last few years. There have always been horses at Penwarne Farm.

In the early days the family would travel to school – Falmouth Grammar and High School – and to church by pony and trap. The Mann family were great riders and huntsmen; the hunt met in the yard on occasions. Members of the family were often seen in the show ring competing in Devon and Cornwall. At the outbreak of the last war, Arthur

Mann owned a chestnut thoroughbred called Fryer, which was commandeered by the military. Shire horses were kept to do the work on the farm; four large shires worked in pairs, while often two foals were reared. Farmers in those days worked long hours and walked miles following the team of horses forward and back across the fields as they ploughed and tilled the land. At lunchtimes the horses would rest and wear a nosebag with food in it.

Corn, wheat, barley and oats were grown, harvested, cut with a binder, put into sheaves and about seven placed in stacks to dry. If rain was expected, shacks would be made into mows. Later these would be carried into the mowhay and put in ricks. At a later date the corn was threshed. This was always a big day, when neighbouring farmers would help one another and the men would come into the farmhouse for dinner – often as many as ten or a dozen including the man travelling with the threshing machine from farm to farm during the season. The corn would be used to feed the cattle in the summer, while the hay was saved for winter feed. The straw was used for bedding. Root crops

Mann Family, early 1900s. Back row: Ellen, Clara, Humphrey, Joanna, Lydia Mary; front: empty chair representing John who died at the age of nine months, Ivor John, Humphrey, Doris, Lydia Harvey, Arthur. Mrs Lydia Harvey Mann died suddenly in November 1912 aged 47.

were also grown, such as potatoes, turnips and kale. The water sugar beet was sold up country, first by lorry and then by train. Turnips and mangolds were fed to the cattle, after being cut up into pieces by a long blade on a wooden stand. A beef and dairy herd was always kept, and ducks, hens and turkeys roamed around the mowhay. It was fun looking for eggs and occasionally a hen would lay out in the hay or corn rick. We would always be surprised to see a brood of chickens arrive. It was always interesting to have sheep on the farm – when lambing, sheep had to be counted twice a day. Cattle were brought into the yard to drink. There was a blacksmith's shop adjoining the piggeries which was used to shoe the horses. There was also a carpenter's shop where gates were repaired. The tower bell was rung by the head gardener to call the men to and from work at 7am, 12pm, 1pm and 5pm. It could be heard some distance away. In the early days people worked every day of the week.

The postman and telegram boy would come by bike. During the war, Mrs Musto walked through Carlidnack to Estray Park and then back through Penwarne to Mawnan Smith every day, delivering mail. The fishermen would travel with pony and trap once a week. The butcher and baker came twice a week by van.

Flour was bought in cwt bags, and salt was bought in large blocks for salting pork. The butcher

would visit the farm to kill and hang the pigs, which were sold at Tresooth Farm nearby. Tresooth also ran a dairy for butter-making for which one received a certificate. Coal was bought in by the tonne for the winter. It came in very large pieces which often had to be broken up before one could burn it. Also, logs would be cut and stored ready for winter use.

Lamps had to be cleaned and filled with oil each day, ready for night time. China hot-water bottles called stone jars were used to heat the beds. A Cornish range was used for cooking and had to be lit every morning, as well as cleaned and black-leaded. The brass (stair rods and cutlery) had to be polished once a week. The wash-house where the family washing was done, had a built-in copper fire which was lit underneath to boil water, while cold water was carried to the wash-house so that the clothes could be steamed twice. The washing was then put through a mangle press with wooden rollers to remove the water, then put out on the line to dry. A flat iron or box and heater were used for the ironing.

The hedges and hills were always full of wild flowers; the mowhay hedge was covered in wild daffodils and snowdrops. Entertainment was singing round the piano or gramophone player, playing games or knitting or sewing. Life was lots of fun on the farm; it was a good life.

Trerose

The manor of Trerose originally comprised all the land between Maenporth and Port Navas (see *The Book of Constantine*) and sits side by side with the manor of Penwarne. There had been earlier settlements there dating back about 3000 years. There are three wells in close proximity to the house and more in the farmland, and a spring rises in the garden.

The first owner of the manor of Trerose was Sir Roger Carminowe, whose son, Sir John Carminowe, gave the manor to his son-in-law William de Whalesbrew in 1313.

On 15 August 1374 the Bishop of Exeter granted a licence to John de Whalesbrewe to celebrate Divine Service in his chapels or oratories within the manor of Trerose; it was this licence that resulted in Mawnan's church, just down the road from the house.

The Whalesbrews kept the manor until 1468, when it passed to Sir John Trevelyan of Nettlecombe, who had married a Whalesbrew daughter.

In 1578 the manor passed in turn to Sir William Killigrew, son of John Killigrew of Arwenack in Falmouth. He was a Groom of the Privy Chamber to King James I and during his ownership the haven of Helford became known as Stealford, due to the number of privateers there.

In 1635 the owner of Trerose was perhaps its most illustrious occupier. He was Sir Nicholas Slanning, who came originally from Devon and was Governor of Pendennis Castle when aged about 30. He became a Royalist General in the Civil War and was one of four leaders of the Cornishmen who defeated the Roundheads at the Battle of Launceston. He was subsequently killed at the siege of Bristol in 1643 and his estate was confiscated by Parliament. It was later re-purchased – reputedly for about £900 – by his son, also called Nicholas, who was later created a Knight of the Bath and a Baronet by Charles II.

During the Slannings' ownership of Trerose their lands in Trebah and the village of Durgan were sold, and the younger Sir Nicholas also later sold Trerose itself, to Brian Rogers, a merchant of Falmouth and through the loss of his ships the Trerose estate had to be broken up and sold to pay off his debts, and in 1706 the house was bought by James Kempe Esq.

By this time much of the early building had been destroyed and stones from it were being used to build the estate's farms and barns. Some of the window lintels can still be seen in the farm and supporting the gate from the farm into the road. The only part not destroyed was the huge chimney and the fireplaces radiating from it, indicating that there were probably buildings to the south and east of the present house. From 1725 until 1925 the existing house was added to from time to time, and now has the overall appearance of a Georgian building. A wing was added in 1925 by an ex-headmaster of Harrow School and the library is still very similar to a headmaster's study. This wing originally had its own front door but there was no connection to the main house, so when the headmaster's wife wished to see him she had to go to the front door of the wing and ring! The two houses are now interconnected.

The Kempes lived at Trerose until Dame Mary Pendarves bought it in 1740. It later passed to the Hoblyn family through marriage.

In the mid-nineteenth century the Laitys, who came from West Cornwall, took over the farm. In the 1851 census Thomas Laity, then 35 years of age, lived there with his wife Mary and son George. He farmed 135 acres and employed seven men, three of whom, William Martin, John Pascoe and William Polkinhorne, lived on the farm. Thomas' brother William Laity was also farming 135 acres there and employed Henry Christophers and Thomas Williams. When the Laitys left Trerose Farm they were followed by the Dunstans and then in the early 1930s John and Mary Benney took over the farm. In time John was succeeded by his son Eustace with his wife Ann, who were succeeded by their two sons, Andrew and James.

The Trerose farm was bought by Mr Fawell, who built a large house in a field overlooking the Helford River. A part of Lower Trerose was sold to Mr Coode, a St Austell solicitor, and he built what we now know as Trerose House. At the entrance gate there was once a small red-tiled stable, used by the Penwarnes to shelter their horses while the family attended church. It became part of the lodge that stands there today.

Caleb Knowles was a farmworker at Trerose before the First World War. He served in the Navy but returned and married Winifred Chinn, a teacher at Mawnan school, daughter of John and Bessie Chinn, builder.

John Henry Christophers with his team of horses on Trerose Farm, 1938.

Chapter 3

HAMLETS & FEATURES OF THE PARISH

Bareppa

After leaving Mawnan Smith on the minor 'back road to Falmouth', as it is locally known, one descends to a sheltered valley and the small hamlet of Bareppa. The earliest known reference to Bareppa is in 1384 as Beaurepper (beau repair), in Norman French, meaning 'fair retreat', as part of the Penwarne estate. From the sixteenth to the eighteenth century it was leased by the Penwarnes to the Barnicots, a family of respected yeomen farmers in the parish of Mawnan. Its origins, however, were probably much older, as indicated by a Bronze-Age pot fragment found in the area, dating back over 3000 years. It is now in Truro Museum. (The tin trade with Brittany at this time would have involved landing at small ports in France and England.)

The old celtic round fortification on the hill above at Carlidnack is Iron Age. It is likely that the people who held it controlled Bareppa and Maenporth nearby on the coast. 'Fine and Brave', the sunken lane to Maenporth above Bareppa, may be a corruption of the Cornish 'Fyn an Bre' meaning 'boundary of the hill'. On the northern boundary of the round it was probably used for

the movement of cattle and by packhorses. Local legend has it that at the time of the Napoleonic Wars when invasion was feared, an enemy ship was spotted approaching Maenporth. As the men were at work in the fields, the women took pitchforks in hand and hurried down the lane to the shore. The French, seeing glimpses of their red petticoats through the trees, thought they were redcoat soldiers and so turned and sailed away. When the men heard of this, they praised the women saying, 'It was a fine and brave thing to do.' Since then the lane has been known as 'Fine and Brave' (see Chapter Nine).

Bareppa House, now a large residence with Georgian-style windows and beautiful gardens running down to the stream on the boundary with Budock, was a fairly simple farmstead when George Barnicot inherited it from his father in the early-eighteenth century. Described as 'the dwelling house lately built in the lower orchard', it would have been 'a rectangular hall house', consisting of two rooms with a cross passage between them, a kitchen and 'hall' or living room. Later that century Bareppa House became the

Bareppa House, Bareppa, 2001.

The rear grounds of Bareppa House during the 1980s.

home of packet captain John Boulderson, who came from London to command the *Earl of Halifax*. With his arrival, the gradual transformation of the house to a gentleman's residence began. The Packet Service was associated with Falmouth for 160 years, carrying mail and passengers all over the world to and from Falmouth. It brought both economic prosperity and interesting people to the town and district. John Boulderson retired to live at Bareppa and later his son was appointed captain and lived in Bareppa until his death in 1831. By 1871 another packet captain, James Bull, lived there. His wife was Josephine, the daughter of Joshua Fox of Tregedna. His brothers were Robert, Alfred and Charles Fox of the Quaker family who founded the estates of Penjerick, Glendurgan and Trebah.

In 1906 local man Albert Bray bought the house. When he was a small boy living with his widowed mother in the cottage below the 'big house' he told her that when he grew up he would make enough money to buy it. After making his fortune in the USA he returned, bought Bareppa House and lived there for 18 years. A bequest left after his death was used to purchase an organ blower for Mawnan Parish Church.

In 1924 the house became the home of Lucy Violet Holdsworth, née Hodgkin, granddaughter of Alfred Fox of Glendurgan, on her marriage to John Holdsworth a Quaker sheep farmer from New Zealand. She continued to live at Bareppa until her death in 1954 and is well remembered by local people. An accomplished writer of books on Quaker life and a fine watercolour painter, she was deaf but a sensitive lip reader.

The Holdsworths employed a housekeeper, three maids, two gardeners and a chauffeur before the Second World War. John Holdsworth, after spending his last years as an invalid, died in 1935. Amy Toy, their loyal, highly-regarded housekeeper, had worked for the Fox family since she was 14 years old – firstly at Trebah and then Treworgan before coming to work at Bareppa House. After the war she looked after the house, helped by her husband Bill Toy and a maid. After her death the Toys went to live in their own house in Mawnan Smith, but took with them Mrs Holdsworth's dogs, a fox terrier and a corgi. During the Second World War two schoolgirl evacuees from the Latymer school in Edmonton, North London, lived at the house for a time. One of them who later returned to live in Mawnan permanently recalled that 'it seemed like paradise'.

By the nineteenth century, the hamlet of Bareppa had become relatively busy, by this time being home to over 60 residents. The 1841 census lists 14 cottages, occupied by 14 farmworkers, a carpenter, his apprentice, a sawyer, a shoemaker and a seaman as well as their dependents.

Left: *A portrait of Mrs Lucy Holdsworth, née Hodgkin.*

Below: *A portrait of Mr John Holdsworth.*

Left: *Mr and Mrs John Holdsworth on their wedding day in the grounds of Bareppa House, 1923.*

Right: *Harry Rowe (chauffeur) and Amy Toy (housekeeper) with the Holdworth's family car at Bareppa House during the 1930s.*

Above: *A portrait of Amy Toy, housekeeper, at Bareppa House, and her husband Bill Toy.*

Left: *Harry Rowe, his wife Emma, and Kenneth Peppin outside Kidley Wink Cottage, then known as Porter's Lodge.*

An abandoned exploratory mine shaft was found in the field behind the row of cottages, where mining is known to have been undertaken in the late nineteenth century. This was later filled in with spoil when the cottages were renovated. One cottage in the hamlet became a roadside alehouse or 'kidley-wink', at this time.

Arthur Rowe, 81 years old at the time of writing, and living in Mawnan Smith, was born at a cottage in Bareppa. His father, Harry, was part-time chauffeur and second gardener to the Holdsworths at Bareppa House. Arthur remembers on car-cleaning day being tipped sixpence to polish the brass grease nipples under-neath the Holdworth's white open Wolesley car.

The Rowes, along with several other local families, lived in Bareppa until the 1960s. The children attended Mawnan school and played together in the orchard and on the narrow winding road beside the stream, there being little traffic thereabouts in those days. Until the 1960s the springs along the stream provided a constant supply of sparkling clean water for drinking and cooking. All household waste was buried or burnt and light was provided by candle or oil lamp.

Today Bareppa remains a fair retreat despite modernisation. Farming continues, supplemented by daffodil growing. The population has declined to about 16 people; three cottages are holiday lets but two small local businesses flourish. Bareppa House itself was let in the 1950s and '60s as Robin Hodgkin the owner, nephew of Lucy Violet Holdsworth, was working in education in the Sudan with his wife (see page 21). They retired in 1977 and returned to live at the house. In 1996 it was bought by a solicitor and his wife, John and Lynda Sissons.

Bareppa Farm was bought in 1977 by Henry Crewes who lived and farmed at Rosmerryn Farm in nearby Budock parish. He sold the farmhouse, as well as some land and farm buildings close to the house but retained the barns and land which his son Neil still farms. A retired Welsh farmer and his wife, Mel and Merle Jenkins, bought the house in 1995. The stables and barns were renovated and their daughter, Angela, now runs her floristry business, 'Riverside Flowers', from there. Mel Jenkins grows some of the plants and flowers for the concern on his land. Keith Penrose, his wife Diana with their two sons Stephen and David run the family builders and under-takers businesses from their home 'Appleshaw' next to the farm.

House at Bareppa, once a Kidley-wink or Beer-shop.

Cottages in Bareppa, c.1950s.

This drainage shute still discharges water from the spring above Bareppa Farm. It lies a few yards from another shute which now no longer exists but at one time was the only source of water for the hamlet.

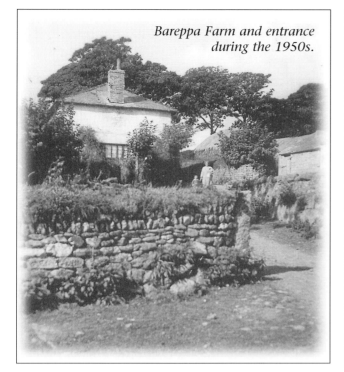

Bareppa Farm and entrance during the 1950s.

Above and left: *Harvest time at Bareppa Farm during the 1950s.*

The Land from Mawnan to Bareppa

Much of the land in this part of the parish was in the ownership of the Vyvyans of Trelowarren. Over the years the ownership passed between many hands, leading to the fragmentation of the area into numerous fields.

In 1803 the rector, Rogers, listed John Boulderson as a tithe-payer at Bareppa. At Carlinnack, Nicholas Pearce was listed at 'Little-in-Sight'. Blackwells Tenement, Barnicoats Part and Walters Meadow were in the ownership of John Peter, while Avis Francis, Richard Edwards, Thomas Humphry and John Downing are listed at Carlinnick. Walter Humphrys had an orchard, John Downmen owned a third of Fine and Brave, while Richard Downmen (who was at Barn Part) owned the remaining two-thirds. At the Norways Tenement was Eliza Edward.

By 1823 the situation had become even more confused. John Boulderson was still at Bareppa. Francis Cheffers payed tithes for Old Sally's field and Job's Part of Carlinnick; Thomas Cock for the first and second part of Fine and Brave, and also Barn Part; Henry Copelin for Little-in-Sight, Shutford's Meadow, part of Wood Close and Nicholas Hill's fields; Sally for Carlinnick Lawry's Part, Norways Tenement and Mr Bath's fields. Walter Humphrys had Carlinnick House and orchard, Ham's Tenement, the Smokey Alley and William's Part.

The 1851 census presents a more in-depth account of the local people. William Skewes lived at Little-in-Sight farming six acres; William Eddy and William Troon, both carpenters, are listed as living in Carlenick Lane. Jane Toy, charwoman, and Richard Downing, roadmaker, also lived in the Lane. Carlenick Common was where Mawnan Poorhouse had been built, which is now known as Gold Martin. There are ten households listed by the enumerator, four of which are uninhabited. It should be noted, however, that this may only be the case because nobody was at home when he called.

Amongst the rest of the Carlenick inhabitants were Francis Cheffers, farming 15 acres and employing two men; William Edwards with six acres and one 'aglab' (agricultural labourer); and Robert Whitlock, with 20 acres and one worker. The residents living in the remaining 13 households included a shoemaker, cordwainer, grocer and copper miner. There were three households in the Norways Tenement: Catherine Saunders, whose eldest son was listed as a 'Mariner R.N.' (the only man serving in the Forces in Mawnan); Phillip Pascoe in the next cottage; and Elizabeth Pascoe, a widow, living in the last house.

A Baptist meeting-house built in brick was recorded by Revd W. Rogers in his private village diary.

By 1950 the Courage family were living at the 36-acre Carlidnack Farm. Between there and Bareppa was a new farm known as West Close, the home of Richard Cobbledick. At Trelyn, Mr Banfil ran a smallholding and the local bus 'Selene'. Mrs Atkinson, who lived at The Nest with ten acres, used to sell the eggs from her flock of hens. Beside Mr Banfil's bus garage, Messrs Arthur and Alfred Chinn, two brothers, had a builders yard. The Norways Tenement had become a smallholding farmed by Edward Sadler, while the cottages and the Baptist meeting-house were his farm buildings. Bareppa House was occupied by Mrs V. Holdsworth, with the Woodgate brothers at Bareppa Farm.

Today Carlidnack Farm has gone and the land has been built on. The same fate came to West Close. Since Mrs Atkinson's death the cottage has been renovated and restored to its thatched glory. Bareppa House's listed stucco front was removed and never replaced. The land of Bareppa Farm was sold and the farmhouse now stands on its own.

Right: Harold Benny, Diane Penrose's uncle, bringing in a load of potatoes from Edward Sadlers' field, late 1940.

Bottom (main picture): *Carlidnack looking towards the valley. Rose Cottage is at the rear.*

Below: *Rose Cottage at Carlidnack.*

THE CHINNS OF CARLIDNACK: AN ACCOUNT BY ROBIN A. HODGKIN

They were the salt of the earth. Originally there were seven children, born in a cottage, St John's at Carlidnack. The father was Edward Backhouses's estate carpenter and handyman at Trebah. Their mother must have been a gifted, determined and deep-hearted character, for the whole family buzzed with humour, patience and good will. 'Patience?' Perhaps 'staying-power' would be nearer to the special kind of gumption that these Chinns displayed on the steep inclines that led up from the Helford River and down to Bareppa.

They had a Methodist background, certainly not Anglican (the gentry), or Roman (best not mentioned in Arthur's hearing), nor Quaker either. Definitely chapel and a bit free-thinking too.

Amy Toy was the eldest sister. Amy, they used to say, was 'the clever Miss Chinn' and Lily (three years younger) was 'the pretty Miss Chinn'. Both married sailors. Bill Toy was an ex-petty officer shipwright and I don't think he ever did much after 1920; battle cruisers dominated his memories and decorated their mantlepiece. He was certainly 'a character' and his loud voice would echo along the corridor beyond the Bareppa green-baize door. A voice like that was often useful as Amy, like her mistress (LVH, Lucy Violet Holdsworth, née Hodgkin, 'Aunt Vi') was deaf. Amy was not stone deaf and was much helped by her primitive electronic hearing aid. LVH on the other hand had been totally deaf since the age of 12 and she relied on lip-reading and LITTLE NOTES.

Amy had gone from Cornwall to Northumberland as a junior housemaid in the large Hodgkin country house where my grandfather, Thomas Hodgkin, had retired from Newcastle. Violet, the eldest daughter, spotted Amy and took her on when the First World War was beginning to make things difficult. They lived in the Constable's Tower of Bamburgh Castle when LVH was working on her 'period' classics, Quaker Saints.

LVH could, at times, be a shade tyrannical. She expected everything to be first class, often when the funds could barely stretch to it. But she and Amy depended on each other to a wonderful degree. One of the great spectacles of the 1930s that Bareppa was to see/hear was LVH and Amy on the telephone. When speaking with A.L. Rowse, for example, who was an old friend, Amy would hold the ear-piece and mouth the incoming words to LVH who would then shout the answer back to Amy and into the shared mouth-piece on the wall. It worked.

When, in 1954–5, I inherited Bareppa, our family owed all those Chinns many debts. Elizabeth, my wife, and I were in the process of retiring from our work in the Sudan. On our first arrival, Lily Tabb (née Chinn), by now a widow living in Carlidnack, agreed to help a little with Catherine, our youngest child (aged five). The comfort was mutual and lasted. Lily even helped us to settle until I found a new job in Derbyshire. Elizabeth, as well as enjoying these friendships and

Left to right: *Samuel Chinn, father of John Chinn; John Chinn, father of Amy, Violet, Winnie, Lily, Arthur and Alfred Chinn; Lucy Hodgkin, 'Aunt Vi', August 1950.*

the help, also picked up a good deal about English/Cornish cooking. Amy's special recipe for Roman Gnocchi still persists in the family repertoire. When Lily joined the household after we arrived she fitted in perfectly but occasionally made the point that she had never been 'in service'.

It's a politically 'sensitive' point to emphasise but Edwardian-Georgian households were sometimes highly educative places. In wartime, when an ethos of 'making do and mending' prevailed, this was a strength. Every bit of linen was appropriately marked and repaired. People were occupied with fine stitching and there was no television to interrupt, although the radio was frequently turned up as Mrs Holdsworth liked to be told if there was any big news.

The Chinn family all loved to lend a hand. Their mother used to say 'every stitch was paid for; every stitch must wear.' It was also a bit of 'Old Cornwall' that still prevailed and which we were privileged to enjoy. Thrift had been the sentiment that guided that family. That, combined with good craftsmanship, guided the two irrepressible brothers, Arthur and Alfred – up the hill.

Alfred and Lily were close in age and were strongly bonded. Though over 60 years of age, Lily was still the pretty one and Alfred provided a fluent ironic commentary on everyday events.

To begin to understand the collective genius of the Chinn family you would need to have visited their workshop – built mainly with driftwood from Prisk beach opposite the red brick house on the north side of Carlidnack Rise. Inside, apparent chaos reigned, although Arthur would always know just where to look for the right board of teak or for a suitable brass screw. All the basic tools were there – somewhere – although many were very old. There was that well-hammered Jack plane for example. The wood fibres on its stern bristled like an old shaving brush. It had probably started life in an earlier creative chaos in a workshop at Trebah. And there were whole families of saws and chisels. The corners and the roof spaces were filled with bits of old timber, or old pieces of lead, slate and tile. 'You never know, do you, when something might come in handy, Mr Robin', Alfred used to assure me. [There were] bits of glass and picture frames – even a few pictures, too.

Right: *Arthur Chinn.*

Below: Left to right; *Alfred Chinn and Arthur Chinn in their workshop at Carlidnack.*

One picture I particularly fancied; a sentimental Victorian coleograph of 'A Delicate Child' – golden haired, treading on the very edge of a precipice. Behind and above was its Guardian Angel. I admired it so often that Arthur gave it to me as a present. My motives, I fear, were base, for the picture was going to be good for a laugh with my climbing friends. Later, it decorated the pantry wall of our narrow Oxford house.

These brothers – helped by young Keith Penrose and Mr Musto – produced excellent, practical joinery and buildings of many kinds.

Towards the end of the Depression (c.1935) when Lucy Hodgkin died at Treworgan at the age of about 90, Aunt Vi had married John Holdsworth and he needed more space and a resident nurse. Aunt Vi wanted space too, for her writing and painting. Extra shelves were essential for all this and for all the books and 'treasures' from Treworgan. So the studio was built by Chinn Bros; 40 feet long by 20 feet wide. They used the best Scandinavian timber from Fox-Stanton yard on a concrete foundation above the old woodshed – soon to become the air-raid shelter. The studio included electric light and plugs for heating, as well as big windows all along the east and north sides. The receipted bill for the whole job was in a desk drawer when we came in 1954 – [it came to] £136.10s.0d. for the whole lot.

The joke about the guardian angel and the daring infant wore a bit thin by the end of the century. But sometimes, when one most needs them, guardian angels do mysteriously seem to be there and they sometimes look rather like Chinns: twinkling, inexhaustible and unique.

Left: Keith and Diana Penrose, née Harris, outside her uncle and aunt's cottage 'Benhar' in Carlidnack Road. now 'The Vyne'.

Below: This present house stands on the site of the Chinns' workshop in Carlidnack.

Carlidnack Farm

The farmhouse was situated at the junction that leads to Bareppa and Budock from the Sampy's Hill road. Among the farm buildings were two that were rubble and cob with a slate roof and the rest were galvanised iron. There were 36 acres of land and the farm was occupied by the Courage family for three generations. They were descended from a French doctor called Corregge, who was a prisoner of war detained at Roskrow. He married a Betsy Roland in Budock, early in the nineteenth century.

Edwin Courage was a farmer and a member of Mawnan's first Parish Council in 1894, which he served for many years as clerk. His son Cecil followed him, and at the death of Cecil, so too did his sons Geoffry and John. In 1950 the farm was sold. The land was built upon, while the old farm-house and buildings were demolished in order to make the junction much safer for the traffic.

West Close

Next to Carlidnack Farm was another farm, West Close. The cattle sheds were constructed from galvanised iron. Mr Skewes owned and farmed the land with the help of two relatives, Richard Cobbledick and Edward Sadler. On the death of Mr Skewes, Richard Cobbledick inherited West Close, while Edward Sadler inherited what is now known as Norways Farm.

Carlidnack Round

The Cornwall Archaeological Society has listed a number of Iron-Age sites in the parish of Mawnan: at Carwinion, at Bosanath, between the Meudon farm and the village, where the Parish Church stands today and at Carlidnack. The name itself has been researched, with the most likely meaning suggested as 'the defended homestead (KER or CAR) above the anchorage'.

Carlidnack Round is considered to be 'the most perfect in the area'. The Celts built a large number of fortifications – cliff-top castles and hill forts – throughout Cornwall as well as the smaller 'rounds'. To defend their homesteads, circular or oval enclosures of about an acre in extent were built. Carlidnack Round is an excellent example of this type of univallote earthwork. Pottery from the first and second century AD has been found there. The 'hill' topped with the earthwork is virtually encircled by the footpaths leading down to Maenporth. The northern boundary is the lane known as Fine and Brave.

Left: *The original wooden house in the round, owned by Colonel Gooden. It has been replaced by a bungalow.*

Below: *Carlidnack Farm, now demolished, is the building in the right-hand corner.*

Durgan

In 1823, Alfred Fox came to the conclusion that this thriving little fishing cove on the Helford River, with its fish cellars, donkey sheds, coal yard, chapel, alehouse and sheltered valley, would make an ideal country estate for his family. He gradually took over the whole cove, demolished the Two Cutters alehouse, improved the dwellings and, with his son-in-law, Sir Joseph Pease, MP for Darlington, constructed a schoolroom on one of the quays, over a fish cellar.

This is the story of some of the families who lived and worked there at the beginning of the last century. Although members of this close-knit community were largely self-sufficient, living on food from the sea, their orchards and allotments, they were certainly not cut off from the outside world. Fishermen in general were admired for their skills and in great demand to crew commercial vessels and sailing yachts all over the world, and the men of Durgan were no exception. A proportion of families had relatives who emigrated to America.

Disaster was never far away; several fishermen drowned in the river. People living at the turn of the last century would have been given first-hand accounts from their parents of the tragedy of the Barnes family in 1845. George Barnes, a coastguard stationed at Durgan, was drowned off Rosemullion Head, together with his three sons and a neighbour, 13-year-old Grace Retallack. They were returning from visiting friends at Swanpool, but when they did not arrive home, Grace's brother rowed out to look for them and discovered the upturned boat. It was surmised that a hat belonging to one of the boys had blown off and they had fallen overboard trying to retrieve it. George was found with Grace's collar clutched in his hand, so he had probably tried to get her back on board.

On the approach road to Durgan, 50 metres before the first dwellings, was the village dump for broken crockery and anything else that could not be burnt, buried, thrown into the sea or recycled on the compost heap. Beside this was a set of steps leading down to the landing-stage on the beach below. When the steps were destroyed in a storm in 1916, the road was completely closed for several days.

The Retallack family moved from the Two Cutters on the other side of the cove into the first cottage when it was built in 1855. They brought up ten children here, including George

Right: *Durgan, c.1960. John (left) and Bernard Badger sitting on the covered over 'shute', next to their father Leo.*

Durgan, c.1900.

Coaster unloading coal on Durgan beach in 1909. In the background is the laundry draped over the bushes to dry.

Left: *Quay Cottage quay before 1900. Meeting place for retired fishermen. Left to right: Granfer Tom, Mr Hare, John Downing, Jose Downing (Granfer Tom's son).*

The Landing Stage, 1928. Back row, left to right: Dorothy Fox, Jinny Eddy; front: Arthur Partington, Doreen James (visitor), Claud Chinn, Percy and Reggie Randlesome, Rosalie Christophers, Gwennie Smith, Florence Eddy, May Christophers, Mary Eddy, Doris Smith, Barbara Rendle.

Far left: *Blind George's house in Durgan.*

Left: *Blind George.*

Below: *Collecting water at the shoot in 1900, watched by young boy and 'Blind George'.*

Left: *Playmates, 1923. Left to right: Mary Eddy, became Mrs Leonard Salisbury, Olive Hendy, became Mrs Percy Forward, Gwen Smith, who died when she was 17 years old.*

Above: *Albert Peters the 'indoor man' at Bosloe and Jinny Christophers on their wedding day in May 1932, outside the cottage at Lower Tregarne. They set up home at 'Sea View Cottage', Durgan, where they were visited by local youths including Ted Smith and Ivor Rashleigh with the 'shellal'. This is the Cornish custom whereby newly-weds are disturbed by the beating of kettles, pans, tea-trays and the blowing of whistles and horns.*

Right: *Laura Smith outside her home – now 'Post Box Cottage', with two of her children, c.1920.*

Outside the first cottage on the approach to Durgan, 1924. Uncle Fred and Aunt Lil arriving from Plymouth by motorbike and side-car. Left to right: *George Retallack ('Blind George'), Uncle Fred, Winifred Rendle, Barbara Rendle, Aunt Lil, cousin Wilfred Cotell (visitor from Falmouth).*

(1864–1941). While still a baby, he went blind. He attended the West of England School for the Blind in Exeter but was homesick and soon returned to his own bit of country, where he was given opportunities to foster his sense of security, identity and collective responsibility, and where he was able to earn a living. When his mother died, aged 92, George was cared for by his niece, Winifred, and her family. He was a talented self-taught musician and dealt with the financial affairs of the local fishermen, but his main source of income came from his tea-selling round. Tea chests were delivered to the cottage, where Winifred weighed out the loose tea and packed it into suitcases before accompanying George on his rounds.

Edward Downing, George's next-door neighbour, was skipper of the *Lady Bee*, Lord Rendlesham's yacht, during the summer months and worked at Bosloe Gardens in the winter. In 1903, he crewed aboard Sir Thomas Lipton's *Shamrock III* in the America's Cup. Edward's wife's daughter, Gladys Sullifan, a housemaid at Bosloe, married Geoff Taysom in 1933. He was an enthusiastic bell-ringer at Mawnan Parish Church, who had come from Hereford to be head gardener at Nansidwell. They met at a dance in the Memorial Hall. As usual, a list of wedding gifts and their donors accompanied the press report of the wedding: 'Lord and Lady Rendlesham – cheque and wedding cake; Mr and Mrs Rendle – sandwich set; Miss Dorothy Gundry – pin cushion.'

At the bottom of the hill is a block of three two-up, two-down cottages. The tiny cobbled

courtyard, edged by three small outhouses, had been a fish cellar. Beyond this space were the brick-built outside 'loos'. The furnishings here consisted of a wooden plank with a hole in it, a bucket underneath and a wad of torn newspapers hanging on a nail. The full buckets were emptied in the sea, preferably not when the tide was coming in!

Mr and Mrs Henry Pascoe returned from America in 1872 with two children and settled in the first cottage. They decided to sacrifice the space in their lean-to and invested in what is now known as a corner shop. An observer standing beside the present-day telephone kiosk will see that an extra storey has been added to the original lean-to (this was done in 1948). Six more children were born to Henry and Ellen. Their only son, Jasper, married Lily May from Falmouth and emigrated to America, where they had seven children before Lily died and the family split up. The first contact between American and Cornish cousins in modern times took place in 1980.

When Henry Pascoe died in 1926, aged 79, the *Falmouth Packet* reported that he was well known and highly respected in the village and neighbourhood; he was considered an authority on shipping and yachting matters. On many occasions he had taken part in the regattas on the Helford River. Chief mourners were his seven daughters – Mesdames Tresise, Prior, Phillips, Hendy, Campbell, Houghton and Randlesome.

After serving in the First World War, Leo Badger, son of Padre J.C. Badger of Falmouth Seamen's Bethel, became engineer on a yacht

*Members of the Pascoe family in Durgan
at the beginning of the last century.
Mrs Ellen Pascoe (left) kept a provisions
shop in the lean-to on the right.*

*Bert Snell, resident of Quay Cottage 1940–1960,
son of a Penryn market trader. In 1948 he was
employed to cut a new path and steps through the
woods several metres from the existing one, which
was in danger of falling away.*

*Left: Durgan, 1947. Left to right: Diane Curtis,
Margaret Badger, Jose Downing, Mrs Curtis. Jim
Curtis, a Penryn builder, his wife and daughter were
summer/weekend visitors to Durgan. Jim hired Leo
Badger's large cabin cruiser Winifred for fishing trips.
On such excursions, Jim's family, together with a
horde of Durgan children and their picnics were
dropped off on a remote beach for a few hours,
while Jim and Leo went fishing off the Manacles.
They picked up the party on their way back.*

*Crew of the Lady Bee, 1920.
Back row, far right: 'Blind George';
front (sitting): Leo Badger, ship's engineer.*

Left: *Durgan, 1932.* Back row, left to right: *Jinny Peters, Lily Chinn, Mrs Badger's sister, Leo Badger holding one of the model ships he made;* centre: *Bernard Badger;* front: *?, Winnie Badger with her baby son, John.*

Durgan, 1946. Left to right, back row: *Ronnie Badger, Sylvia King, Margaret Badger, Leonard Salisbury;* centre: *Yvonne Snell, Carol Chinn, Heather Sandford, Richard Sandford.*

Above: *Lucky Girls, August 1959. Elizabeth and Linda Badger in their boat* Shrimp *built by their father, Bernard. He later built* Kingfisher *so that the girls each had their own boat.*

Above: *Bernard Badger on the left with his friend and neighbour Denis Smith, 1946.*

Jose and Harriet Downing celebrate their Diamond wedding anniversary in 1949. After his fishing days were over, Jose let his boat to Cyril Taylor, a farmer from Tehidy, and Arthur Moss, a Falmouth builder, for regular fishing trips. They eventually bought their own boat, which they kept at Durgan and Jose looked after it for them. When a brand new cinema, the Odeon, opened in Falmouth in 1936, (now Tescos), the management offered free tickets to anyone who had never been to a cinema. Jose's two friends put his name forward and a car was sent to collect him and Harriet, but they refused to go!

Durgan, 1948. Mr Stevens, butcher from Constantine, delivering meat. Doris King and Winnie Badger are waiting with their plates for their meat ration. Margaret Badger (now Mrs Giles of Penryn) is in the foreground.

belonging to the new occupier of Bosloe, Lord Rendlesham. He was given lodgings at Durgan and soon met a young lady on the river. Winifred Chinn worked at Bosahan and, on her days off, rowed back home to Helford. Leo, Winifred and one-year-old Bernard moved into the Pascoes' cottage, where four more children were born – John, the twins Margaret and Ronald, and Peter. Only two families lived in the house in 100 years!

Seaview Cottage, the middle one, was the home of Mrs Tresise. Her husband, a fisherman, had drowned in the Helford River when he was quite young. She lived on to the ripe old age of 92.

After Mrs Tresise had moved away, Seaview Cottage provided temporary accommodation to Mr and Mrs Hare's daughter and grandson, Mrs Parkinson and Arthur, until they were able to join Mr Parkinson, who had emigrated to America. Albert Peters and Jinny Christophers started their married life in the cottage in 1932. Albert was 'an indoor man' at Bosloe. Jinny enjoyed the company of young Bernard and John from next door; they appreciated surreptitious sips of the homemade wine that Jinny excelled in making.

At the end of the yard, Violet and Arthur Randlesome lived with their sons, Percy and Reggie. Violet was one of Mr and Mrs Pascoe's daughters.

The main square, which was in the parish of Constantine in 1900, was a busy place. Fishermen would be tending their craft, going out to fish or mending their nets in the cellars. When it was time for 'barking' (preserving the nets) a fire would be lit behind 'the shoot', where a cauldron of preservative was heated. Nets were immersed and boiled before being draped over the walls of the quay to dry. There was often a queue of women at the shoot, gossiping while waiting to collect water in pitchers and buckets from the primitive water supply – the stream from the pond at Glendurgan. The donkey sheds, where the animals were kept in winter, the coal yard and the large boathouse for the Fox family boats were all labour intensive. And there were always children playing happily in the area. Crab pots were stacked on the quays alongside fishing gear, washing lines and benches, where retired fishermen would spend many hours recalling times past to visitors and youngsters.

31

Beach Cottage and Quay Cottage were built at the same time as the schoolroom (1876) on the site of the Two Cutters public house, which Alfred Fox had acquired just after 1861 from Thomas Hill and his daughters, Eliza James and Mathilda Morcumb. The first cottage here – now Beach Cottage – housed one of the Downing families. Granfer Tom had been a fisherman, and his wife Martha, who died in 1914 aged 71, regularly walked to Penryn Fish Market and Fish Cross with her husband's catch. Their son Jose brought his bride, Harriet Retallack, here where they led a very thrifty life. Jose's only luxury was the evil-smelling shag tobacco for his pipe, although they had some nice pieces of furniture which had been bought at local house sales.

Two villagers lost their lives in the First World War. One of them was Norman, the son of Jose and Harriet. He was a typical, popular youngster. Jose's nephew, Sid Pascoe, who lived next door, served in the Royal Navy.

The Smiths did not come to Post Box Cottage until 1920, when fishing was no longer a thriving industry. Alfie Smith was one of the new breed of local workers who found employment with owners of the new estates. These people usually brought the staff from their previous homes with

Trebah Pier. A temporary jetty was designed for the Normandy assault on 6 June 1944. It allowed the landing craft to approach Trebah Beach and tie up with prows down so that military vehicles could be driven aboard from the shore, which had been laid with concrete matting. During its construction German raiders took more than a passing interest in it. At 6pm one sunny evening, children who were playing on Durgan beach watched in amazement as several aircraft skimmed up the river and dropped a stick of four bombs on the workmen. Luckily no one was injured. The pier was dismantled c.1952.

them but gradually took on local workers. Lord Rendlesham at Bosloe engaged fishermen to crew his yacht and gardeners such as Alfie to develop his hobby of daffodil hybridisation. Three families lived in the little group of present-day holiday lets known as Rose Cottages.

Jack Downing (Jacker) was the village elder and father of Edward, who lived across the cove. He had been a fisherman and skippered the *Lady Bee* before his son. He was looked after by two daughters, Mildred and Tilly. They earned a living by doing the laundry for Glendurgan House. Peter Eddy, son of Glendurgan's head gardener, was killed in the First World War, and left a widow, Rosina, with five young children to bring up in the middle cottage. A brother and sister lived in the end cottage – Billy and Grace James. Billy crewed for Lord Rendlesham in the summer and worked in Bosloe garden during the winter months. They kept open house to their nephew and nieces, Jack, Bessie and Mabel Hall. The Jameses were typical of Durgan families at the beginning of the last century, who had lived and worked in the cove all their lives; they were intensely proud of young relatives who moved on to professional careers. Three families, including the James family, provided Mayors for various towns.

The last building on the right in the lane leading out of Durgan was divided into six tiny homes. Mr and Mrs Hendy and their young daughter Olive lived in the first house (now Chyandour), next door to Mrs Hendy's sister Millicent and her husband, George Houghton. The elderly Mr and Mrs Hare lived in the top house, Clare Cottage. They had retired to Durgan from Falmouth, where they had worked for a member of the Fox family. Mrs Hare liked to tell her neighbours the latest news of her daughter and family in America. Backing onto the Hendy's property were the other Hendys – Sid and his wife. Her broad Norfolk accent never left her! The last two cottages were knocked into one for the Johns family in 1892, when they moved down from Bosloe Lodge with four young children. They were a quiet family who did not often mix with their neighbours, which was quite understandable as they were comparative strangers to such a close-knit community. Seven years after the eleventh child was born, the fourth daughter, Violet, temporarily returned to Durgan with three daughters of her own. Durgan children have welcomed many more Johns grandchildren back during school holidays.

Rashleigh Cottage, on the coastal footpath, has been completely modernised. It was originally a cottage with a shed at one end, on the seaward side, and a fish cellar on the other end. There is a record of a Wesleyan Methodist Chapel at Durgan in 1867, which was situated above the fish cellar.

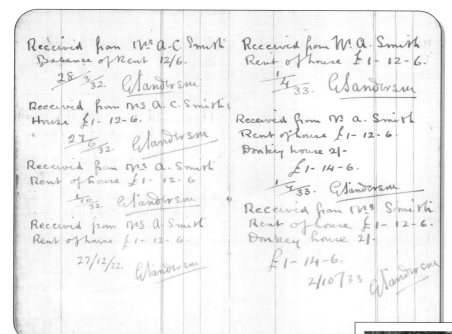

Left: A page from the Rent Book for Post Box Cottage and Donkey House. By 1932 the Donkey houses were being used as storage sheds. It was one of the head-gardeners duties to collect the rent for Mr Fox of Glendurgan – here it is Mr George Sanderson.

Right: Message left by French fishermen on a crab pot at Durgan in the 1950s.

Below: Farewell party on Durgan beach for Glendurgan's gardener, Keith Moyle, 1996.

The Schoolroom

Sir Joseph Pease opened the schoolroom in June 1876, having arrived on his steam yacht, *Roseberry*, amidst much rejoicing. It was to be used as a school for the younger children of the cove, as the older children attended the National School in Mawnan. Pupils at the school included the four eldest Pascoe children, George Rashleigh, Mary Eddy and two children from Helford Passage, Sarah Rowe, daughter of a coastguard, and Sophia Downing, the innkeeper's daughter. William Downing, aged eight, and ten-year-old Bessie Rashleigh transferred to Mawnan school in 1888, probably when Durgan school closed. Jose Downing talked about those days to his niece, Winifred Rendle, in 1950:

You paid 1d a week for school. It was not compulsory and many boys didn't go if something more interesting came up. The schoolroom was also used as a church and the parson came down and took services. When free education came in, every child went to Mawnan school and the one at Durgan was turned into a Reading Room and Library. The men paid 2s.0d. per year, had games such as draughts and bagatelle and the Western Morning News *was delivered each day. When the fishermen were out fishing at night, a light was left on in the Reading Room. As the Durgan men came in, they went into the school and stayed up 'till all the boats were in. Then they all helped pull them up. In 1900 there were nine fishing boats operating from Durgan:* Milly, Secret, Shamrock, Dora, Ganges, Fleetwings, Stella, Mabel *and* Two Sisters. *On the wall outside the door of the schoolroom was a barometer.*

In 1930, however, everything changed when the First Gold Hill Troop, Bucks, camped nearby. As their Scoutmaster Mr Paine was a musician, they were used to performing in public and so staged a variety concert in the schoolroom, much to the delight of the local population. It was decided to form the Durgan Scout Troop, followed soon after by the Durgan Girl Guides. One of these Guides, Barbara Rendle, wrote in 1998:

It was due to the Gold Hill Scouts that our school-room was opened to children. It became the Scout and Guide HQ and monthly whist drives and socials became popular up until 1940.

The summer visits from the Gold Hill lads were eagerly awaited, with several lifelong friendships being formed with Durgan residents. In August 1934 the *Falmouth Packet* reported:

A wonderful concert was given in Durgan school-room, in aid of the camp funds of the Durgan Troop. The concert was organised by Group Scoutmaster Paine of the First Gold Hill Scouts who are in camp at Durgan. The cream (so to speak) of the concert was the excellent performance on the violin by Miss Pauline Crothers of Penryn, who is a famous concert artiste in both London and the provinces... Other performers were Mr Owen Crothers, G.S.M. Paine and Mrs Paine. Lady Rendlesham was present with friends from Bosloe.

Wedding receptions were frequently held in the schoolroom. On Easter Saturday, 1933, the Pascoes' granddaughter, Olive Hendy, and her husband, Percy Forward, were driven from Durgan to their honeymoon destination by young Llewellyn Medlyn, and two days later Gladys Sullifan and her bridegroom Geoff Taysom were supplied with a guard-of-honour by the Durgan Scouts. In 1945 the schoolroom was the venue for a grand VE-Day party. The last event took place in the late 1940s, when another party was held for the whole village, this time hosted by Mr and Mrs Cuthbert Fox on their return from a holiday in South Africa, where they had met General Smuts. Shortly afterwards, the children watched workmen convert the schoolroom into a dwelling, while the adults shared out the card tables, chairs, books and unique, distinctive crockery.

Trebah Lane or 'Rocky Walk'

Durgan was an ideal deep-water anchorage for the Romans who traded for tin. They would have walked to the mining areas around Wendron up the steep-sided rough track, which, in the Middle Ages, was part of the network of paths connecting the important estates of Trerose and Trebah. Later still, when Durgan was a thriving fishing village, the wives of the fishermen led their donkeys up the lane, to hawk their husbands' catches around the neighbourhood. From 1828–42 it was the path used by the pupils at Sarah Fox's school. During the first half of the twentieth century Durgan housewives had to negotiate the rough track to catch Mr Banfil's bus at Trebah Crossroads, in order to do their shopping in Falmouth.

People have continued to live, work and play happily here since Durgan was handed over to the National Trust by Mr and Mrs Cuthbert Fox and their son Philip in 1962. The metamorphosis of Durgan from a busy fishing cove to the thriving tourist attraction of today has been a truly worthwhile and acceptable one.

Durgan, 2000. Durgan resident, Mr Frank Womak, on Schoolroom Quay.

Left: Durgan, c.1910. Schoolroom Quay.

Durgan Regatta, 2001.

HELFORD PASSAGE: A PERSONAL VIEW BY HUGH DAVIES

My wife and I live [at Helford Passage] right at its heart in a little compact house comprising numbers 1 and 2 Coastguard Cottages, occupied for most of a lifetime by Ernie and Elsie Rickard in No.1, and Bill and Jane Williams in No.2. Mrs Carrie Ham has lived at No.3 for many years, while Hartley and Lance Peters are at No.4. Nos 5 and 6 at the western and uphill end of this little terrace were occupied for some 50 years by the late Mrs Ursula Martin.

It has not been ascertained when the coastguard cottages were built, but we believe from certain details of construction and finish that it was around 1850, perhaps a bit before, but not much. We have lived here for 15 years and the view from our front windows cannot have changed in any particular for hundreds of years. The beautiful place has utterly captivated us, and we know we are very lucky.

Looking at several old charts (we have one in the cottage dated 1692) it's not all that easy to define precisely where Helford Passage actually is. The name appears on old charts variously upstream or downstream of today's Ferry Boat Inn. However, it seems probable that the term 'passage' refers to the passage of the Ferry from Helford village to the beach on the northern side of the river and, as far as I can ascertain, bounded to the east by the beginning (west end) of the Kessell family's field, and to the west as far as the shore immediately below Heyle. Indeed, old charts define the beach immediately below the Ferry Boat Inn as Passage Cove, and the shoreline below Heyle as Gate Beach. During the passing of time, the area has expanded somewhat.

Bar Road, not much more than a farm track before the Great War, gradually became the major development of houses we know today, and includes Helford Passage in its postal address. But at Trebah crossroads, that little group of properties comprising Brynn, Trebah Wartha, Virginia Cottage and the Tower House, uses 'Trebah Wartha' as part of the address, not 'Helford Passage'. These dwellings were, in fact, included in the Trebah estate and tenanted by estate employees. Tower House was the estate laundry and the tower itself accommodated the tanks of fresh water for laundry purposes.

The ferry has been operating since medieval times. At one time it belonged to the Bishops of Exeter. Its landing places were variously Passage Cove (the Ferry Boat Inn beach) and Bar Beach on the northern side of the river; and on the southern Helford (village) side, The Shipwrights – perhaps Helford Point, and certainly Treath. Until the turn of the last century, horses and carts were carried –

the cart on the ferry, and the horses towed swimming behind. Horsemen travelling, say from St Keverne to Falmouth using the ferry, would save themselves some 20 miles of winding country lanes.

What would travellers landing at Helford Passage have found in 1850? They would have seen the row of coastguard cottages (and the coastguard station), with their little outhouses and privies (still there, but used only for storage now!), a couple of substantial cottages comprising the Ferry Boat Inn, the old boathouse, the tiny cottage on the corner now called 'The Hideaway' but then 'The Watch House' (used by the coastguards) and a cottage behind, now much enlarged (today's 'Watch House'). The horses would be rested after their long swim, watered (there was a well) and the travellers would continue their journey up the hill, and on through Mawnan Smith, where they might stop for a noggin or two at the Red Lion (I would!) and on to Falmouth or Truro.

Later, the pub was enlarged and became quite a posh small hotel (dinner jackets for dinner). It was visited by the smart, the rich, the famous and the infamous. To name but a few: Edward VIII and Wallis Simpson, Generals Eisenhower and Patton and later (in 1946) by that endearing actor, David Niven. The infamous visitors included the German Ambassador to the Court of St James', Count von Ribbentrop – need I say more!

Today's Ferry Boat Inn, a tied house of St Austell Breweries, is excellently run by Steve and Leslie Brown.

From our bedroom window we can see just about the whole yacht mooring area and most of the dozen or so fishing boats, to which the river is a home port. We hear the fishermen depart in the early morning and we enjoy watching their return in the evening, garlanded by gulls wheeling and diving as the catches are cleaned and prepared for market. The river is often a safe haven for fishing boats from other ports, seeking shelter in bad weather. The yacht moorings have grown in number and are probably now at a maximum, but there always seems to be room for visiting yachts. The Helford, apart from its own special delights, is a very useful point of arrival and departure – for France of course, for the Scillies, for Ireland, for the Azores and far beyond. The French are our most frequent visitors, but we see Scandinavians, Germans, Dutch, Belgians, Americans and even Swiss!

Oh dear, I nearly forgot the monster! Carrie Ham has seen it. On 4 September 1991 Carrie was sitting in her front garden and saw what she at first thought was a capsized yacht. She ran into her cottage for her binoculars. The object sank and resurfaced twice; then something like a long arm came out of the water 'seeming to be shaking something at the end of it'. Was it Morgawr? For further sightings watch this space!

I can't leave today's Helford Passage without mentioning my friends Arthur Eva and Simon and Tina Walker. Arthur's been here near enough forever. One-time motor mechanic, boat builder, designer and builder of the famous Anarth series of dinghies, raconteur, he and his dear wife Anne are friends to all who live and visit here. Arthur embodies the spirit of the place.

Simon and Tina are ground landlords of the whole ferry boat site, own and run the ferry to Helford Point, hire out small boats, and administer all the moorings. Their meticulous management of the area, car parks, gardens and swimming pool adds distinction to this lovely place.

Has Helford Passage changed? Well yes it has – and again, no, it hasn't! The Ferry Boat Inn is bigger and the hotel itself has given way to a substantial development of self-catering flats, so that the population at peak (during the school summer holidays) is around 160. The winter residential population is about 23 – not much different from 150 or 200 years ago.

Does a population of 160 ruin the place? Undoubtedly some would say 'yes', but we who have our homes here have learned to live with it. We do not feel that our privacy is invaded. Many of the people who come here year after year have become friends, and each year we look forward to their arrival. We tend to keep our bedroom windows closed until the last reveller, frequently a local, has left the Ferry Boat Inn on a Saturday night! The sort of families who come to stay at Helford Passage, and day visitors too, come because they love it for what it is. They come to walk, to mess about in boats, to relax on the beach, have a pint in the pub; and above all to immerse themselves in the beauty, the peace, and the tranquillity of the place.

The Ferry Boat Inn

The Ferry Boat Inn dates back certainly 300 years, perhaps even longer, and the ferry itself goes back to the fifteenth century. An inn has stood on the site for generations, marking the ferry crossing to the Helford over the river.

The rich, famous and even the bomb-weary came to Helford Passage to stay at the newly built Ferry Boat Inn during the Second World War. The new owner, Commander Douton, planned the new inn like a ship: long, low and snuggled into the cliff, and the bedrooms were named after sailing clippers.

The war years, events, dramatic moments, and characters are what people remember about the Ferry Boat Inn. However, even before the war Maud Rickard, who worked as a parlourmaid and waitress, recalls many Lords and Ladies visiting the inn. The staff would work long hours, starting at 7am and working late into the evening. She also recalls the coming of the war and how the hotel was blacked out on the Friday before war was declared on the Sunday.

Nora Butler, who also lived through the war years at the Ferry Boat Inn, recalls arriving with a stream of people flowing through the inn. There were regular holiday-makers looking bemused, along with a host of French and Belgian people hoping to take refuge. There were camp beds in the drawing room and the dining room and emergency rations were distributed.

The kitchens were wonderfully equipped with masses of cupboards and work surfaces, and the latest in pre-war electrical gadgetry, including a huge washing-up machine. Nora recalls rowing across the river with the housekeeper's three children, and a plane swooping down and shooting at them, before zooming off down the river.

Admirals, Air Marshals and Generals all stayed at the inn. General Montgomery stayed for three days before going to the Middle East. Captain Slocum, Operational Head of Naval Intelligence, also stayed at the Inn. One wonders what drew a man like this to the Ferry Boat Inn.

Ronnie, the ferryman-cum-part-time barman, would take a boat up the river to the Calamansack Estate, belonging to Commander Warrington Smythe, and arrive back laden with mounds of fresh produce and baskets of flowers. The crews of the ships spent many hours in the bar, and as by a freak of the licensing laws the Shipwrights Inn on the other side of the river Helford had to close at 9.30pm but the Ferry Boat Inn could stay open until 10.00pm. Some officers would ring for the ferry to go over and pick them up for a final drink at the Passage Inn (its original name).

The Ferry Boat Inn is now run by St Austell Brewery, one of whose greatest strengths has been that it is in essence a family business – not only in ownership and management but in all aspects of the brewery's operation. One generation has followed upon another; the Managing Director, Piers Thompson, is a descendant of Walter Hicks, who founded the company in 1851.

The main bar, with its unrivalled view of the river, still has a feel of ships and the sea. Its French windows open onto the terrace, where food and drink can be enjoyed in the sunshine, in the same way that it was enjoyed by the characters and guests of previous years.

Mawnan Smith grew up where two ancient track-ways met. One led to the church of St Mawnanus on the cliff and the other to the ferry at Helford Passage. The ferry has linked the Lizard Peninsula with Penryn and Truro since the thirteenth century according to records and was maybe used earlier. At that time it was owned by the Bishop of Exeter and was probably used by clerics and pilgrims as a safe and quick way to reach the Celtic Christian centre at Lanhevrau (St Keverne).

A fleet of helicopters, probably from Culdrose, flying over the Helford Estuary. At the bottom right Helford Passage and Trebah Beach can be seen, with the road built by the Americans during the Second World War. On the left of the picture is the village of Helford. The passenger ferry operates between the two.

The Coastguard Cottages at Helford Passage, c.1900.

Apparently, in the early nineteenth century, the ferrymen took advantage of there being an inn on both sides of the passage (The Shipwrights Arms at Helford and The Ferry Boat Inn) and were often drunk, which made the ferry unreliable and dangerous. In the late 1800s Miss Fox of Penjerrick felt so strongly about the delays that she had a wooden house built on the Lizard side of the water to ensure that passengers would have shelter and not be forced to spend money and time in the inn.

In the 1930s the inn was rebuilt and enlarged from the old cottage it had been. American officers adopted the inn when they were based in the area before the D-Day embarkation in the Second World War.

Left: Helford Passage early 1930s, before Wilfred Pascoe built the present day pub.

Below: The Ferry Boat Inn, c.1947.

Today the inn is a popular meeting-place for locals and tourists alike. The passenger ferry service runs from Easter until October, both to a timetable and on demand.

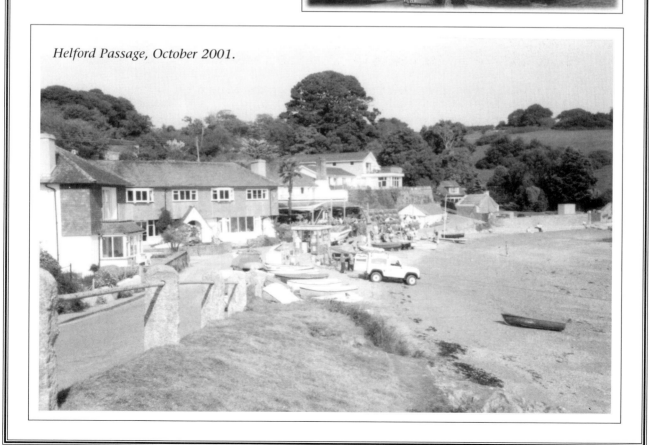

Helford Passage, October 2001.

Above: *Horse bus. This was usually called a horse ferry, because the horse and wagonette was brought across the river on a ferry.*

Left: *The Coastguard Officers Quarters, Helford Passage.*

Anna Maria Mine

Although the Helford River was not noted for its mining, it did operate on a small scale. The most documented and apparently most extensive mine in the area was Wheal Anna Maria (named after Anna Maria Pender of Budock Vean). Anna Maria Mine, or Pedenpoll Mine, at the head of Porth'naba Creek, dates from around 1833–35, and produced silver, bournonite and copper for several years.

The following comes from the *Falmouth Packet*, May 1907:

On Whit Monday, 200 people, including farmers, carpenters, blacksmiths, fishermen, labourers and a number of women and children, assembled near the mine to witness the arrival of two large boilers.

They arrived in Penryn and were conveyed to Anna Maria by a large traction engine by the way of Mawnan and in descending Budock Vean Hills very careful handling of the engine was necessary, owing to the narrowness of the road. The engine got into the hedge by some means, and it was a

little time before it could be released. It was at first thought that the best way to bring the boilers to Anna Maria would be via Port Navas and Trenarth Bridge, but this was found to be impracticable as the road was not wide enough to take a traction engine.

At the bottom of the field adjoining the shaft, a large oblong space was dug out and when the trucks containing the boilers were drawn in, they were levered off on the top of the pit where they will remain until the foundations are completed. The proceedings were eagerly watched by the large crowd.

More labourers were engaged; a counting house and tool house were planned and the winding engine was about to be brought from Penryn Railway Station. A year later, the mine employed 14 men, including experienced engineers from Falmouth. The mine captain, Mr Teague, was delighted that they had reached the third level. But by 1912, dismantling operations were taking place and the mine closed down.

Chapter 4

PRINCIPAL PROPERTIES

Boskenso

The earliest written reference to Boskenso was in the 1327 Mawnan Subsidy Roll when Marina and John Boskenso were assessed as having to pay 17d. in tax. The homestead was beside an ancient track passing Boskenso, Tregarne, High Cross, Polwheveral and Nancenoy, continuing on to Helston. During the fourteenth century Boskenso was held by the manor of Penrose (near Helston), which continued until the mid-eighteenth century. In 1371 John Penrose was granted a licence 'to celebrate in his chapel at Boskenven'; the presence of a resident cleric suggests that it was at that stage a place of some importance.

In 1541 after the death of Thomas Penrose, a document mentions Boskinso Dreffe (now Drift Farm), Tregarne and Penpoll being under the feudal jurisdiction of John Trevylyn 'as of his manor of Treros'. Richard John, a Breton chaplain living at Boskenso, became involved in a land dispute between Thomas Penwarne and John Trevylyn in the early-sixteenth century. Thomas Penwarne alleged that Richard John of Boskenso and James Clarke of Tregarne had grievously assaulted his servant Erne Piers who 'kept the bestis' in the three closes under dispute, and their hounds had killed 21 of his sheep. This long-running dispute came before the star chamber in 1516, when the local justice (Sir John Trevylyn's cousin) refused to uphold Thomas Penwarne's complaint.

With the exception of Boskenso and Tregarne, most of the land in Mawnan parish was divided between the manors of Trerose and Penwarne (*see Chapter Two*). This lead to disputes between the families, especially as the Trevylyns no longer lived in Mawnan by the sixteenth century.

Boskenso remained part of the manor of Penrose until 1729 when it was sold to Ambrose Thomson of Penryn. In 1797 Sir Michael Nowell of Penwarne bought Boskenso and it remained part of the Penwarne estate until 1946. Sir Michael died in 1802 without an heir, and the condition in his will for his nephew to inherit caused something of a scandal. He could only become owner of the estate if he did not marry a certain Miss Frances Bawden of a Falmouth brewing family. If the match took place, his brother, Revd Robert Michael Nowell Usticke, was to inherit. However, although the couple lived together, they did not marry, so Stephen duly inherited. Later the brothers healed their differences when Miss Bawden's relations became troublesome. Stephen left all his property and land to his brother and Miss Bawden was cut off with just one shilling! When Revd Robert died unmarried, the estate passed to a nephew, Revd Michael Nowell Peters, and on his death to his daughters, Mary Tonkin and Lydia Borlase. Lydia died in 1886 aged 58. Mary Tonkin, wife of Revd John Tonkin, lived at Penwarne until her death in 1924.

The old Boskenso farmhouse burnt down and was replaced in the 1850s by a much larger and grander house. It was thought to have been intended for John and Lydia Borlase and their daughters but after John Borlase's early death, Lydia and her children lived at Bareppa House for some time. In the 1830s Anthony Retallack took over the farm as tenant and by the time of the 1841 census he was a widower with six children and three live-in servants. He married again and had three more children. The Retallacks lived at Boskenso for nearly 20 years.

Robert Crowgey became tenant farmer in 1856. Robert, his wife Mary and their two sons had previously lived in Constantine and Wendron. In the 1871 census the farm was listed as being of 155 acres. Robert Crowgey employed three men and his brother-in-law, John Lawrence, as well as two dairymaids, Elizabeth Tremaine and Sarah Cock, who lived in with the family.

John Gilos farmed there in the 1880s and '90s, followed by John Roberts and his son Frederick. Mr Edward Matthews originally from Mousehole and his wife Florence (née Gwennap) settled in Boskenso in 1933 with their son Stewart taking over in 1946. Richard, one of Stewart's sons, carries on the family tradition.

Bosloe

View of Bosloe, 2000.

For over 150 years a house has stood on the site of Bosloe overlooking the Helford River. Tracing the history of Bosloe and its occupants reveals much about life in the parish of Mawnan.

The land on which Bosloe stands was once part of Bosveal Farm and of the Trerose estate until that was broken up in the last century. The house was originally known as Chatham Cottage and retained that name until it became the home of William Ward in the 1890s. It is believed to have been named in memory of the much admired eighteenth-century statesman William Pitt, Earl of Chatham. The house is unlikely to have been a cottage as we know it; by the late-eighteenth century it had become fashionable for well-to-do people to build country retreats for themselves and call them cottages.

Chatham Cottage is said to have been occupied in 1837 by a Captain Manderson, but by 1841 when the census was taken, a retired Army officer, Captain Gillett, aged 50, was living there with his father, Thomas, and son, James. However, they were not the owners of Chatham Cottage. The 'house and plantation' and adjoining land running down to the river was owned by James Treweek, a mine agent from Gwennap.

James and Elizabeth Treweek and their family most probably came to live in Mawnan in the late 1840s. Their youngest son George was born in Mawnan in 1848, and the names of Elizabeth Treweek and six of her children are recorded in the 1851 census: James, who was a 19-year-old 'freehold farmer of 60 acres'; Francis, 14; Jane, 9; Elizabeth, 7; William, 5; and George, 2. Their father and his eldest son Nicholas may have been visiting mines abroad at this time. The family accompanied him sometimes; Jane and Elizabeth were born in Cuba in 1842 and 1844 respectively.

James snr soon retired from the mining industry – an 1856 directory lists him as a retired mine agent – but he continued to be involved in other concerns. By the time of the 1861 census he was a 'land and railway prospector' as well as a farmer. (The Falmouth railway opened in 1863.) James and Elizabeth Treweek both died in 1882 and were buried in Mawnan churchyard. The inscription on their ornate tomb also records their son Nicholas who died in California the same year.

After James Treweek's death, Chatham Cottage became the home of John Peter, a retired solicitor from Callington in east Cornwall. Although Callington is some way from Bosloe,

Bosloe House, 1909.

Bosloe House, 1909.

Above: *The fireplace in the main room of Bosloe House, 1909.*

Left: *The main room of Bosloe House, 1909.*

Above: *Indoor staff at Bosloe, 1934.*
Left to right, back row: George Walton, ?,
Janie Orchard, Doris Smith, ?; front: ?,
Albert Peters. One is Mrs Fenton (Cook).

Left: *Albert Peters, indoor man, at*
Bosloe in 1930s. He later lived in
the Square at Mawnan Smith.

Below: *The Wards enlarged Bosloe, 1896–1903.*
The picture shows workmen engaged on
the project, together with tools of trade.

The Rendlesham family, with guests, staff and crew of the Lady Bee at Durgan, before sailing to Port Navas to see the Prince of Wales, June 1921. Back row, second from left is Mrs Winifred Rendle and baby Barbara Rendle.

John Peter may have become acquainted with James Treweek, and Bosloe, through his father, who had been a wool merchant and had also been involved in the mining industry.

An interest in sailing may have been the main reason why the Peter family wanted to live on the Helford River. When they moved to Chatham Cottage, John Peter arrived at Durgan in his yacht. Having been much involved in local affairs in Callington, he was largely responsible for the opening of the gas works in 1852, and was Clerk of the Turnpike Trust, the town's Portreeve and for many years a churchwarden. Now it was Mawnan's affairs that interested him and in particular, the formation of the first Mawnan Parish Council. A photograph taken in 1894 shows the nine members of the Parish Council in front of Chatham Cottage. When John Peter and his wife, Margaret, came to Chatham Cottage, they brought with them from Callington their young gardener, George Johns and his wife Anneta, to live in the lodge. The Johns settled happily in Mawnan bringing up a large family who attended the village school. When the Peters returned to East Cornwall, the Johns chose to remain in the parish and various members of the family lived in Durgan for many years.

In 1886 William Welsford Ward and his wife Charlotte came to live at Chatham Cottage. William Ward, a Bristol solicitor, had married Charlotte Rogers, the second daughter of Reginald Rogers of Carwinion, on 4 March 1886 in St Michael's Church. The *Falmouth Packet* reported that Mawnan was 'all astir' for this happy occasion. The villagers erected an archway of evergreen over the gate leading to the church and waited there to greet the bride 'so long known and loved by them'. St Michael's was a particularly appropriate venue, for it had been largely through the efforts of the bride's uncle, the Revd William Rogers, that the house of worship had been built and consecrated in 1874. The four stained-glass windows had been given in memory of Charlotte's grandfather, Canon John Rogers, Rector of Mawnan from 1807 to 1838, and of her father, Reginald Rogers who had given the land on which St Michael's was built.

At Chatham Cottage, the Wards enlarged and improved the house, which they renamed 'Bosloe', adding a substantial west wing in 1903. William Ward, like John Peter before him, became involved in village affairs and in 1902, when Mawnan school was placed under the administration of the County Council, he became one of the school's new managers. It had been through the efforts of Charlotte Ward's grandfather, Canon John Rogers, that Mawnan National School had been established in 1833.

The Wards left Bosloe after the First World War and the death of their only son Francis. He was on holiday at Bosloe when war broke out in 1914. He returned to Bristol, where he was articled to a firm of solicitors, and joined the City of Bristol Regiment. He died in action in Flanders on 9 October 1917, leaving a wife and daughter. Three cousins, Reginald and Gordon Rogers and Neville Fox, with whom he would have spent many happy hours at Bosloe, also lost their lives in the conflict.

Bosloe next became the property of the Gage family who leased it in 1919 to Lord Rendlesham, a member of the Thellusson family. Peter Thellusson, a Genevese merchant, came to England in 1762 and bought Rendlesham White House in Suffolk. He traded with the West Indies and became very rich. Peter had a dream of a descendant who would be extremely wealthy and powerful, so in his will, £100,000 was left to his wife and children, with £600,000 invested at compound interest for the grandson of the eldest male of his three sons. This would accumulate to quite a fortune! The will was contested, but confirmed by the House of Lords after eight years. In 1856 the last of the grandsons died – then more litigation followed. Who was the eldest male descendant? Finally the heir was named as the fifth Baron Rendlesham, a grandson of the third son of Peter Thellusson. The dream did not come true. Due to the mismanagement of the estate and two costly law suits, there was just the original £600,000 remaining. As a result of the scheme, an Act of Parliament was passed – The Accumulation Act of 1880, also known as The Thellusson Act – which prevented property being left to accumulate for more than 20 years.

Frederick Archibold Charles Thellusson, the sixth Baron, succeeded his father in 1911. He sold Rendlesham White House (by then known as Rendlesham Hall) and moved to Bosloe. It was his love of fishing and sailing which brought him to live by the Helford River, where he kept a yacht called *The Lady Bee*. Bosloe was also an ideal place for his other great interest – gardening – and, in particular, the growing of prize-winning daffodils. A regular exhibitor at the Royal Horticultural Show in London, he won 21 prizes in 1934. In 1897, J.C. Williams of Caerhays had begun to grow new varieties of daffodils which would appeal to the public and have strong constitutions, suitable for the flower markets of London and the Midlands. He was an extremely successful hybridist and Lord Rendlesham built on his success and made further progress in producing new daffodils.

Lord Rendlesham was also a keen sportsman and attended all the local cricket matches. In 1924 he gave land in Carwinion Road for a Bowling Club and became the club's first President. (Until matches could be held at the new club, members played on the lawn in front of Bosloe House.) Lord Rendlesham died at Bosloe in July 1938. He was twice married: first to Lilian, the daughter of Joshua Manley of Jamaica, and secondly to Dolores, the widow of Mr Henry Harcourt Williams of Pencalenick, Truro. The title passed to his brother, Percy Edward, aged 63.

The first Lady Rendlesham is well remembered in Mawnan as a benefactor and a friend whose interest and active support in improving local amenities added considerably to the quality of village life. She was much involved in the fund-raising for the Memorial Hall in 1923, she gave land for a children's playground in 1928, and established a Nursing Association to provide a District Nurse for the community. When the nurse's bungalow was sold in 1982, the Rendlesham Trust was set up and run by local people to help the elderly and those in need in the parish.

Lady Rendlesham was also President of the Mawnan Women's Institute for many years, during which time the organisation went from strength to strength. The WI garden parties held at Bosloe every June were long remembered. After her death in 1931, a tablet to the memory of Mawnan's 'generous friend and helper' was placed in the Memorial Hall. Today her portrait hangs beside it, presented to the village by Lord Rendlesham.

The Gage family lived at Bosloe until 1951 when it became the home of the Tucketts. Then in 1978, it was acquired by the National Trust. Today a footpath through the property is used by the public, whilst the gardens are often open for local charities. The house is divided into three spacious holiday apartments, and a tiny 'Bothy' (former potting shed) is a popular holiday hideaway. Tony Lugg, the National Trust North Helford Warden, manages the estate, together with his wife Margaret.

Inset: *Frederick Archibald Charles Thellusson, Sixth Baron Rendlesham, 1868–1938.*

Budock Vean

Budock Vean's earliest recorded name was Eglos-Budock-Vean, meaning Little Budock Church. The name dates back to celtic times, that is to say to some date prior to AD800, when it was a small religious centre. After that date, the Saxons began to over-run Cornwall and to overwhelm the old celtic church. It was quite a small religious house – hardly substantial enough to be really called a monastery – but had its own chapel, its Holy Code, and its own burial-ground. It was dedicated to St Budock, the Breton Saint who eventually became Bishop of Dol! The site of the church was set among the trees to the north-west of the present building, but no remains now exist. However, within the past century, human bones have been dug up from what was once the graveyard.

After the Norman Conquest in 1066 Cornwall was divided up between the great lords and a vast area went to the Bishop of Exeter. This expanse of land included the whole of the Roseland Peninsular, the present parishes of Falmouth, St Gluvias, Penryn, Mabe, Mawnan and Budock, with Manaccan and St Martin on the far side of the Helford River. Budock Vean was also included, although it was really in the parish of Constantine, because it went with the ferry rights at Helford Passage. The passage on each side of the river was then called Treath (meaning 'ferry') although it was known by this name on the far bank only. The ferry rights were of great monetary importance to the Bishop since all goods passing to and from the Lizard went via the ferry and so tolls were considerable. Budock Vean was therefore a place of material importance.

It is not known exactly when Budock Vean ceased to be a religious establishment and became a small manor, but it must have been at a very early date. In 1260 we find that Richard paid six shillings and three sheep and did ploughing and sowing service on the Bishop's demesne at Penryn like other tenants.

In 1349 another Richard and Elizabeth, his wife, who were registered in the area died of the Black Death. In 1538 records show that the property was held jointly by John Penwern, Richard Retyn and John Carane, each of whom rendered to the Lord of the Manor of Penryn, 9d. for a sheep, 2d. for aid, 1¾d. in lieu of ploughing and ¾d. for reaping.

In 1613 Budock Vean passed to the Langfords who were great Puritans – so much so that in about 1660 John Langford was included into the Benefice of Gwennap, the Royalist rector having been evicted. He in turn was thrown out after the Restoration. His son Thomas however continued to be a violent Puritan and was an ardent supporter of Monmouth at the time of his rebellion. Orders were issued for Thomas' arrest, but he appears to have weathered the storm, for it is recorded that he was still living at Budock Vean in 1709.

Early in the eighteenth century, Budock Vean passed to the Pender family, who built a fine house on the site. This trend of costly building projects occurred across Cornwall during this period. The Penders' new home was recorded as being the largest house in the parish. They retained it until after the First World War, when it was sold to the then tenant, Mr Dunstan, who sold part of the estate as building land, while the house and the rest of the property were sold to a Mr Taylor, who intended to convert the house into a country club.

Mrs Susan Dunstan, founder of Mawnan Women's Institute and her husband John, 1920.

BUDOCK VEAN HOTEL

One of the West Country's most popular hotels, is Budock Vean, yet in 1929, this was just an old rat-infested, decaying manor farm. Behind the intriguing tale of the unexpected growth of Budock Vean lies the determination of Mr Harry B. Parkinson ('Parky') and his friend, Mr Ezra Albert Edward Pilgrim ('Eddie'). Here is Parky's story:

If you belong to the present generation of cinema patrons, you may have no idea of the revolution brought about in the industry by the invention of 'talkies'. I worked within the early film industry and the idea of a moving picture fascinated me, but a talking picture seemed to reach the limit of imagination. I could not compete with this invention, so I abandoned my interest in films and looked for new worlds to conquer.

I went to stay with Eddie Pilgrim, whose firm was developing the Budock Vean Estate (now Budock Vean Lane), and joined forces with him. He was a building developer and together we built roads and installed mains services. The River House was partly built and our first job was to complete it. More houses and bungalows were constructed and sold without difficulty. We then turned our attention to the manor house itself and converted it into a country house hotel. At that time there were very few quality hotels outside of towns and this was perhaps the first of what was to become a new and very popular classification of hotel. In my former work of producing and directing films, I spent half my time in hotels – good, bad and indifferent. Many a time I had been annoyed, mostly by little things, which I felt ought never to happen in a well-run hotel. Now my chance had come!

In six months, with local labour directed by an old Cornish foreman, George Lowry, and his two sons, Jack and Cecil, the conversion was completed. Eddie was an architect by training and designed all this new work, creating a notable feature of the dining room, with a fine minstrel's gallery over a wide, open fireplace. This was indeed a beautiful room, and to see it filled with guests at dinner, always in evening dress, was one of the joys of hotel management.

The engagement of staff who would respond to our ideas proved fruitful. Where would you have found a housekeeper like Miss Hodges, or a gardener/ handyman like Bill Williams? His orchids won the admiration of even our most well-travelled visitors.

At this time work had also been taking place on the outside of the hotel. The first task had been to lay the lawns and make a pathway to our private beach. Next came the nine-hole golf course, planned for us by James Braid. A bowling green, tennis courts and putting greens followed. Boats

and cars for visitors' use, plus a separate garage and chauffeur's quarters were added to meet the demand. The cabin cruiser was a most successful investment. With it went skipper, Leonard Salisbury, from Durgan, who would take 12 guests on a fishing daytrip or just exploring on the river.

Cabinet ministers as well as stage, screen and radio personalities stayed with us. Bud Flanagan and his wife were among the guests we were always glad to see. Bud possessed a magnificent set of golf clubs, presented to him by Billy Cotton, which he kept permanently at the hotel.

In 1935, when I returned to London for a couple of years, Eddie's wife, Alice Rose Pilgrim, arrived to look after things. She soon got a liking for hotel life, so they bought a nearby property and converted it into another country house hotel – Nansidwell. It was at this stage that an old friend, Harry Whiteside of peanut fame, appeared on the scene and I went back to the hotel as Managing Director. In years to come the hotel was owned and run by Harry's sons.

During the war, we never knew where we were. Without warning, some 60 or 70 sailors would drop in, straight from their ships in Falmouth, and every room would be occupied, yet the next day we would be empty. Before D-Day, Budock Vean was put out-of-bounds to all civilians, with armed guards on point duty. Consequently we became a glorified restaurant for service personnel. Early each morning, the telephone would ring, 'May I have a table for 12... for 20... for 35... ' and so on. It was fantastic. Night after night we were packed to suffocation. From about six o'clock onwards, Army vehicles of all shapes and sizes conveyed men and women to our door. I had to ration whisky to two doubles per person. We served three sittings for dinner and dancing went on all the time. After D-Day, although rail travel was still restricted, requests for accommodation came from all ranks of the Forces and from civilians. We could not take even five per cent of the applications. On the night that peace was declared, a few of the younger guests, including a honeymoon couple, were dancing to long-playing records in the dining room, when one of our lady guests rushed down the stairs in her dressing-gown, having heard the news on her radio. Well, naturally, everyone went mad with joy; it was drinks on the house and champagne all round.

One cold, dark night in the winter of 1947, Nye Bevan, then Minister of Health, arrived with his wife Jenny Lee, plus a doctor, as Nye was very ill. On their departure, Miss Lee thanked me for all that had been done for them. In her own words, 'it was simply perfect'. A year later, after many happy years at Budock Vean, my thoughts of retirement were clarified by an offer from Harry Whiteside. I sold him my share of the business and retired with my wife to our Kensington flat.

BUDOCK VEAN COTTAGE

Budock Vean Cottage is believed to have been built around 1900 and is first shown on an Ordnance Survey map of 1907. There may have been an old building on the site at one time, but this does not show on earlier Ordnance Survey maps. It is now one house, but is believed to have originally been two cottages, built by the owners of Budock Vean Manor Farm (now part of Budock Vean Hotel) and originally known as Trebawartha Cottages (referred to as such in a deed dated 1928).

When built, each cottage appears to have had four downstairs rooms and an entrance hall, plus four bedrooms and a bathroom. This is much more accommodation than a farm worker would normally have expected 100 years ago. They may have been built for the farmer's sons who worked on the farm.

The cottages were sold in 1929 by a developer called Taylor who had acquired the farm with the intention of building a country club/hotel, presumably to raise cash for the projects. Deeds therefore start from then. They were re-sold in 1931 to Mr and Mrs Johnson, who paid £1350. They converted them into one house, and in doing so made considerable structural alterations. The Johnsons lived in the house for many years and it was also lived in by Mr and Mrs Davis for about ten years until 1979; at the time of writing, Beryl Davis lives in Budock Vean Lane. She remembers her husband laying parquet flooring in a downstairs room that had previously had a mud floor. There is a well in the garden which was in use around 1970 when the water pressure dropped during the holiday season.

Nansidwell House. Grade II listed building built for Sydney Rowlatt designed by Leonard Stokes, c.1905.

Nansidwell Beach.

Right: *This sun chalet was built at Bream Cove in the 1930s by Mr and Mrs Pilgrim for their guests at Nansidwell Hotel. It was neglected until 1999 when the National Trust cut through the undergrowth and renovated the building. Nowadays it is used by visitors to the beach and walkers on the coastal footpath.*

View from the terrace of Nansidwell across Falmouth Bay.

Carwinion

Carwinion supposedly means 'camp of the white people'. The earliest written references to Carwinion in the parish of Mawnan date from 1297 (when it was referred to as Caerwenkein). In the 1327 Mawnan Subsidy Roll Rado de Caerwengen was assessed to pay 1s.11d. in tax. The Cornish name, however (along with other local place-names, such as the field known as The Berries), suggests that a homestead was probably established on the site much earlier, in Celtic times. 'Caerwenkein' can be interpreted as 'the defended homestead (caer meaning Round) of Wenkein.'

The Cornwall Archaeological Society has listed Carwinion among the Rounds to be found in the parish of Mawnan, placing it to the west of the present nineteenth-century Carwinion House, in the field behind Mawnan's school. The hedge on the right-hand side through which the foot-path from Bosveal first passes would appear to have been built on the remnants of an earthwork.

Early settlers arriving in the Helford River probably followed the stream inland from Porth Sawsen, as the footpath does today. The lower part of this valley is listed as ancient woodland. A homestead on this site would have been conveniently situated between the ancient trackways that developed along the ridgeway: one to the Round where the Parish Church was to become established, the other to the Helford River and the ferry to Meneage.

A conveyance dated 25 March 1814 was signed between William Williams of Crogeth Saint Keverne and William Edwards of Mawnan, for a term of 500 years for the tenement farm called Carwinion. William Williams leased to William Edwards 'all the Carwinion plot', which contained a meeting-house in the north-west corner of the Smith field with a proper road leading to it, plus a garden of one fifth of an acre. A note was made that: 'William Edwards shall from time to time dig, raise clay or clobb stuff, [he] also has the right to build houses.'

In this early conveyance land is transferred to Carwinion, resulting in the estate that we know today. The National Trust are the present owners, having received Carwinion as a gift from Cecil Rogers.

Mawnan Chapel and Wesley Cottage.

Staff of Carwinion House, Mawnan Smith, c.1890's.

The Woolcock Family

From the early-Middle Ages to the eighteenth century, Carwinion, together with most of the land to the south and east of the parish, was part of the Trerose estate. One of the families that lived and farmed there, as tenants of Trerose, was called Woolcock. A good deal is known about this family. These yeoman farmers are frequently mentioned in local records during the seventeenth and well into the eighteenth centuries, when they were of some standing in the community. Some of their wills and inventories have also survived.

In the 1641 Mawnan Protestation – a document drawn up shortly before the outbreak of the Civil War to assess the loyalty of the parishioners to the King – William Woolcock's name is included in the separate list of parish officials. Later in the century his son, Thomas, was among the signatories of the document drawn up by the rector, the Reverend Joseph Trewinnard, to deal with the problem of intramural burial, when it was agreed that the constant disturbance of the church floor should be controlled. A fee of 30 shillings would be levied for the privilege of burial within the church. In the 1660 Poll Tax Returns, William's son Robert was assessed to pay the quite large sum of eight shillings; only seven others in the parish – all listed as 'gentlemen' – paid more in tax. Thomas, who was also living at Carwinion, paid 4s.2d. Both Robert and Thomas were yeomen.

The Hearth Tax Returns for Mawnan, whereby householders were taxed according to the number of hearths in their houses, suggests that the Woolcocks' farmhouse (with four hearths) was quite large and comfortable. Of the 60 houses listed in Mawnan only five had more hearths, all of which were homes of well-to-do gentlemen: Penwarne had ten, Nansidwell, Bosveal and Trerose six, and the Sanctuary (the Rectory) five.

The medieval farmhouse of Rado de Caerwengen would have been much simpler – probably a hall house – a rectangular building divided into two rooms, a hall and a smaller service area with a cross passage running between. However, by the seventeenth century many houses had been rebuilt (this was the time of the 'great rebuild') and it is likely to have been the Woolcocks who enlarged and improved their farmhouse at Carwinion.

Although the house no longer exists, it is interesting to note the details of the inventory that was drawn up after Thomas Woolcock's death in 1671. Nine rooms are listed. In the hall (the main room) there were two tables and five chairs; in the buttery (where beer and ale were made and stored) there were two barrels and various tubs, seven brasses and a corn chest; in the lower chamber there was a bed ('furnished', i.e. with bedding), a table and forms as well as the family plate and table linen. Until the seventeenth century and often much later in country districts, rooms were generally furnished in a haphazard way, and not kept for specific purposes such as dining or sleeping. On the upper floor there were three chambers (bedrooms). In the chamber over the hall there was a 'furnished' bed, a table and a chair; and in the middle chamber over the kitchen there was a 'furnished' bed, one trunk and two chests. There was also a man's chamber with one bed, perhaps for a younger son or a servant. The inventory also lists a number of horses, sheep, young bullocks, cows, calves and pigs.

The Rogers Family

By the end of the eighteenth century most of the Carwinion land had been acquired by the wealthy Rogers family of Penrose near Helston, who built Carwinion House and established the attractive gardens. The Rogers, who were originally from St Breward, had prospered when they moved to Breage in the 1590s at the time when the mining industry experienced a revival in Cornwall. John Rogers had become the Steward of the Coinages in Cornwall and Devon in 1700, Deputy Supervisor of Blowing Houses in 1714 and Deputy Recorder General of the Duchy in 1724. In 1790 his son Hugh bought Penrose and on his death two years later, Hugh's son John – 'the Second of Penrose' – inherited the estate at the age of 22.

John married Mary, the daughter of Francis Bassett of Tehidy and had 19 children – 13 daughters and six sons. The eldest, the Revd John Rogers, was to become the rector of Mawnan.

The Revd Rogers was much involved in Mawnan's affairs for nearly 40 years. On his arrival in the parish, in 1807, he had found the church building and churchyard in a very poor condition and at once set about attempting to prevent any further dilapidations. In July 1807 he announced that he would not permit any graves to be dug 'in the future, within three feet of the walls of the church.' Although parishoners had been discouraged from burying their dead within the walls since 1678 – a fee of 2d. being levied for the privilege – many graves were placed as near the walls as possible, causing the foundations to be undermined. The whole church was, in fact, in a very poor condition and a certain amount of restoration (not entirely well advised) was eventually agreed by the Rural Dean, but not until 1826.

John Rogers was a man of wide interests. He was a distinguished Hebrew and Syrian scholar, and produced papers on botany and mineralogy. He was particularly interested in the improvement of education and agriculture and he was personally involved in the improvement of Mawnan Glebe.

In 1832 John Rogers set in motion a plan to establish a school in Mawnan. Working with the National Society, he acquired the meadow behind the Red Lion for five shillings, in which the school was built. The three trustees named in the Indenture signed by the Revd Rogers on 1 February 1834 were the rector at Mawnan, the vicar at Constantine (the Revd Edward Rogers), and the Revd John Sheepshank, Vicar of St Gluvias and Archdeacon of Cornwall. They received the school building, one acre of land on which they had the right to build (any profits from which was used for the children of the school), and an endowment in three per cent consolidated bank annuities which had been purchased by the rector. Seven cottages were built on the land, the rents went towards the teachers' salaries and school equipment and heating. The last of these cottages was sold in 1929.

Although schools were beginning to be established throughout the country, the Revd Rogers' gift of land and an endowment made it possible for a school to be built in Mawnan much earlier than in many other Cornish parishes.

As Chairman of the Parish Vestry (a nineteenth-century Parish Council) he was also involved in many other Mawnan affairs. The Vestry was responsible for dealing with the levying of rates, the relief of the poor and the maintenance of parish officers – churchwardens, overseers of the poor, constables and waywardens (who worked on the roads and footpaths).

After Revd Rogers' retirement to Penrose in 1838, his family continued to be involved in local affairs. He had married Mary Jope, the daughter of the Revd John Jope of St Ives and St Clear, and had five sons and one daughter. The eldest son, John Jope Rogers, a solicitor, became the 'Fourth of Penrose' when he inherited the estate on his father's death in the 1840s. His third son Reginald, who inherited Carwinion, was responsible for building the attractive Carwinion House, probably in the late 1840s. (The house is not listed in the 1841 Mawnan census.)

The Carwinion farmhouse was then occupied by James Humphrey, his wife Mary and baby son James, as well as a servant, Grace Saunders, and a farm labourer called Thomas Trugeon and his 70-year-old mother, Philippa.

In 1851 a number of households are listed, one of which was that of farm bailiff Francis Pascoe and his family. Three other cottages were

Mary Rogers.

occupied – one by farm labourer Thomas Pellow and his family, one by a widowed nurse, Katherine Philips, and another by a coastguard, Adolphus Jenkins, his wife and eight children (born in various coastal towns and villages in Devon and Cornwall). Carwinion House would have been built by this time but may not yet have been occupied by Reginald Rogers and his family. However, by 1861 he was living there with his wife Mary and children, Reginald, who was seven, Augusta (six), Hugh (three) and Charlotte (one). Reginald was listed as a solicitor and Notary Public, as well as a farmer employing four men. The household included a cook, Eliza Harvey, a house servant called Jane Buckingham, and a housemaid called Mary Holman. There was also a nurse, Jane Harris, and coachman, James Harris. Two cottages were occupied – one by farm bailiff Francis Pascoe with his wife and family and the other by Francis Jenkins and his wife.

Revd Rogers' second son, William, had become the rector at Mawnan in 1842 and remained in this role until his death in 1889. Like his father before him, he played an important part in the life of the parish. As a school manager for 47 years he knew the village families well. He was a frequent visitor to the school; on Monday mornings he took a service and, in the afternoon, scripture lessons, and his wife also taught geography, drawing and needlework.

When he died it was recorded in the school log-book that he would be greatly missed. Some years before he had been instrumental in realising improvements to the school building and replacing the dangerous open fires with stoves.

It was largely through Revd William Rogers' efforts that St Michael's Church in the village was built in the 1870s. At this time the Anglican Church was at a low ebb across England, and Cornwall was no exception. The Mawnan villagers had always faced a long walk, in all weathers, to the Parish Church on the headland or to one of the lively Methodist chapels in the village or at Carlidnack. A number of small churches, sometimes called Mission Churches, had already been built in the county when the Bishop set in motion a plan to build St Michael's on land given by Reginald Rogers of Carwinion. An architect, James Piers St Aubyn, was appointed, and builders Messrs Oliver & Son of Falmouth were employed. The foundation stone was laid on 28 May 1873. A bottle containing information to this effect is said to have been placed in the wall near the pulpit.

The Bishop of Truro – a personal friend of William Rogers – consecrated the new church on 15 July 1874. It was a great day for Mawnan; people who bought a ticket for 2s.6d. were able to attend a luncheon in the Public Rooms (the Reading Room next to the church) followed by a Public Tea (9d.) and a service at 6.30pm at which the preacher was the Revd Edward Collins.

The Rogers family had given generously to St Michael's Church. As well as providing the land, Reginald Rogers gave the carved oak pulpit and his wife Mary had made the altar cloth. The three stained-glass windows in the chancel were given by the family as a memorial to their father, the Revd John Rogers, 'for 21 years Rector of Mawnan', and when Reginald died in 1877 his family also gave the window on the south wall, behind the choir stalls, as a memorial to their father. The magnificent window also on the south wall but in the main body of the church was given in memory of the Reginald Rogers who died in 1923. It was probably designed by a cousin, Eleanor Fortescue Brickdale, a noted artist and book illustrator.

Three stained-glass windows in the church were also given by the Rogers family as memorials. The colourful window above the altar was given in memory of William Rogers who died in 1889 and the window on the north wall depicting the Virgin Mary and St Luke is a memorial to Mary Rogers who had been born on St Luke's Day in 1828 and died in 1905. As a memorial to her husband, Reginald, the plain glass in the thirteenth-century lancet window in the chancel was replaced with patterns of coloured glass around a lily.

During the 1880s William Rogers became involved in further restoration of the Parish Church and with the re-casting of the bells in the tower. Originally dated 1675 and 1760, two of the three bells now bear the words 'Recast by John Warner and Sons, London 1858'. In addition on one of the bells is inscribed 'Laus Deo 1888' and on another 'W. Rogers, Rector, 1888.'

Many years after the dedication in April 1889, an amusing description of the ceremony by three of the young people at Carwinion – Jane, Agnes and Frances Rogers, William's nieces, came to light. The solemnity of the occasion had been somewhat spoilt when it was discovered that the collection bag had been mislaid and the churchwarden, James Skewes, had insisted on using his hat!

Reginald Rogers, the Revd William's nephew,

Admiral Hugh Hext.

was mainly responsible for the planting and design of the Carwinion Gardens in the latter part of the century, probably in association with the Fox family at Glendurgan and the Hexts at Trebah. Reginald had married Mary Hext in 1880. It may be that they helped finance some of the improvements from which the garden benefited.

The Rogers family also became involved in village affairs. Early in 1914 Reginald proposed that a club or meeting-place should be built for the young men of Mawnan and although the outbreak of war prevented this being carried out at that time, a Village Hall was eventually built as a memorial to the young men of the parish who had died and to those who had served in the First World War.

The Rogers lost two sons, Reginald and Gordon, as well as two nephews, Nevil Fox and Francis Ward. Reginald, the eldest son, a schoolmaster, was 34 when he died on the Somme in 1916. Gordon, who had been in partnership in the family firm of solicitors, had joined the Army on the outbreak of war and was killed in a motor accident in April 1916. He was 29. Nevil Fox, the son of Mr Fox of Crownhill and Mrs Agnes Fox (one of the Rogers daughters who contributed to the poem about the dedication of the bells) was 23 when he died in action with the Welsh Regiment in France in July 1917. Francis Ward was the son of William Welsford Ward and Charlotte Ward (née Rogers) of Bristol and Bosloe who had been married in the new St Michael's Church in 1886. He was 30 when he died in action in Flanders in October 1917.

Soon after the end of the war, a committee was formed to build a village hall under the chairmanship of Reginald Rogers. Five trustees were appointed and a site chosen on what is now Sampy's Hill (no roads in the village were named until 1960) but the project moved slowly until the newly-formed Women's Institute, of which Mrs Rogers was a committee member, came forward and offered to raise funds. Within a few weeks work began and the foundation stone was laid.

The official opening of the hall on 23 July 1923 was a great occasion, attended by the Lord Lieutenant of the county, Mr J.C. Williams, the Bishop of Truro, Dr Guy Warman, and the President of the County Federation of Women's Institutes, Lady Molesworth-St Aubyn. Sadly, Reginald Rogers did not live to see the completion of his plans for a meeting-place in the village. He died on 9 June 1923.

The Chairman of the committee for the building of the hall, Mr P.H. Horton, paid tribute to Mr Rogers, saying he was a man much respected in the area, who would be greatly missed. He stated that the Rogers family had suffered a greater loss in the war than any other in the parish. His only surviving son, Commander Hext Rogers, was invited to preside. Another son, a midshipman, had died at sea shortly before the war began.

Most of the £2000 required to build the hall had already been raised in various ways – the most enjoyable by village entertainments. Garden fêtes were especially popular, none more so than the event in Carwinion Gardens on August Bank Holiday, when £84 was raised.

The *Cornish Echo* gave a full account of the fun and games; there were various stalls; a bran tub and hoopla; a baby show (the best baby, judged by Dr Enid Smith of Falmouth, was Arthur Rowe); sports for all (including a slow cycle race for men, boys and girls); and even a men's hairdressing competition, won by two members of the Gundry family.

The following year, Mrs Mary Rogers gave a memorial tablet, which listed the names of the fallen. She presented it at a meeting of the hall committee on 5 November 1924, when it was agreed that it should be placed in the centre of the chimney breast, over the mantelpiece. Later, when the hall was extended, two tablets, the second of which included the names of all the Mawnan men who had served in the war, were placed on each side of the main entrance.

During the Second World War, Carwinion was in the forefront of local news when a bomb fell in the grounds. Carwinion House was not damaged but a bungalow nearby was completely demolished and its occupants killed. During this period vegetables and fruit were grown in Carwinion Gardens as they had been during the First World War when a number of Land Girls had been employed. In the 1950s, a visitor to Mawnan realised that his aunt had worked as a Land Girl at Carwinion in 1916, so lent an album of photographs taken there at the time for local people to see.

In 1969, Cecil Rogers gave Carwinion, including its wooded footpath running through the valley to Porth Sawsen, Chynalls Farm plus an endowment of ten acres, to the National Trust. After his death Anthony Rogers, a great-grandson of Reginald Rogers, came to live in the house with his family and for over 30 years has been replanting and restoring the gardens. Of particular interest to the many visitors, who come from all over the country to walk in the grounds and enjoy a cream tea, are the 120 species of bamboo, for which the garden is well known. Today Carwinion is recognised as one of the premier bamboo collections in Britain.

The Rogers family of Carwinion, 1886. Left to right, gentlemen: *William R., John R., Reginald R., Wilson Fox, Hugh R., W.W. Ward, Arthur R;* ladies: *Mrs F. Fox, Miss F. Rogers, Mrs R. Rogers, Mrs Wilson Fox, mother of Mrs R. Rogers, Mrs Ward, Mrs Fox;* seated: *Grandson, Reginald Rogers.*

Chenhalls

Chenhalls means 'the house or place by the cliffs'. Included in this holding was the small tenement of Treworgan and names on documents identified with this farm included Cosworth Martin of Mullion, his son John, his wife Duanee (who as a widow married Edward Seccombe), Robert Were Fox Junior and James Leverton, stationer of Penryn. A Leverton was later to become the rector at Mawnan.

On 28 September 1867 Reginald Rogers of Carwinion and James Kempthorne signed an agreement for a term of 14 years for the rental of Chenhalls, at a rate of £52 per year. It was this James Kempthorne's daughter, Nancy, who emigrated to the USA to marry her neighbour Walter Humphry who emigrated to America from Nansidwell Farm.

William and Edward Orchard were the next tenants to sign a lease for 14 years at £60 per annum. They were followed by Mr and Mrs Tippet, with her brother William Christophers and they signed their agreement in the 1930s and farmed there until the National Trust became the owners. The outbuildings were converted into holiday lets, and the land rented to local farmers. Chenhalls, like many farms of a similar size, had by this time become uneconomical.

Left: Left to right: *William Christophers and Edward Sadler at the sale of Chenhalls, during the 1970s.*

Below: *Chenhalls Farm, May 2000.*

Glendurgan

Notes by Charles Fox, November 2001

In the beginning the land at Glendurgan was moorland on which but a few trees grew. This, together with bogs and scrub, was typical of Cornwall's ancient landscape. The two plants that grew in proliferation and which would have been appreciated by the people were gorse, which was used for fuel, and willows, which were used for making crab pots and baskets. Even in the early-twentieth century the character of a Durgan allotment would be marked by a bed of withies. Around the hamlet was a handful of orchards which must also have contributed to the villagers' subsistence.

The garden was started in the early 1820s by Alfred Fox, who by 1826 had built a small thatched cottage at the top of the valley. In 1837 it was the victim of a serious fire, as is so eloquently recorded by Barclay Fox, son of Robert Were Fox:

Was engaged to Grove Hill to dinner, but at 4 o'clock was met by the intelligence that Glendurgan was on fire. Rode there directly with Uncle A. We found the tragedy there concluded and the four smoking walls with a smokeless chymney at either end all that remained of its former magnificence. The crowd of villagers there assembled were eager in their condolences with his Honour (Uncle A) who showed himself the hero throughout and caused, I imagine, admiration and wonder. He was the merriest of the party, looked on the bright side of it and gave all the operatives some porter, which was the finest trait of all. We found nearly all the furniture saved and stowed away in the loft over the stable. Nobody knows how it happened. The thatch caught first and it is conjectured that it was occasioned by a spark. It was not insured.

The house was then rebuilt on a slightly larger scale with a caretaker's cottage at the back. It was extended by Alfred's son George Fox in 1891, the year after Alfred's widow had died. Planting was continued by his descendants Cuthbert and Philip, followed by the National Trust to whom Glendurgan was given in 1962.

The garden is one of three valley gardens created by three brothers, the other two being Trebah and Penjerrick which respectively were the inspiration of Charles and Robert. Alfred was a man of business, Charles a man of letters and Robert a man of science – he invented the dipping needle which pinpoints the centre of the earth. All three brothers were partners in the family businesses, which at that time included timber, fishing and mining interests, as well as the Falmouth ship agency. All three gardens have views of the sea; it is not known if this was designed to enable the family to see any potential business which might come sailing over the horizon.

In due course with the expansion of their families and maybe a sense of crowding, and too much activity in Falmouth, some members of the family felt inspired to invest in properties outside the town. Although this was principally for recreational activities there is no doubt that the productivity of the land, such as orchards at Durgan, would have entered the equation. There was another magnet: at one time G.C. Fox & Co. had serious interests in the fishing industry, particularly pilchards. A natural diversification was to invest in fish cellars all round the coast of Cornwall and it is just possible that the hamlet of Durgan on the Helford provided this outlet. At Glendurgan there are pilchard-pressing stones to be found along the School Room Walk. In 1923 a Durgan man, John Downing, then in his eighties, recalled how the reading room's quay walls were the same as the old cellar; it had a big door on the south side for rolling pilchard casks over a staging on to a vessel for shipment.

What is more relevant to the expansion of the Fox gardens was the family's shipping connection, which meant that the partners of the business were able to commission ships' captains to bring them interesting seeds from all over the world. For example it is not known if he was specifically instructed but it is said that William Lobb imported from South America the seeds which grew into the monkey puzzle trees at Penjerrick. An apocryphal story is that the introduction of tree ferns to this country was the result of some trunks that had apparently been destroyed in a bush fire near Adelaide in South Australia. Then used as ballast in a ship that came to Falmouth, they were observed to have sprouted. Later on George Fox records that he and other members of the family were recipients from an Italian fishing contact (the firm exported pilchards to Italy) of a gift of olive trees, a genus which the National Trust has recently re-introduced with considerable success.

Members of the family also acted as consuls in an honorary capacity for up to as many as 36 different countries, which may also have deepened their relationships abroad, as well as making them, and their properties, amenable to visitors. In the summer of 1848 Alfred Fox wrote:

… a steamer brought 39 German captains and wives of three of them to Glendurgan to dine with us, in all about 64 at dinner on the lawn. A delightful day.

Left: *Picnic at St Mawes for Glendurgan staff, 1937.*
Left to right: *Mary Stuart and Nellie Williams of Mawnan.*

Below: *Glendurgan House, 1936.*

As is being increasingly realised, the collection of plants and the gentle art of gardening can lead to feelings of peace and contemplation. As an extension of this it fast became a Quaker tenet to establish a Heaven on earth, perhaps rather a loose interpretation of any biblical instruction to cultivate a garden. This predominant and common characteristic, this quest for the divine, may account for the countless garden appraisals which include words such as peace and heaven. As if to confirm the various appraisals there is a part of Glendurgan known as the Holy Corner, or Heavenly Bank, which features trees such as the Judas tree, the tree of Heaven, two types of the tree of the crowns of thorns and the Glastonbury thorn.

Alfred's nieces, Caroline and Anna Maria, founded the Royal Cornwall Polytechnic Society for the education of the underprivileged. It is said they took the word from the French, 'poly-technique'. Many members of the family lectured there on subjects ranging from mackerel to mining. Having a large family, Sarah Fox, Alfred's wife, must have been acutely aware of the value of education. She might also have felt privileged to have been in a position to educate children; it was very much part of a Quaker, as well as a Victorian, upbringing to exercise the mind. It would therefore have been a natural step coming from such a background, steeped in philanthropy, to start in 1829 the first school in Mawnan Smith. As Alfred said, it became 'the object of her care'. It was run in the woods at the end of what has become known as the School Room Walk, until the summer of 1842 when it closed. It subsequently became a cider-house: the cider press is there at the time of writing. The decision to close the school was a very difficult one for Sarah, but it may have led to her son-in-law Joseph Pease building a proper school house in Durgan in 1876. What presumably would have pleased Sarah is the fact that in 2001 the National Trust constructed a replica of the original – better suited these days for the educative needs of small visiting children.

It is my sincere hope that Glendurgan will continue to give pleasure to other families as well as to my own.

New Street Adult School, Falmouth and Friends at their first treat at Glendurgan, 19 July 1886.
Falmouth Adult School was established in 1884. Classes were held at the Friends' Mission Room, New Street, Falmouth on Sundays 9–10.30am. Lessons in reading, writing and biblical instruction were given. A library, savings bank and sick benefit fund was also connected with the school. The officers included Mr G.H. Fox of Glendurgan. The following are included in the group some of whom lived in Mawnan: Ed Goldsworthy, J. Mosney, Jas Dromstick, Chas Baltons, Bennett, John Pascoe, J.H. Hughes, Ronald Cundy, Ronald Uren, J. Davey, Jas Rogers, Jas Williams, Jas Boundy, Wm Pascoe, Skinner, Chas W. May, Chas Hughes, Phil H. Hall, Rd Davies, R.A.V. Bailey, Rob Hein, A. Sisson, H. Coward, Hughes, Stan Andrews, Chas Martin, A.F. Fox, Wm Maguire, Wm Hodge, Davis, Thos Painter, Jas Emmett, Josh Read, Geo Cock, W. Alway, W. Wilce, Frank Jose, Skinner, Fiddick, Ronald Bu, Obad Nicholls, H. Martin, J. Pluit, Fred Gilson, Holland, A. Mountstephens, J.K. Stephens, E. Thomas, W.H. Tregidgo, Geo Wood, H.J. Holland, Geo Devonshire, Wm Morrison, Geo Goodman, Martin, E. Wordsdell, G.H. Fox, J. Godsworthy, Dan Trevarthen, J.E. Downing JP, H. Tuke, Chas Bray.

The Foxes of Glendurgan
by Philip H. Fox

It is reported that my great-grandfather, Alfred Fox, bought the land above Durgan in 1820, where he built a thatch-roofed cottage on the hill, looking across to the far southern shore of the Helford River, and where he started creating the garden now visited by thousands of people every year.

From a marriage certificate in my possession, I read that:

On the sixteenth day of the fifth month, in the year one thousand eight hundred and twenty-eight, Alfred Fox and Sarah Lloyd, daughter of Samuel and Rachel Lloyd of Birmingham in the county of Warwick, appeared before an assembly of Friends, commonly called Quakers, in their meeting house in Birmingham where he, the said Alfred Fox, taking Sarah by the hand declared as followeth: "Friends, I take this, my friend Sarah Lloyd, to be my wife, promising through divine assistance to be unto her a faithful and affectionate husband until it shall please the Lord, by death, to separate us."

Sarah declared likewise and both signed a certificate which was witnessed by some 100 other friends, including such names as Cadbury, Fowler, Edwards, Wilson, Pumphrey and many Lloyds and Foxes – all presumably good Quakers.

In the years to come, they had 12 children – six boys and six girls – all born in different months. These were: Alfred Lloyd; Theodore; Rachel Elizabeth, who married Philip Debell Tuckett; Sarah Charlotte, who married Robert Nicholas Fowler; Mary, who married Joseph Whitwell Pease; Howard, who married Olivia Blanche Orme; Helen Maria, who married John William Pease; Lucy Anna, who married Thomas Hodgkin; Charles William; George Henry, my grandfather, who married Rachel Juliet Fowler; Wilson Lloyd, who firstly married Augusta May Rogers, and then Constance Louisa Grace Rogers; and finally Sophia Lloyd.

I can just remember great aunt Lucy, who lived at Treworgan, Mawnan Smith, as well as Howard and his wife Blanche, who survived him. They lived at Rosehill in Woodlane, Falmouth. I can also clearly remember my great uncle Wilson and his second wife, my aunt Connie, who lived in Carmino, Falmouth. I also have fond memories

Members of the Fox family taken two days after the outbreak of the First World War. Left to right, back row: Ella Pease, George Henry F., Rachel Juliet F., Howard F., Annette F., Wilson Lloyd F., Connie F., Blanche F., Orme F.; centre: Stella F., Lily Gresford Jones, Helen F. (Pease), Lucy F. (Hodgkin), Rachel Elizabeth F. (Tuckett), Violet Hodgkin (Holdsworth); front: George Romney F., Michael Gresford Jones, Ivy F., Meg F., Erica F. (Laity).

of a very dear cousin, whom I called 'Uncle Barclay' – Robert Barclay of Grovehill, Falmouth – after whom we named our first and third sons.

I was brought up in Wodehouse Place, Woodlane, Falmouth – surrounded by relations until 1936, when we moved to Glendurgan.

My eldest son, Robert Hamilton, now living in Dallas, Texas, USA, with his wife Lisa, has a son called George Henry Hamilton, and a daughter named Sophia Isabella. George Henry was named after my grandfather, who was born on exactly the same day 150 years earlier!

George Henry the First, my grandfather, and his wife Rachel had seven children: my father, Cuthbert Lloyd; Barnard; Romney; Annette; Margaret; Erica; and Dorothy. Father and Uncle Romney could never quite agree on how many first cousins they had. While one was quite certain it was only 69, the other was positive it was 72! My mother, Moyra, knew she only had 18 – but, when adding these to my father's, and assuming average productivity from those who were married, I suppose I must have a couple of hundred second cousins! My wife Rona and I had three sons, Robert Hamilton, Charles Lloyd and William Barclay. Robert, as I have said, has two children. Charles and his wife Caroline have three daughters, Meriel, Stella and Roselle. Stella was born on my 70th birthday with half an hour to spare. One day soon I hope Charles and his family will be living at Glendurgan.

My great grandfather Alfred, who started the Foxes at Glendurgan, was born in 1794 – sadly my father never knew him. But how proud Alfred would be to see Glendurgan now, nearly 200 years on and still in good shape, largely thanks to the stewardship of the National Trust, to which it was bequeathed in 1962.

DURGAN SCHOOL, 10 OCTOBER 1828

While Alfred Fox was engaged in matters of horticulture and garden design, his wife Sarah started the first school in the area. It opened in 1828, with Matilda Hill being engaged as mistress followed by Lavinia Chinn in 1832. The school closed in 1842. At the onset of her employment Matilda Hill noted:

I agree to undertake the instruction of the children who may be admitted by Alfred Fox into the school which he is about to establish on his premises, and to teach them spelling, reading, writing and cyphering, also needlework and knitting to the girls, at a rate of £9 per annum. Each child shall pay me one penny per week. A. Fox or myself shall be able to put an end to this agreement on giving three months notice. A. Fox to regulate the hours of attendance and every other matter connected with the school, also the period when the school is to be first opened.

Record was also made of some of the regulations in the school:

A mark to be put down against those who do not sit still and pay attention during the time of reading and questioning, or who go in a disorderly manner to and from their places. All talking to be avoided, and signs to be made by the children instead of speaking. A good mark to be put down on the list for every child that has attended divine service, and for those who repeat the first four lines of a hymn correctly.

A replica of the schoolroom is now in place on the border with the Trebah estate.

Victorian school replica. It was rebuilt by the National Trust and officially opened as a summer-house by Charles Fox, great-great grandson of Alfred and Sarah Fox, on 26 September 2001.

Children of Mawnan School in Victorian costume at the official opening of the Victorian school replica in Glendurgan Gardens, 26 September 2001.

ALFRED FOX'S DIARY EXTRACTS, SELECTED BY L.A. HODGKIN (NÉE FOX), 1911

1830

3/8 I went to Penryn Election and rode round by Glendurgan to see the new pond down in the valley at the end of Pascoe's orchard.

6/8 Assisted masons at Glendurgan who are making the new fishponds. From 1–8pm with R.W. Fox at Boyers cellars trying experiments on spouting fluids: found resistance underwater, same as in air. A revolution has broken out in France.

13/8 Went off (in a boat) three times to see the tucking of pilchards. Was joined at Coverack by Sarah and her brother George Lloyd, Anna Maria and Barclay.

21/8 Went to see Frank Stevens at Cairnky near Half-way House and caught 100 fine trout and 25 small ones. Will put 20 in new pond at Glendurgan and 105 in large pond.

25/8 I rode in company with Barclay to Glendurgan. Called in at Joshua's – saw his specimens found at Pennance and sat up until 12 midnight at home smelting three and four of the said specimens which yielded 1 gram of silver.

30/8 Sarah and I went to Glendurgan and Trelow where we met Sir R. Vyvyan. Lord and Lady Vernon arrived today in their yacht, Harlequin, and sent me a brace of partridge.

10/9 Dr Hodgkin came to see Fred Fox who is suffering from an aneurism. I took Dr. H. to Glendurgan and we dined at Canon Rogers' Mawnan Sanctuary with Dunstanville.

(NB. Fred Fox died on 21/9)

12/11 Sarah and I did some gardening after breakfast. I rode to Glendurgan. The most beautiful meteor I ever saw fell near me as I passed Mawnan Poorhouse.

1831

1/3 Sarah and I spent the whole day at Glendurgan; Sarah at the school and I cutting down trees and planting new ones.

27/4 Charles bought Trebah.

13/5 The pigeon arrived here this evening in 51m from Lostwithiel, announcing the poll to be: E. Pendarves 1542; Sir Chas Lemon, 1524; Sir R. Vyvyan, 794.

18/7 Admiral Coddrington with 13 ships of war in sight all afternoon and evening. Sarah appointed Lavinia Chinn as the new mistress of Glendurgan School.

19/8 We came to Glendurgan to stay.

21/8 Sarah and I rode to and from Falmouth. We walked in the Trebah fields by moonlight.

1832

8/3 Completed the cutting down of trees in Glendurgan. In all, about 4000–5000.

23/3 Went to Glendurgan; busy planting silver and spruce firs. The next day walked in 56½ minutes from Glendurgan to my house in Falmouth and on 30th walked from the cottage to my house in 55 minutes.

29/6 There was an extraordinary meteor at 11pm. It illuminated our rooms with candles burning and appeared equal to the sun in power. It was visible in Falmouth and elsewhere. It appeared to burst over Durgan into stars like a rocket.

1833

2/10 Cholera very severe at Falmouth – 48 deaths.

9/10 59 deaths from cholera and 180 cases.

1/11 I rose at 5am and went on the water until breakfast. The men are still busy with the labyrinth.

1834

9/9 40 years old today. I rose as usual at the cottage at around 6am. Engaged until 8am in thinning the plantation. I took six hives of bees today.

1836

1/1 New years day. Two days ago, Charles bought Rosemerryn Estate (404 acres) for £1600.

1837

14/1 I went with Barclay to Glendurgan for dinner and took plans of orchards that have now been planted close to Durgan. Engaged all day planting apple and pear trees in my meadow, late Pascoes' next to Durgan and in Lashbrook's steep hill next to Cornish's orchard Durgan.

8/4 Our cottage caught fire at 1pm in the roof. It spread rapidly and burnt everything except the major part of the furniture. Our neighbours cordially sympathetic and worked to save our goods and offered asylum to John Peters and family.

5/6 My mother and I journeyed from London to Falmouth to hurry to the deathbed of my dear sister Elizabeth. We left at 10.30am on the 1st June in my mothers carriage. Reached Amesbury (85 miles) at 9pm. Slept. On the 3rd we set off at 3am from Okehampton with four horses and reached home before 2pm (85 miles).

1838

1/6 We slept last night in our new cottage at Glendurgan.

1/8 Negroes in our colonies free, glorious thought awakening gratitude.

1840

American, Danish, Greek and English captains, etc. dined with us.

1841

5/4 A fine daughter arrived weighing 8½lbs – my eighth child. Mama and babe quite prosperous for which favour it is difficult to feel sufficiently thankful.

5/10 John Sterling's lecture on the Advantages of Knowledge was a brilliant display of oratory and intellectual superiority.

27/10 I registered our baby under the name of Lucy Anna.

1842

23/9 Sarah and I walked to the Sanctuary and called on the new rector, William Rogers.

29/9 Our school finally broke up after 13 or 14 years continuance. A sad day.

27/10 I went to Windsor to sleep for the first time in my life. I climbed to the top of the tower in Windsor Castle.

1843

11/3 I bought my first pair of spectacles.

28/5 We are much charmed and affected this evening by the fidelity and affection of a rook for a dead companion.

6/6   I called at Selley's hotel on M. Lamonsoff, the Russian minister at Rio and his two secretaries, Barons Freytag and Knovica. (Emperor Nicholas is in London.) They agreed to dine with us but the weather improved and they left at 5pm. Captain Sullivan was our only guest.

13/6   My beloved Sarah confined of a fine boy, Charles William, our ninth child; a favour which claims a grateful heart.

7/9   One or two whales have lately been seen in Helford river and at Coverack, etc. One was 60 feet long.

4/10   I shot a rabbit from my window last night and seven pigeons at one shot this morning.

1844
One of my Jersey pears weighs 19ozs.

31/10   Barclay and his dear bride Jane arrived at Perran last evening and were received by the assembled multitude with demonstrations of joy etc.

19/11   I planted 60 pear trees in Birdis orchard.

1845
16/5   Rose at 5am. Went by rail to Bristol.

17/5   Again in London. Sir Charles and I called on Captain Beaufort about the railway crossing at Penryn creek also at the Admiralty and on the Board of Trade. Saw Sir G. Clark and J. Shaw Lefevre about oyster beds in the harbour.

4/6   Cornwall Railway passed in Committee.

16/6   Again in London on railway matters.

29/7   I went in a boat to Tregothnan to meet Lord Falmouth and other gentlemen. Rode to Truro to attend a large Railway Committee who fix plans forwarding again to Parliament for a railway from Falmouth to Plymouth. Omnibus to Penryn and on my pony to Glendurgan. A good catch of six mullets and mackerel in my trammel tonight.

27/9   My precious Sarah was confined at 8.15am of a noble boy – our tenth child, George Henry.

1846
16/6   I labelled pear trees and planted 76 Pinus Austriaca and Pineasters on school room meadow edge.

8/7   I start tomorrow for London about Cornwall railway.

17/7   The Lords Commission decided the railway ought to be made from Falmouth to Plymouth.

25/7   The Lords Commission today gave us the preamble of the Cornwall Railway Bill – a great fact resulting from a contest and exertion since 1839 when W.H. Bond and I first resolved in London to use every effort to get a railway through Cornwall after the scheme of 1836 utterly failed.

5/8   Dull am. Very fine pm. Sarah and eight of our children went with me to see the Queen's four yachts which started at 8am for Mounts Bay and Scilly.

6/8   The Queen and her suite arrive here, 7pm.

7/8   I went on board the Black Eagle *and breakfasted with C.E. Anson and Colonel Grey. Prince Albert went to the United Mines and stopped at Polytechnic where Sir C. Lemon, W. Gay and I were on the steps to receive him but he did not come in. I went on board the* Victoria and Albert *with minerals, etc. for the Duke of Cornwall and some native copper for the Princess Royal. By command I went in the Queen's barge to Swanpool to prepare for drawing a ground sean. The* Fairy *came to us and I went on board and then came with the Queen. Prince Albert, Sir Jas Clarke, Colonel Grey and R. Taylor came in another barge but we caught nothing.*

4/10 Alfred yesterday began to learn Italian with Robriou de la Trehonais: £15 per year.

1847
27/1 Our sixth son, Wilson Lloyd was born. A dear babe, he is our eleventh child.

21/2 My dear Sarah came downstairs for the first time to dinner.

11/5 In 1847 there was a great scarcity of food and the miners rose up in a multitude – there was great anxiety. 60–80 soldiers arrived at Falmouth with two guns in consequence of the miners' threats and acts. The firm sold about 1800 quarters of wheat today at 95/ – nearly 9000 pounds worth. A nice supply for our millers in this time of need.

9/6 A messenger from the Mayor of Penryn announced the approach of 4000 miners. I walked with Barclay and Wm Crouch to meet them and dissuade them from their folly, but it proved to be an erroneous report.

16/6 Extremely busy at office till 11.30pm. 160 vessels arrived with grain; 40 came yesterday.

21/6 241 vessels arrived for orders, of which 74 have wheat. Still very busy; at office 'til 10.45pm.

21/12 I saw 190 vessels in the bay this am.

1848

26/1 About 20 Captains invited to dinner but owing to the stormy weather only three came.

28/1 Heavy fall of snow.

22/9 Dear Juliet married Edmund Backhouse. 44 at dinner in Bank dining room, plus a few in another room. Partook of an excellent dinner. The party went to Perran to tea.

28/9 My beloved Sarah presented me this am with our twelfth child: a blooming daughter – a sign of mercy (Sophia Lloyd).

30/10 I went early to bank and found my precious mother sinking. Witnessed the peaceful happy close without a sigh or struggle, within three days of 30 years since my darling father died – touching thought.

1850
24/6 I bathed today, the first time for a year or two, with six of my children at Gyllynvase. Delightful.

2/7 George Croker Fox, my cousin, died, aged 65.

28/12 34 captains of many nations invited to dinner. About 24, 12, or 13 nations dined with us.

1851
1/5 At the Exhibition (London) 9am. The Queen arrived at noon and walked twice from one end to the other. The Duke of Wellington and the Royal family cheered enthusiastically. 2500 persons were present. Such works of art will never again be brought together in all probability.

1853
20/1 We are deeply interested about our dear Rachel and Sam Fox who are much attached to one another.

23/6 Mary married Joseph Whitwell Pease and has gone from us forever. How thankful we should be to resign our precious daughter to the care and love of one whom we so highly esteem, deeply as we feel our loss.

25/7 *Minnie accepted Joseph Pease this evening. My Sarah saddened by the prospect of losing Minnie.*

8/8 *Helen gone to Frenchay school.*

1855
25/1 *Our dear Charlotte gave us our first grandchild, a fine little girl of 7lbs 10ozs.*

31/3 *Received a letter from Egypt appraising us of the death of our dear Barclay on the 10th at a pyramid in Egypt. A grievous blow to us all. J. Hodgkin arrived.*

30/4 *Josephine Fox engaged to Captain Bull, R.N.*

20/8 *My dear Sarah, Howard, Helen and Lucy started with me per* Ordine *steamer for Portsmouth en route to Paris. We stopped at Plymouth in consequence of the leaky state of the ship which had been on the Wicklow Bank. We took tea at our kin cousin H. Fox's.*

Glendurgan Staff & Gardeners

New residences such as Glendurgan, Trebah and Bosloe provided regular employment for many people, and for some such as Miss Caroline Bouts, it was a job for life. She died at Glendurgan in 1914 aged 92, after 55 years as 'a most faithful and devoted maid and friend to Mrs Tuckett and her family.' Miss Mary Stuart, housekeeper in the late 1930s and a long way from her native Stirlingshire, appreciated walking along the cliff paths on her afternoons off. She recalled that, among the many invited visitors to sample the delights of Glendurgan, Matron and the nurses from Falmouth Hospital were given a special welcome.

As the local estate owners would be the first to admit, they were served by excellent gardeners. Such was their reputation that one young man, Mr Harry Smith, was persuaded by guests at Glendurgan to return to America with them, in order to manage their estate, Norberts, in Pennsylvania. Unfortunately it was a short stay; he travelled back to England with his wife and baby, Alan, on 2 January 1915 aboard SS *Haverford*, for he had become very ill.

It was the head gardeners who were instrumental in making the neighbourhood famous for its unusual gardens, as Mr Cuthbert Fox wrote on the death of Mr George Sanderson: 'Mr Sanderson was one of a succession of head gardeners who have done an immense service to horticulture.' Other gardeners included Harry Thomas and Charles Day of Trebah, William Rashleigh of Bosloe, and Jim Vague of Carwinion. All these are

names never to be forgotten among Cornish gardeners. Mawnan churchyard bears the gravestone of John Peters, for 56 years head gardener at Glendurgan. He was followed for a further 50 years by William Eddy, and he in turn by George Sanderson for about 50 years. George was a Northumbrian, and came down to the South West to work for the Tuckett family, who were tenants of the property. He married Kate Eddy, daughter of William Eddy.

By the time Mr and Mrs Cuthbert Fox and their son Philip had given Glendurgan to the National Trust, Jack Nancholas was the head gardener. He had started his career at Ruses' Market Garden in Falmouth, and like his predecessor, married the daughter of another head gardener.

Glendurgan continues to attract the freshest gardening talent in the country, with Steve Porter becoming the youngest ever National Trust head gardener in 2000. He took over the position from Rob James who was also the previous holder of the youngest head gardener's accolade. Keith Moyle moved on to further training at the Royal Botanic Gardens in Kew, and now has a permanent position there – the most important botanic garden in the world. At Glendurgan, Steve is in charge of two full-time gardeners, a careership trainee and volunteers who all help to keep the garden in its magnificent condition.

There are still a few former tenants of Durgan, now at least 80 years old, who remember

Inset: *Alethea Daniels from Redruth, the Glendurgan cook, 1936.*

roaming through the grounds to pick snowdrops, lent-lilies, primroses, violets and bluebells. It was a point of honour that trees and shrubs were never touched! On Saturday mornings these erstwhile children joined Miss Dorothy Fox and her companion, Miss Marsh, for fun and games in the grounds. Christmas parties with treasure hunts were eagerly awaited, as were George Henry Fox's birthday parties. On these occasions, each child in the cove was presented with half-a-crown.

Other family celebrations were shared with the Durgan folk. These included marking the wedding of Mr George Romney Fox to Miss Barbara Twite in 1929 and Mr Philip Fox's marriage to Miss Rona Briggs in 1948. Philip and Rona were welcomed back to Glendurgan with a party on the lawn, and were presented with a silver salver on behalf of the tenants, by the oldest Durgan resident, Mr Jose Downing.

Members of the Fox family were often at sea with a variety of craft coming, going or moored in the Helford River, not far from the shore. Equipment and gear were stored in the large boathouse, which still stands at the Durgan entrance to Glendurgan. In the 1920s and '30s it was the popular meeting-place for the retired fishermen, who repaired and re-painted ready for the next season – a workplace, yes, but a cosy, welcoming one, where more time was spent in gossiping than working. The young lads, keen to earn some pocket money, sandpapered and varnished the spars of the yacht *Dreva*.

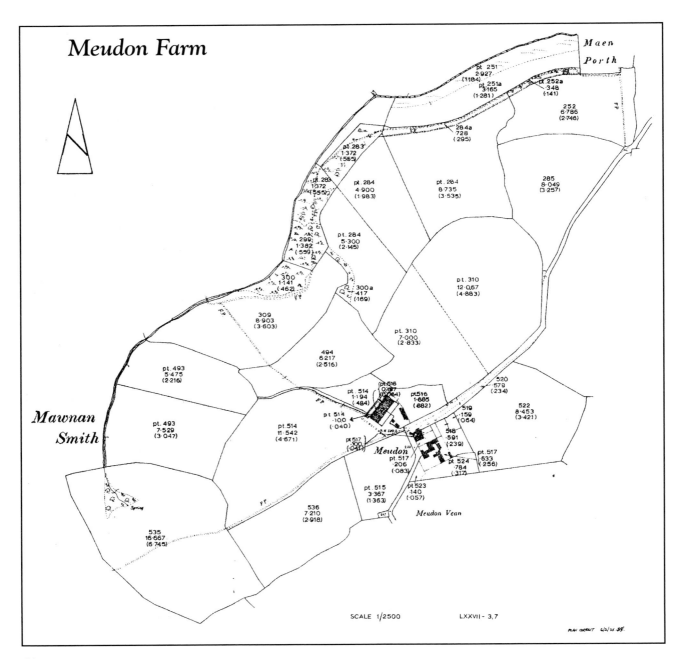

Meudon

The first mention of Meudon is in a document dating from 1250 which includes, amongst other witnesses referring to the benefice of Constantine, an Adam Meuthen of Meudon in Mawnan. Then in 1558 Richard Gerveys Esq. made a settlement of his manor of 'Mewthen' and other lands to provide marriage portions for his four daughters.

Robert Shutford of Kea in his will dated 8 November 1680 gave the poor of Mawnan 10s.0d., while to his executrix he gave 'that part of Mudon which I bought of my brother-in-law Henry Mason.' His will states that he had 'household goods at Mudon – £3.0s.0d., stock and corn in the ground at Mudon – £20.0s.0d. and Estate in the tenement – £20.0s.0d.'

There were various other holders of the manor until John Kemp bought the lease from a relative, who was Lord of Trerose, and between 1700 and his death in 1711 he built the mansion with its farmhouse and ancillary buildings. His widow Mary married Francis Gregor of Trewarthenick and on her death he inherited the estate.

Richard Johns paid the tithes for Meudon from 1814 until 1827, and in 1821 an entry in the Mawnan Parish Register dated 25 July records that Jane Johns married Jose Lorenzo de Trinidade of the City of Lerora Cidadi in Portugal.

The manor was leased by Thomas Willoughby until his death in 1837. His two sons, Thomas and Henry, and his daughter, were all married on 29 January 1838 at Mawnan Church before emigrating with their mother to Adelaide, South Australia. The eldest son had already emigrated to Texas.

An advertisement in the *Cornwall Royal Gazette* on 2 March 1838 reads:

To be let by tender, the capital Barton and farm of Meudon consisting of capital mansion house, walled garden, a capacious farmhouse, barns, stables and other convenient outhouses, 160 acres of arable meadow pasture land and orchards, 25 acres of productive crofts and waste. An excellent lime kiln complete, conveniently situated, also the right to the taking of seaweed and sand from Bream Beach.

In the 1841 census George Fox, aged 50 years and of independent means, is shown as residing in the mansion at Meudon. His servants were Caroline Chinn, aged 15, Ann Chinn, aged 55, and Jane Chinn, aged 12. In the farmhouse was Barnabas Northcott, aged 30 years, his 24-year-old wife Philippa, their son William, aged two, and their daughter Philippa, aged one.

William Armstrong, aged 36, a retired Major of the Dragoon Guards, and his wife Charlotte, lived in a new dwelling known as Meudon Vean at the time of the 1871 census. By the census of 1881 William Northcott, aged 42, with his wife Eliza, son William and daughter Margaret were occupying the farmhouse. During those years part of the orchard garden and plantation situated in the valley that runs down to Bream Cove was divided from the Meudon estate.

In 1893 *Kelly's Directory* listed John Cock as farmer at Meudon. John Tremain was listed in the 1897 directory and in both 1902 and 1906 the farmer was John Wesley Julian. In 1910, ten acres of the Meudon estate were conveyed to Robert Barclay Fox, and it included the lime kiln at Maenporth.

In 1909 the Meudon estate was sold to Joseph Thomas Julian by Robert Fox and Henry Backhouse Fox. The contract included an easement to lay two telegraph cables by the Direct Spanish Telephone Co. under the footpath leading from Maenporth to Mawnan and Meudon to Mawnan.

During the First World War, there was a scheme for purchasing smallholdings and allotments for returning soldiers and in May 1919 Cornwall County Council presented a valuation of Meudon Farm to the Small Holdings Committee. The area of the farm was then 204,081 acres but it was in a very poor state, the hilly areas having been neglected for years and there being no good permanent grazing. The conditions inside the manor house were no better, although there were eleven bedrooms and three sitting rooms as well as the usual kitchen, dairy, etc. There were also two small cottages and various outbuildings, all in bad repair. The County Council offered £3600 for the lot but this was rejected by the owner, Michael Holman of Restronguet Farm, Mylor, who had recently bought the farm from Mr Julian. Finally Mr Holman suggested that he keep over 50 acres of the cliff land and sell the remaining part of the farm to the Council, which was agreed.

In the draft plan the County Council announced that John Rickard, returning soldier of four years' service, would have the No.1 holding. Richard Ruberry, with two sons returning from the war, had No.2. Peter Porter had No.3, while Mr Houghton had accommodation land of eight acres. Mr Eva had nine acres. Mr Trudgan of the Borough Bakery at Penryn, had one acre of land and a bungalow.

Meudon Vean

Meudon derives its name from the nearby Meudon farmhouse, which was first mentioned in 1250. In 1796 Robert Were Fox leased the land for a period of 99 years from James Kempe and Francis Gregor, merchants of Falmouth, and in 1802 started building a house on the site.

In 1864 the Fox family sold it to Miss Elizabeth Ann Barclay for £200 – a lot of money in those days. Elizabeth Barclay had been a nurse and for many years was to be seen driving a wicker carriage around the area, ministering to the needs of the sick in the parish. The Barclays sold the house in 1895 to Charles Francis Cole, whose brother John Cole bought the next-door property, Treworgan, and another nearby property, Rosemullion. He also bought the foreshore to the lowest water mark, from south of Rosemullion to Bream Cove, from the Duke of Cornwall (who later became King George V). However, in 1905 he sold the foreshore to his brother Charles and Justice Sidney Arthur Taylor Rowlatt, KC, of Nansidwell. Charles Cole lived at Meudon Vean for many years and died in Naples in 1925.

Mrs Alice Constance Watts bought Meudon Vean in 1922. It was sold in 1936 to Major General William Henry Snyder Nickerson, VC, CB, CMG, a keen cricketer. In 1943 Lady Edith Worley bought Meudon Vean from Mr Michael Bickford Smith. Lady Worley came from Surrey and she brought with her Eddie, her head gardener, who had been a judge at the Chelsea Flower Show. Together with other gardeners, including George Folkhard and Joe Hojek, she brought the gardens back to the glories they had known in the days of the Foxes and Barclays. The house was expensively furnished and Lady Worley entertained many friends.

However, she could be somewhat eccentric. For example, on one occasion she returned from a visit to Egypt to be told that during her absence a donkey that she owned, called Friar Tuck, had jumped over a fence and hanged itself on its tether. It had been buried in the gardens by the then head gardener, George Folkhard. Lady Worley did not believe this story and thought that the donkey might have been sold, so she demanded that it be dug up so that she could satisfy herself that the animal had indeed died.

In 1964 after Lady Worley died, the contents of the house were put up for sale and the catalogue of this sale shows how expensively and lavishly the house was furnished. The items sold included a number of Kazak, Persian, Wilton and Axminster carpets and rugs; Dresden, Worcester, Wedgwood and Minton china; a vast amount of cut glass; and

antique furniture including Hepplewhite, Queen Anne, Regency, eighteenth-century Italian and seventeenth-century Dutch. Amongst the more prosaic items were a copper coal scuttle and Hoover vacuum cleaner, two shoe scrapers and a green linen garden umbrella with a metal stand.

In 1966 the name of 'Vean' was dropped when Mr and Mrs Harry Pilgrim bought the house and opened it as a hotel. This was done because the couple thought it would be confused with other places that had similar names. Since then a new wing has been built alongside the old house and the hotel is now managed by their son, Mark.

A feature of Meudon is the Tower House, which was built c.1900 as a garden folly. It was enlarged in 1908 and a second floor added to accommodate the head gardener. The Tower House was occupied for a time by the round-the-world yachtsman, Sir Francis Chichester, who used it as a retreat for a few weeks before he died in 1972. It then fell into disrepair and became derelict, but at the time of writing is being restored.

Robbie Nash and Muriel Folkard with donkey 'Friar Tuck'.

Nansidwell Farm

According to Charles Henderson there is only one meaning of the name of this manor: the Church of Saint Sidwell, a holy sister reputedly born at Exeter. There is only one other manor that carries this name, which is near Launceston. He could find no trace of any ancient chapel, nor did the local people remember any such holy place or well.

In the sixteenth century, Nansidwell was the property of the Newcourts, but very little is known about them. William Newcourt married Phillippa Penkievel at Saint Minve, she being the daughter of Sir Francis Penkievel of Roscrowe. He died on 12 July 1620 and was buried in Mawnan Parish Church. A small oak tablet bearing his Arms of Devon design was displayed on the wall of the church, but was later removed.

The tithe account book states that Edward Seccombe and Francis Rowe paid the tithe for Nansidwell in 1805. Walter Humphrey paid it in 1823. However, the latter also paid for a house and orchard, The Smokey Alleys, Harries Tenement, part of the Williams Tenement, all of which were at Carlinick.

On 14 October 1849 Walter Humphrey, with his wife Ann and children Elizabeth, William, Sampson, Frances and Catherine, embarked on the SS *Java* for New York. They then travelled to Iowa where Walter, the eldest surviving son, was waiting for them, as he had gone ahead to purchase land for them. (James, the eldest son, had died at the age of 28 in London where he was Secretary for a Lord Cavendish.)

Later, Nancy Kempthorne, whose father farmed neighbouring Chenhalls Farm joined Walter junr in Iowa and they were married. Walter senr (1788–1869), his wife Ann (1793–1888), their son Walter (1827–70) and Nancy his wife (1826–77) are buried in Illyria Community Church cemetery, in Fayette County, Iowa, USA. Other members of the Humphrey family were buried at Mawnan Parish Church; their head-stones are on the left of the path as you enter the churchyard.

On Monday 29 July 1850 at two o'clock at Selley's Hotel in Falmouth, the desirable farm of Nansidwell was put up for auction. It included 63 acres, of which five were orchard and four young plantation. There was also an excellent walled garden with an ornamental building adjoining, which could be converted into a house. The farmhouse was commodious, the outbuildings recently erected.

In the 1851 Mawnan census, Richard Bolitho (aged 36) was the farmer at Nansidwell. In later years the Hodge family farmed there for two generations. In its last years as a farm Hellyar Tremaine was the occupier.

Nansidwell Farm mowhay and farm buildings.

Penpoll

The first mention we have of Penpoll is in 1675 when the Revd Quarme signed a parochial document fixing the intramural burial fee at £1. With him on that day was John Newcourt of Nansidwell, R. Penwarne of Penwarne, George Ley and Henry Quarme of Bosveal who were all gentlemen with the right to bear arms. Henry Quarme rented Penpoll, and it is unlikely that the Penpoll he rented bears any resemblance to the Penpolls we know today.

The 1823 Mawnan Parish Tithe Account shows that Walter Humphrey occupied Penpoll Wollas (Lower Penpoll); Anthony Warren occupied Penpoll; John Prisk occupied Penpoll Crease and John Pascoe occupied Penpoll Mill.

By 1823, John Manuel was resident at the Penpoll Mill, with 63 acres of land. F. Pender had 12 acres of Penpoll, Newy Treliggan paid £41 in tithes for her part of Penpoll and James Hill paid £14 for his part.

In the 1851 census of Mawnan Francis Hearle was shown to be farming Higher Penpoll, with 63 acres. James Hill was also farming Higher Penpoll, with 30 acres. John Jose, an agricultural labourer, was living as head at Lower Penpoll. There was also a blacksmith, called Anthony Rail.

Between 1950 and the year 2000 two of the Penpolls were absorbed into larger neighbouring farms. However, Lower Penpoll still exists as a unit. The road from Durgan Cross to Higher Penpoll used to continue past the farm, going across the Downs and joining the road near Bosaneth. Another road led from Higher Penpoll down to the creek, passing through Lower Penpoll. Both roads have now disappeared.

Penpoll Mill has become a small engineering factory and is now known as Trenarth Bridge.

Lower Penpoll

The Small Holdings and Allotments Act of 1908 gave the County Council the power to buy land for re-letting to young farming people; so enabling them to farm on their own account in Stithians (see *The Book of Stithians*). Menerdue (The Black Hill) was purchased for this purpose and split up into four holdings, each of about 40 acres. When Frederick George Benney married Elizabeth Annie Gluyas of Stithians, they acquired one of these farms. Much later, Menerdue was flooded to create Stithians Reservoir.

In 1913, when the time came to move to a larger farm, Mr and Mrs Benney rented 80 acres at Lower Penpoll from the Penders of Budock Vean Farm (now the hotel). Mr Benney's sister, Mrs Susan Dunstan and her husband, were the tenants of Budock Vean Farm. There were seven Benney children: Edward Henry (b.1906); William (b.1909); Dot (b.1912); Mary (b.1915); Audrey (b.1916); Betty (b.1921); and George (b.1918), who took over the farm with his wife Phyllis Spargo of Mabe. Their son Edward is, in 2001, the occupier. Lower Penpoll was a typical farm of the last century – sufficiently small to be entirely a family concern. The fields were not large, perhaps about three acres on average and protected by Cornish stone hedges.

With such a large family and such demanding work, it was important to keep to a routine. Monday was washing day, when at least five double-bed sheets had to be washed, dried and ironed. On Tuesday, Mrs Benney did the baking – mostly bread, yeast buns and heavy cake. Wednesday was pasty day throughout the district, and Lower Penpoll was no exception. At school one Wednesday, Audrey chided a friend, Percy Randlesome, for throwing away the end of his pasty, 'You might be glad of that pasty one day.' Percy often recalled these words when he was a prisoner-of-war from 1941–45.

George Benney (1918–1997), helping his father at Lower Penpol, c.1930.

Saturday was an exceptionally busy day for everyone. Willie and Harry were up very early to drive the cattle to Penryn to be weighed, before taking them back to be slaughtered at Bickland Killing House, where the carcasses were sold to the butchers – Medlyn of Constantine and Warrens in Arwenack Street, Falmouth. The early-morning journeys through Budock caused havoc – cows would stray into cottage gardens, with the house-holders shouting and screaming abuse at the two young drovers. Mr Benney travelled to the Killing House to bring the boys back home in the pony and trap.

Mrs Benney was up at 6am every day, even though she rarely went to bed before midnight. By 7am there was a row of clean shoes warming up in the fender for the children. On Saturdays, she went shopping in Falmouth. On a spring Saturday she would purchase all the family's summer clothes in West End Stores, and all the winter garments on an autumn Saturday. (For the girls there were Chilprufe strapped bodices at 5s.0d. each and directoire knickers at 4s.6d.) When Mrs Benney arrived home at teatime, the children accompanied their father to Falmouth. They went to the cinema while he watched the boxing in the Drill Hall, Berkeley Vale. On 16 September 1932 he would have seen Eric Berryman, lightweight champion of Cornwall, defeat Albert Ryall on points in a splendid ten-round lightweight championship. In the afternoon, before going to 'the pictures', Willie went out to set his gin traps in the hedges. When he got back from Falmouth at 10.30pm he had to check them, so his younger sister Audrey held the lantern, while he carried the sack for the unfortunate rabbits. Audrey enjoyed this late-night excursion, as it gave her an opportunity to carry her brother's lantern instead of her own. Willie's lantern had a very bright light as, unlike his brothers and sisters, he kept the glass clean.

On Sundays, the family walked across the fields to Mawnan Chapel, where Audrey and Betty were in the choir and where Mary played the organ. The choirmaster was Mr Albert Cheffers of Carlidnack Lane, head gardener at Bosloe. The girls had to attend choir practice one evening each week, which necessitated another journey across those nine muddy fields.

Mr Benney owned a threshing machine in partnership with two other farmers from Cury, where the machine was housed. At harvest time, he took a team of horses to meet the machine half way. Early in the day, the engine-man cycled over from his smallholding at Porthkellis to light the fire and get up steam. Most of the work, however, was done by members of the family, with occa-sional help from neighbouring farms. When an observer remarked that Dot was as good as a man

at pitching, the reply was: 'Well, she has to do a man's work!' Betty handed the sheaves to brother Willie to build the hayricks in the mowhay. Back in the farmhouse, Mrs Benney was baking apple tarts and brewing up kettles of tea for 'croust time'. Her husband insisted that tea stayed hotter in a kettle. It was Mary's task to carry the heavy kettles of tea out to the workers, with Audrey struggling alongside with the basket of apple tarts, cream and spoons.

All work and no play was not practised at Lower Penpoll. There seemed to be plenty of time for leisure pursuits. The girls belonged to the Girls' Friendly Society, which met weekly in the Memorial Hall. The leader was Miss Cooper, who lived at the newly-built Heyle in Helford Passage with her brother. She was driven to meetings by her chauffeur, Hewett, but always drove herself home. Miss Cooper was rather deaf and is best remembered for having a large ear-trumpet.

In the summer, Audrey and Betty swam in the creek at Porth-naba (known as Anna Maria Creek today). At that time it was a perfect spot for swimming, because it was not silted up with mud as it is now. The grassy bank along the length of the creek was a favourite picnic spot for local families, who rowed up in their dinghies. Later on, the girls walked further afield to join school friends on Grebe Beach. The children participated in all the village activities – flower shows, sports events, concerts, dancing lessons, etc. George in particular was a fine all-round sportsman. During the 1930s, he regularly won the men's half-mile race at the Cottage Garden Society's sports event and when Mawnan outclassed Perranwell in the Wheatly Cobb competition in February 1939, George scored four of Mawnan's eleven goals.

When the boys left school they worked full time on the farm. Mary and Dot's first under-taking was to attend butter-making classes at Constantine, and from then on they cycled round the district on a milk round. This proved to be such a successful venture that Mr Benney had to invest in an Austin 7 to get to the Port Navas and the new Budock Vean Estate. At 14, Audrey was enrolled at Miss Trounson's Girls Collegiate School in Clare Terrace, Falmouth. The two Miss Trounsons, Rose, a large lady, and Annie, were ardent supporters of Pike's Hill Chapel. Audrey travelled to Falmouth by bus every day, arriving back home at 3pm in time for a late lunch.

Although this is a short account of a specific family in the early part of the last century, it was typical of rural life at that time, when families lived, worked and played together and were an integral part of village life.

The Sanctuary

The Sanctuary is an old L-shaped stone house whose walls have mellowed into a silver-grey by the passage of many years. It is said that the house is over 300 years old. The front door and fan light above are Adams, as also is the wide staircase. Many of the passages are made of large blocks of granite and the kitchen floor has very old red tiling and granite slabs. Rumour has it that long ago there used to be a secret passage leading from the kitchen floor right down to the beach; evidently a lot of smuggling went on in those days. This passage appears to have led under the fields to reach the beach at Toll Point. There is also a very old cellar with built-in alcoves. All the walls of the house are about three or four feet thick. In the Sanctuary garden there is a very old well, which is said to be a Holy Well. Its age is unknown but there is a stone gargoyle above the door, which certainly looks ancient. The garden has a magnificent old wall about 15 feet high, built in grey Cornish stone, with a slate roof covering the top of the wall. Here and there it has large granite buttresses.

A 1678 terrier (a register or roll of a landed estate) of the parsonage of Mawnan states that the Sanctuary lay almost east and west with a cross roof pointing towards the south, covered in part with slate and in part with thatch. It comprised five ground-floor rooms and six chambers. Two of the ground-floor rooms were floored with deals, none wainscoted or ceiled. Besides the barn and stable there was an outhouse.

The 1746 terrier shows the Sanctuary to have been enlarged to include six ground-floor rooms and seven chambers. Two of these were still floored with deal, the others with lime and stone, while one was ceiled with paper. The house was stone and covered with slate; evidently the thatch had been replaced by this time. The barn and stable had not been changed, but an outer kitchen had been added.

The Sanctuary.

Trebah

This Celtic place-name suggests that Trebah Farm stands on a site that was settled nearly 2000 years ago. The situation, in a sheltered position with land running up to the crest of the hill (Trebah Wartha, meaning higher) and running down to the river (Trebah Wollas, meaning lower) is typical of those chosen by the Celts when they moved out from their hut circles and fortified rounds in the late Iron Age or early Dark Ages.

As has been mentioned, there is evidence of a number of rounds in the area; and there is one only a short distance from Trebah above Porth Navas creek. Perhaps Trebah's first farmer came from around Porth Navas to Durgan Cove, made his way to the head of the track we now know as Rocky Lane and cleared land to make a homestead.

The track running up from the cove was probably established in even earlier times. Local legend states that it was known and used by Phoenician traders who came to Cornwall in search of tin. A flourishing tin trade was certainly enjoyed during the first and second century BC, although it is more likely that continental merchants, acting as middlemen for the Mediterranean market, bought the tin that was carried down to the Helford River from the tin-producing areas inland. Tin traders probably continued to use the ancient track during the Roman era; a quantity of Roman coins have been found in the parish of Constantine.

The ancient name of Trebah, Treveribou (and sometimes Trevraybou or Treveriba) may be interpreted as the celtic 'Trev' meaning a homestead, plus the personal name of the man who first lived there. Later the occupying family took the name of the homestead; one of the taxpayers listed in the 1327 Constantine Subsidy Roll is Roger Trevraybou.

Early Records of the Trebah Estate

The first written reference to Trebah is in a charter witnessed by Laurence Halapps in 1313 at Treveribou. Laurence was the son of Oliver de Halapps who is listed in a rental of Penryn Manor. Trebah lay within the great manor of Penryn and from the time of the Norman Conquest was under the feudal jurisdiction of the Bishop of Exeter. In the centuries that followed, the freehold tenancy of the Trebah estate passed to various local families, usually by inheritance or marriage. Some will have lived there; others with property elsewhere often sub-let to tenant farmers. Records give only a few tantalising glimpses of these people.

The co-heiresses of John Resewyk of St Keverne inherited Trebah in 1469. One of them, Joan, married Thomas Enys of Enys near Mylor, but it is not known whether her sister crossed the river to live on the land she had inherited. And what of Thomas Vela? The 1538 Penryn Manor Rental shows that he was the freehold tenant of Chiecoys (Chycoose), the Passage, Penansary (Pennance) and Rosemerryn as well as Trebah. And who was Richard Tresegher who sold Trebah Wartha to Edward Humphrey of Philleigh in 1558? In 1574 Edward gave it to his daughter on her marriage to Thomas Rise and when Thomas died in 1613, it was acquired by Sir William Killigrew, already owner of Trebah Wollas and the adjoining Trerose estate.

After the Reformation in the sixteenth century and the repression of the Collegiate Church of Glasney in Penryn, the ancient Manor of Penryn passed into the hands of the influential Killigrew family of Arwenack. Sir William Killigrew, one of the younger sons of John, governor of Pendennis Castle, was said by Richard Carew in his *Survey of Cornwall* to be 'the most kind patron of all his country (i.e. Cornwall) and countryman's affairs at court'. He was for many years a loyal and trusted servant of Elizabeth I and later James I, who appointed him Groom to the Privy Chamber.

Trebah & the Civil War

Sir William died in 1622. In 1635 his son Robert sold Trebah, together with Trerose, to the Governor of Pendennis, Sir Nicholas Slanning of Bickleigh in Devon, who is said to have wanted a country residence in the district. However, Sir Nicholas did not live very long to enjoy his Cornish estates. On the outbreak of the Civil War, the young man raised a Cornish Foot Regiment for the King and led it to victory at Braddock Down, Stratton and Lansdown, before he was fatally wounded outside the walls of Bristol in July 1643.

Sir Nicholas' heir was born on the day his father fell, and in the years that followed the defeat of the Royalists, much of the land he inherited was sold on his behalf to pay the large fine of £999.5s.0d. demanded by Parliament. By 1649 part of Trebah Wartha had been sold to Parliamentarian Lord Robartes of Lanhydrock and part to John Langford of Budock Vean, who later also acquired Trebah Wollas from Walter Hele of Plymouth. Sir Nicholas had sold Trebah Wollas to the Heles just before the outbreak of the Civil War.

The next recorded transaction was in 1709 when Thomas Langford of Budock Vean and John Kessell of Manaccan sold the whole of the Trebah estate to Richard Williams of St Keverne. In a deed dated 4 March 1709, 'the lands called Treribo Wollas and Treribo Wartha' were sold to Richard Williams and his heirs for £331. John Nicholas of St Keverne acquired the estate on his marriage to Prudence Williams, the daughter of Robert and Sibylla and the granddaughter of Richard Williams. Prudence and John were married in Constantine Church on 30 November 1763.

Trebah Farmhouse

It seems most likely that John Nicholas was responsible for building the main part of the present Trebah Farmhouse. He was probably the first owner to live on the estate since the early-seventeenth century. The house was almost certainly built on the site of the original farmhouse. Few, if any, new houses were built with courtyards in Cornwall in the eighteenth century and where such a layout is found – as at Trebah – the new house invariably stands on a very much older site.

The medieval farmhouse was probably in a very poor state by the eighteenth century and it would not have been very large. The Constantine Hearth Tax Returns (1662 and 1664) give some idea of what it had been like a few hundred years earlier. The farmer who lived at Trebah in the 1660s, Edmond Bright, was assessed to pay tax on two hearths, which suggests that it was a traditional small, low building with one room on either side of a central passage and unheated bedrooms above, partly in the roof beneath the thatch. This would have been a typical home for a Cornish tenant farmer, although Edmond Bright might have been expected to have had a somewhat better house. Fairly prosperous, he employed several farm servants and paid a Poll Tax of 6s.5d. His wife Elizabeth also paid 2s.6d. and his daughter Gertrude paid 1s.0d. (As a comparison, Thomas Woolcock of Carwinion paid a poll tax of 4s.2d. and lived in a house with four hearths, obviously enjoying a higher standard of living.)

Edmond Bright's servants each paid tax on one hearth in their one-roomed cottages at Trebah (long since gone) and paid 1s.0d. in Poll Tax. These farm-workers – Nicholas Hugoe, John Short, Anthony Dawe, Sidrack Hugoe, Matthew Julyan and Samuel Coome – were Mawnan people. Their baptisms, and in some cases their marriages, are recorded in the Mawnan Parish Register. Samuel Coome was the son of Francis Coome, the Mawnan blacksmith whose smithy at the crossroads most probably gave rise to the name of Mawnan Smith. Anthony Dawe may have been the son of John Dawe, one of the three Mawnan men who joined the local company under Captain John Penwarne in Sir Nicholas Slanning's Cornish Regiment.

Trebah in the Eighteenth Century

John Nicholas's fifteenth-century farmhouse is typical of the period; a neat façade with regularly-spaced windows and narrow brick chimneys at each end of the roof. The layout of the house – full-sized rooms on both floors at the front, and smaller rooms fitted under an extended roof at the back – is one that was especially popular in Cornwall at the time. Although houses were at this stage being built to a 'double plan' (two rooms deep, unlike the old style where rooms, one deep, were arranged in a row), the Cornish very often showed a preference for this 'linhay' or 'lean-to' plan.

John Nicholas's wife Prudence died in 1776 after 13 years of marriage, and their two children, Dorothy and Richard, both died in infancy. When John died in 1788, Trebah passed to his nephew, William Nicholls, who lived there until his early death in 1803 at the age of 39. Memorials to John Nicholas and William Nicholls embellish the south wall of Constantine Parish Church. William, a wealthy merchant of Falmouth, was almost certainly responsible for the building of the Trebah house, on land adjoining the farmstead.

The Foxes at Trebah

In 1826 Robert Were Fox, of the enterprising and energetic Quaker family of Falmouth, bought the Trebah estate, the farm and the new Trebah house for his son Charles. Charles took possession in 1842 and, presumably because the Nicholls residence had been unoccupied for some years, chose to build a large new red-brick house for himself at the rear. The fifteenth-century buildings at the front became the servants' quarters.

In September 1858, Charles Fox of Trebah was visited by his sister's three daughters, Lizzie Tuckett the eldest, Mariana aged 18 and Charlotte (Charley), who was still a schoolgirl. The long journey from their home at Frenchay near Bristol included an uncomfortable steamer trip from Plymouth to Falmouth. When they reached Trebah they marvelled at the roomy house which had taken the place of the cottage, admiring the small stained-glass windows in the porch and the wonderful serpentine chimney-piece in the drawing room. In the daytime Mariana often walked to Trebah Beach and back with her aunt, and she found the east wind, which often blows there, most exhilarating.

In the 1840s the Trebah farmhouse was occupied by the tenant farmer Pascoe Ellis and two servants, but by 1851 Richard Trevaskis, the Fox's bailiff, was living there. Then, some time before 1861, Charles Fox leased the farm to John Gundry of St Buryan.

When the 1861 census was taken, the farmhouse was occupied by John Gundry, aged 35 (described as a farmer with 96 acres), Margery his wife, also 35, their sons (Richard, who was seven, and John, who was six – both scholars), and ten-year-old daughter Mary. Also living in the house were John Downing, aged 19, and William Downing, aged 16 (both farm servants), Grace Spargo, aged 19 (a housemaid) and Fanny Jones, aged 13 (a churnmaid).

A comparison of the Constantine Tithe Map and the first Ordnance Survey Map of the area, made in 1878, show changes brought about by Charles Fox and his son-in-law, Edmund Backhouse. The farmhouse was enlarged for the Gundry family, some new farm buildings were erected and a drive made from the main road, where a lodge was built.

Trebah in the Twentieth Century

Sir Jonathon Backhouse, Edmund's son, sold the Trebah estate to Charles Hext in 1906. The Hexts, a Devonshire family, had first settled in Constantine in the sixteenth century. The gardens planted by the Fox family attracted many visitors; the Prince of Wales and Mrs Simpson were among guests entertained by Mrs Hext in the 1920s and '30s. Trebah Farm was sold to the Gundrys when the estate was split up after Mrs Hext's death in 1939 (Charles Hext died in 1917). Members of the Gundry family still farm Trebah today.

During the Second World War, Trebah house and gardens suffered badly. In June 1944, 6500 men of the US Infantry Division embarked from Trebah Beach for the D-Day landings in Normandy. This event has been commemorated in recent years at a memorial placed above the beach.

In 1949, shortly after the property had been acquired by Mr Martyn, fire caused considerable damage to the main house. The only part that remained was the old Nicholls house, which had been used as the servants' quarters for Charles Fox's red-brick mansion. This became the main house again. Trebah changed hands several times in the years that followed. From 1961–71 it was the home of Donald Healey, CBE, the rally and racing driver and designer of the Healey sports car. During that time he carried out extensive restoration work, clearing the beach, building a boathouse and restoring the lake in the garden.

A new era began in 1980 when the Hibbert family bought Trebah and, after further restoration work, opened the gardens to the public seven years later. In 1990 the Hibberts gave the estate to the Trebah Garden Trust, a registered charity, which will ensure that the 26 acres remain forever open for the enjoyment of the public.

Trebah Farmhouse.

Above: This house at Trebah Crossroads was originally the Trebah Estate's laundry. The tower was used for water storage.

Right: A cottage at Trebahwartha occupied until the late 1930s by farm workers at Trebah Farm.

Mr Richard Peters, horseman at Trebah Farm. He moved to the above cottage, now demolished, at Trebah Crossroads in 1904 from Job's Water, Constantine. He was trampled to death in the stables in 1926. His children included: Jack, Ellen (Mrs Cocking), Janie (Mrs Thomas, then Bray), William, Thomas (emigrated to Canada), Laura (Mrs Smith), Albert, Hilda (Mrs J.H. Christophers), Alma (Mrs Burley).

Tregarne

Tregarne Farm and Mill lay within the manor of Boskenso which was held by the Penrose family of Helston under the feudal jurisdiction of the lord of the manor of Trerose. In the Mawnan Subsidy Roll of 1327 Nicholas de Tregarn and Rado de Tregarn were each assessed to pay 11d. in tax. The site is typical of celtic farmsteads; situated on granite uplands near the coast with land running down to the valley below, it was settled when people moved out from the enclosed camps, 'rounds', in the Iron Age or early Dark Ages. A possible Iron-Age site can be found near Tregarne at Bosanath.

In 1541 after Thomas Penrose died, John Trevylyan Esq. was said to hold Tregarne, Boskenso and Penpoll. During the early part of the sixteenth century there were disputes between the Trevylyans and the Penwarnes over land at Carlidnack. In 1816 a dispute came before the Star Chamber when Erne Piers, servant of the Penwarnes, was attacked and grievously wounded by servants of John Trevylyan, and Penwarne animals were killed or turned loose from their fields at Carlidnack. Thomas Penwarne is said to have won his case. His son acquired the lease of the farm and mill and it remained in the hands of the Penwarne family until well into the eighteenth century.

It was sold in the 1730s or '40s to Captain Robert Lovell and the farm of 216 acres was divided into four tenements. A map drawn in 1771 for Captain Lovell names his three tenants, all of whom were women; Margaret Hill had 8.3 acres, a dwelling house, which still stands, outhouses and courtilage, an orchard and two gardens 'below the way' (referring to a track which passed through the farmstead across the parish boundary into Constantine); Jane Rose had 8.2 acres, a dwelling house, courtilage and adjoining meadow; and Bridget Stephens had 34.2 acres, a large meadow and a 'little field above'. No house is mentioned so it appears she must have lived elsewhere. Captain Lovell presumably lived in Tregarne Farmhouse. When he died Tregarne passed to his nephew Robert Lovell Gwatkin of Killiow, who sold it in the 1790s to Sir Michael Nowell of Penwarne. It was to remain part of the Penwarne estate until 1934.

In the 1860s Revd Michael Nowell Peters of Penwarne divided the farm into Higher and Lower Tregarne and built a new farmhouse at Higher Tregarne. It was leased to Benjamin Hocking from St Just. Revd Peters was also vicar of Madron in West Cornwall until he died in 1888. He had many West-Cornwall family connections which is perhaps why Thomas Lawry from Morvah in West Cornwall came to Tregarne as a tenant in 1889. The Lawry family remain at Tregarne in 2002. A new farmhouse was built for them in 1903 by Mary Tonkin, daughter of Revd Peters. When the Penwarne estate was sold in 1934 the Lawrys bought Lower Tregarne.

Aerial photo of Lower Tregarne Farm, 1972.

Right: *Reggie Lawry and granddaughter Suzannah at Lower Tregarne farmyard. The old house has been demolished.*

Above: *Lower Tregarne, c.1949.*
Left to right: *Mrs Irene Lawry, Humphrey Harvey (with push bike), Mr Scantlebury, Noel Christophers.*
front: *Percy Lawry.*

Above: *The hounds meeting at Tregarne Farm, January 1958, with Mr Reggie Lawry in the foreground.*

Left: *Reggie Lawry on his hunting horse 'Dan' by Tregarne Cottage.*

Below: *Lower Tregarne Farmyard with the well in the background, 1949. Left to right, back row: Noel Christophers, Joanne Hurst, Stephe (prisoner of war working on the farm), Peter Christophers; front: Percy Lawry and Edward Christophers.*

Above: Left to right: *Thomas Lawry, of Lower Tregarne, with Mr Nicholls and Mr Gundry.*

Treworgan

An agreement for the sale of a portion of the tenement of Treworgan and Chenhalls by Mrs M.F. Rogers of Carwinion and Mr R. Rogers of Falmouth to Mr C.F. Cole of the Salisbury Club, St James Square, London, was signed on the 17 May 1892 for an area of ten acres. The price was £1600.

The house we see today was built and occupied by Mr and Mrs C.F. Cole. Mr Cole's brother lived adjacent, at Meudon Vean. The Coles were fond of boating, so employed a boatman, and constructed a slipway to facilitate the use of their boat. By 1912/13 Mr and Mrs Hodgkin were in residence, but Mr Hodgkin died within months of occupying Treworgan.

Almost at once followed the four years of the war. One of their sons was in the War Office and another son daily expecting imprisonment as he was an 'Absolutist Conscientious Objector'. Yet both found their mother unfailingly able to understand both points of view. The interests of the village of Mawnan Smith occupied much of Mrs Hodgkin's time. The nursing committee and other village efforts always found her to be a warm supporter, while her love for children led her to buy a piece of land for a children's playground so that they could play in safety. She opened the playground in August 1928. Cornwall County Council accepted the gift of land and agreed to be responsible for its upkeep. The playing field still exists albeit in somewhat smaller form, as a portion was taken for a telephone exchange. When the telephone exchange was moved further along Carwinion Road some years later that portion of land then had flats built upon it, St Michael's Court, as can be seen in 2001.

In February 1922 at the Friends' Meeting House in Truro, Mr and Mrs Hodgkin's daughter was married to Mr John Holdsworth of New Zealand, son of the late John and Martha Holdsworth of Eccles. There was no reception at Treworgan, but Mrs Hodgkin entertained the wedding guests in an adjoining room of the Meeting House. It was requested that wedding presents might take the shape of contributions to the Russian Famine Fund or to the recently started Friends' School at Wanganui, New Zealand.

In 1931 Mrs Hodgkin celebrated her 90th bidthday at Treworgan, surrounded by three generations of family. She lived until 1934 and was buried at the Quaker's burial-ground in Falmouth.

The house was then sold to Mr and Mrs Lane. It was reputed that his family helped King Charles during the Civil War. There were two children, Jane and Thomas. Mr Lane died early and Mrs Lane remarried Colonel Sanguinetti. During these years there was an indoor staff of three, with two more workers in the gardens. After the family left, that style of life ended at Treworgan. After many changes of ownership Mrs Martin Oliver bought the property, and on her death Mr and Mrs Hugh Scully became the present owners.

Lucy Anna Hodgkin

Lucy Anna Hodgkin (née Fox), who died at her home, Treworgan, on 26 December 1934, was born at Falmouth nearly 100 years before. Although during the 51 years of her married life Northumberland was her chief home, she loved to re-visit Cornwall and remained always at heart a Cornishwoman. After the death of her husband, in 1913, she returned to spend the remaining 21 years of her life in her native place, and she died and was laid to rest as she wished, in Cornwall.

Lucy Anna Fox was born on 5 April 1841. She was the eighth child and the fifth daughter of Alfred and Sarah (Lloyd) Fox of Wodehouse Place, Falmouth. On 7 August 1861, she married Thomas Hodgkin, the second son of John and Elizabeth (Howard) Hodgkin, of Tottenham. Shortly before, her elder sister Helen had married John William Pease of Darlington. Together the

Mrs Lucy Hodgkin (left) with her daughter Mrs Violet Holdsworth.

two brothers-in-law and their partners succeeded in founding the bank of Hodgkin, Barnett, Pease, Spence & Co., well known for many years in the North of England and finally amalgamated with Lloyds Bank in 1902. Thus the two Cornish sisters were transplanted early to the North, where for many years they lived in neighbouring homes, Pendower and Benwelldene, on a hillside high above the river Tyne, overlooking the beautiful Derwent Valley. Here, at Benwelldene, Thomas and Lucy Hodgkin's seven children were born, and here they spent nearly 30 years of happy married life, filled to the brim with an ever-increasing tide of interests: family, business, socialising, philanthropy, literature and religion.

In 1894, Thomas Hodgkin, at the age of 63, feeling the need for more leisure in which to complete his history, *Italy and Her Invaders*, partly retired from business. He moved with his family first to Bamburgh Keep, on the Northumbrian Coast, and afterwards, in 1899, to Barmoor Castle, Lowick, nearer the Tweed. Here, in 1911, Thomas and Lucy Anna Hodgkin celebrated their golden wedding, surrounded by children, grandchildren, and many neighbours and friends: 'A delightful, exhausting, joyful, sad, back-looking, trembling, exalting, humbling day,' wrote Thomas Hodgkin in his diary.

Two years later, at the ages of 81 and 71 respectively, Thomas and Lucy both felt the need to live in a warmer climate. They spent a trial month at Treworgan, near Falmouth, and from the first moment were delighted with the house and lovely valley garden sloping down to the sea.

They looked forward, with almost youthful zest, to spending their remaining years together 'by the side of the dear Cornish sea.' But this hope was not destined to be realised. Thomas Hodgkin, who had been in failing health for some time, died suddenly on their first Sunday morning at Treworgan, as his wife was waiting for him in the carriage which was to have taken them to a Friends Meeting in Falmouth.

All her life Lucy demonstrated a genious for sympathy. Everyone brought their troubles to her, so sure were they of her ability to offer words of cheer, counsel and comfort. She had 'a heart at leisure from itself, to soothe and sympathise.' When, in 1909, Lucy accompanied her husband, with a son and daughter, on a year's travel among the scattered members of the Society of Friends in Australasia, this gift of sympathy proved invaluable. She won in a few short days or weeks, a place in the hearts of many, both young and old, that no intervening space of years and distance could dim. On her return from this journey, when her own family with two other members of the deputation were reporting their experiences to a meeting, Lucy by her own wish remained silent. Few who were present will forget how, when pressed by the clerk, she rose at last, and said just one sentence: 'Trust utterly. God is better than all your fears.' Speaking in public was always a great effort to her and only in her later years was she able to overcome this and minister to them more frequently. She offered words of prayer or praise that sank deep into her hearers' hearts and contributed largely to the unity of the little meeting.

The Thatched Cottage, Sampys Hill, Mawnan Smith

The following account is adapted from the Women's Institute scrapbook, Mawnan, 1965:

When the 1841 Mawnan census was taken the thatched cottage at Sampys Hill was occupied by the Pascoe family – Sampson Pascoe, a 33-year-old blacksmith, his wife Mary and their three children, George, James and Sampson. In 1861 Sampson, by this date 53, was living in the cottage with his sons Alfred and Edward, who were agricultural labourers, and Sarah 13, Stephen 9, Francis 7 and Lucy 5, all of whom were at school. The family continued to live in the cottage until late in the century when Sampson, by then an old man, became well known for walking up the hill each day to his 'plantation' where the Memorial Hall now stands. When the village roads were named in the 1960s it was decided to name the road 'Sampy's Hill' after the blacksmith who had lived for a long time in the thatched cottage.

The cottage itself is estimated at being between 330 and 335 years old. The earliest mention in papers we have contains a reference to it as two cottages within the estate of Sir Michael Nowell of Penwarne. However, the cottages had been converted into one long before we bought it in March 1963. The only amenity at that time was mains water and this was from a tap outside the front door.

We have attempted to modernise the interior whilst trying to preserve the old Cornish cottage exterior. The outside was cleaned and re-painted, the thatch was covered with wire to keep out the sparrows and the derelict doors on what used to be the stable were replaced by a Cornish stone wall, on which grows a fuschia hedge. The old wooden gateposts had rotted and were replaced with granite and an oak gate. A scullery and outhouse at the back were pulled down and replaced with an extension comprising bathroom, toilet, laundry room, food store and sitting room.

The old part of the cottage had many problems. The upstairs floor had to be strengthened as even our small dog caused the floor to shake when he ran across it. Electricity had to be wired in mineral cable to reduce fire risk. The Cornish range was removed and an oil-fired boiler installed. The clomb oven was partly closed and the top half was formed into a recess behind the sink unit. Water was taken into the cottage but the roof space wouldn't take a storage tank so a boiler had to be fitted. This heats the water through a coil, which gives constant hot water without a cylinder at mains pressure. All the plaster is being removed and the walls are to be replastered. We are gradually getting the cottage redecorated.

At the time of writing, the owner of the thatched cottage is American-born Lorna West from Boston, Massachusetts. On the oak gate is now inscribed 'A Centre for Inner Peace'. Lorna West is a trained and practising psychotherapist as well as a composer and photographer.

The Thatched Cottage.

Inglenook fireplace in the Thatched Cottage.

Cornish range in the Thatched Cottage.

Chapter 5

PLACES OF WORSHIP

Carlidnack Chapel

After John Wesley's death in 1791, there was some dissent within Methodism. Most groups had little influence in Cornwall, but the Bible Christian Movement (1815–1907) had many followers in the West Country. It was successfully organised by a wealthy farmer from Luxylyan, called William O'Bryan, hence the popular name for its followers, the Brynites.

For several years up until 1887, the Bible Christians had been preaching in the old chapel, which had previously been used by the Baptists, but had been closed for a considerable time. This building still stands – immediately next to Norways Farmhouse. As the congregation grew, it became necessary to build a new place of worship. Sir Vyell Vyvyan provided a suitable site on the other side of

the road, for a term of 80 years at five shillings a year. The *Daily Mercury* of Saturday 8 October 1887 reported on the opening of the chapel:

Thursday was a bright day at Mawnan, on the occasion of the laying of the foundation stones of a new Bible Christian Chapel by Miss Fox of Penjerrick, and Miss Barclay of Meudon Vean. The weather being fine, a great many visitors attended from Falmouth and Penryn. At 4.30pm tea was provided for about 160 seated people in a tent kindly lent by the Falmouth Town Mission. At 7pm, a public meeting was held in the tent, Mr. C.B. Kelway took the chair and addresses were given by Messrs Lomas, Badger, Pollard & Dale.

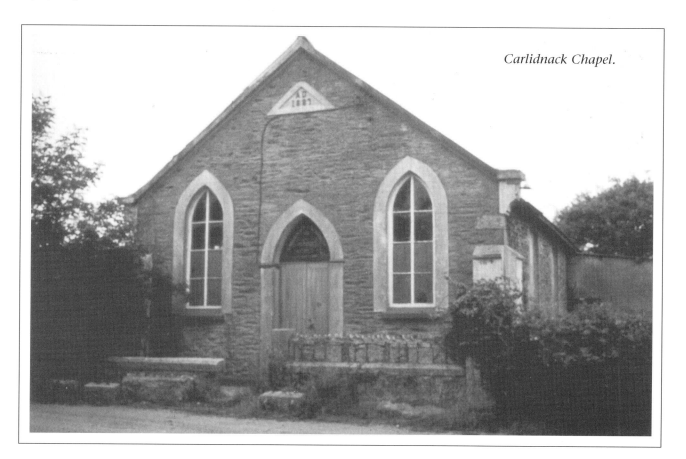

Carlidnack Chapel.

The builder, Mr S. Eva of Falmouth, completed his contract by Christmas, and so the chapel was opened on Thursday 29 December at 3pm, followed by tea in the old chapel. The chapel seated 140 people and the total cost was about £190. The trustees were favoured with a loan of all the money they needed to borrow at a rate of 3 per cent. The old chapel became the room for the Sunday school.

In 1907 when the Bible Christians joined with other churches to form the United Methodist Church, Carlidnack's Chapel was renamed Mawnan United Methodist Church.

Several members of this church joined the Army to serve in the First World War, including Mr Charlie Tallack, the superintendent. Walter Francis Sara enlisted in the DCLI in 1915 and was killed a year later aged 25. He had been employed by Mr Black as a gardener at the Crag.

In February 1918 a Bible and Hymn Book was dedicated in memory of the following local preachers and leaders: James Chappell, Richard Benny, Henry Hodge, Francis Jenkin and John Roberts. Philip Chinn was also included in this list, as he died in 1911. He was aged 76 and died after a severe case of sunstroke when the temperature rose to 103°F in the sun and 80°F in the shade.

The chapel had a thriving congregation, with the usual well-organised social events such as tea treats, outings and anniversary services. The photograph (below left) shows one of the Carlidnack tea-treats, led by the Mawnan Brass Band; they are passing through the village to a field where an outdoor tea was provided. This was in 1913.

Two men who made significant contributions to the life of worship in the village deserve a special mention: George Retallack and Charlie Tallack. Mr

One of the Carlidnack Chapel tea treats lead by the Mawnan Brass Band passing through the village to a field where an outdoor tea was provided, c.1913.

George Jenkin and Christobell Penrose on their wedding day, 24 March 1956. They were the first couple to be married at Carlidnack Chapel, since it was built in 1887. Lady Tuker decorated the chapel for the occasion.

Members of Carlidnack Chapel, c.1950. Left to right, back row: *Charlie Tallack, Bessie Tallack, Edna Ferris, Christobell Penrose, Beryl Musto, Lena Rundle, Mrs Berryman, Mrs Chinn, Mrs Tresidder, Mr Ferris;* centre: *Christine Musto, Leslie Moore, David Rowe, Geoffrey Peppin, Rosemary Forward, Diane Harris, Kathleen Jenkin;* front: *Anne Tallack and young son, Margaret Christophers, Janet Peppin, Susan Christophers, Mary Cocking, Kenneth Peppin, Linda Peppin, ?, Mary Woodgate, John Barrington, Christine Bailey.*

Tallack was one of the volunteer local preachers and Sunday school superintendents for about 50 years until 1959. He was a large, bluff and genial character, who attempted to show in his daily life an example of the christianity he preached on Sundays. He was a keen member of Mawnan Band and his drum became a permanent fixture in the Sunday school porch. He lived with his wife and four children in one of the cottages at Carlidnack, above the red-brick house, and was actively involved in many other village activities. Mr George Retallack ('Blind George') walked to the chapel every Sunday evening on his own from Durgan, a distance of two-and-a-half miles each way. He was forced to stop when the traffic got heavier in the 1930s as it was considered too dangerous for him. George had a good bass voice and sang in the choir and he often played the organ at services. At home he was able to play hymns on his harmonium and listen to his large selection of records on his gramophone (including brass bands, male-voice choirs, Paul Robeson, Dame Clara Butt, as well as more humourous records such as 'Eleven more months and ten more days').

The chapel was not licensed for weddings for many years. The first wedding to take place there was that of George Jenkin and Christobell Penrose on 24 March 1956, with a registrar in attendance. The last baptism to take place in the chapel was of Susan Helen Jenkin on 29 November 1964. The chapel was closed shortly after this, in 1967, and a house now stands on the site. Built into the base of the front wall are the two foundation stones of the chapel.

Mawnan Chapel from 1814

The following is an extract taken from the deeds of the Methodist Chapel dated March 1814:

A plot of land one fifth of an acre, part of the estate of Car-winyon in the parish of Mawnan has been leased at a yearly rental of twenty shillings to William Williams Esq. and William Edwards (Gent). The said plot of land shall include a certain meeting house there in the north west and known as Smith's field. The said gentlemen may peacefully and quietly, have, hold, occupy, possess and enjoy the said plot and can dig as much earth, clay or clob stuff as shall and may be necessary and wanted by them to build every house or houses that may be hereafter erected or built on the said land.

A licence to hold religious services at the place known as the Meeting House at Mawnan Smith was granted in March 1815 to Thomas Truscott by the Lord Bishop of Exeter.

In August 1844 another transaction is recorded. It was known as a release of land, in an exchange between Reginald Rogers Esq. and George Laity (a farmer). The land exchanged was known as Cross Close, Smiths Close and Long Close and was part of the same said premises granted to William Williams and William Edwards in March 1814. The fee was five shillings.

Four years later, in June 1848, 'The First Trustees Deed' was formed. The said gentlemen, William Williams and William Edwards, signed an indenture appointing several men of the parish as trustees of the premises. The following were some of the names included in the list: Humphrey Harvey, Barnabus Northcote, John Odgers and John Kempthorne. In 1879 these or successive trustees purchased a further plot of land measuring four-and-three-quarter poles from Mr S.

Lugg for £13. The said plot was to be hedged in on the south side by Mr Lugg.

In or around 1887 extensive renovations were undertaken. The gallery was removed and the chapel reseated. The woodwork of the old pews was used to line the walls as a dado. At this time the entrance door was at the side with a vestry door over the porch.

The Sunday school was opened in 1902. It was then necessary to close the side door of the chapel and make the entrance at the front. The superintendents at the time were Thomas Harvey and Henry Thomas and the scholars numbered 80.

In 1930 Miss Russel of Little-in-Sight, presented the trustees with a plot of land at the back of the premises. This was enclosed by a wall; the Friends and Sunday scholars provided the blocks at 6d. per block.

In the early days the singing was led by a flute and later an harmonium was installed; for several years there was a string orchestra consisting of one bass viol, one cello and several violins.

There is no record to show which denomination worshipped at the first Meeting House, but from 1814 it has been a Wesleyan Chapel named after its founder John Wesley. Such chapels are grouped together in circuits; Mawnan is one of 18 which form the Falmouth circuit, reaching all the villages for seven or eight miles. There are four ministers and a team of 50 local preachers. As there are 36 pulpits to be filled each Sunday it can be seen how much Methodism depends on its local preachers. This work is entirely voluntary. In days past when transport was difficult these men walked many miles to reach the village chapels and they were given hospitality each week. The circuits are grouped in districts (there are two in Cornwall) and the supreme authority comes from an annual conference with a president who holds office for one year only. During his year of office he holds John Wesley's original bible which is now over 200 years old. In 1934 the Wesleyan United Methodist and the Primitive Societies were amalgamated and their own titles were merged, so that they are now known as just 'Methodists'. This amalgamation service was broadcast. Its first president was the Revd Dr Scott Lidgett, who lived for over 92 years.

During the Second World War the Methodist schoolroom was used as the official rest room and storeroom for emergency blankets and mattresses. The evacuated children from London and Bristol used it for extra schoolroom accommodation. In May 1941 the windows and roof were damaged by a blast following enemy action. They were repaired and the chapel redecorated in 1948. The St John's Ambulance Nursing Division consisted of about 12 women from the district, with Mrs Jackson of Falmouth as tutor, and had now made it their headquarters and first-aid centre, meeting each week for training.

The Guides and Brownies meet regularly in the Sunday school room.

There is a chapel rota for flowers each Sunday. After the service, they are taken to the sick and bereaved in the village.

Many people have worshipped at both chapels for generations. The following are just a few of the others who lived in the district and were devoted workers in the chapels and the Sunday schools: Benjeman Webster, John Chinn, John M. Harvey, John and Charles Roberts, William Houghton.

Leaders of the Sunday school are, in 2001, Mrs Caroline Mitchell and Mrs Rosemary Curtis. The children attend church for the first part of the service, then go to the Junior Church in the adjoining Sunday school room. All the children are remembered with a card and small gift on their birthday and each receives a book token. A special centenary was celebrated in July 2001.

The children sing to the congregation most Sundays and perform in the Harvest celebration. They organise the Nativity Sunday activities for the whole congregation and on Easter Sunday they present members of the congregation with posies of flowers. Members of Mawnan Chapel are very fortunate in having such generous Friends who donate time, money and expertise to their chapel.

The Catholic Church

Like many Cornish villages, Mawnan has an old tale about the building of its first church. The story goes that many centuries ago the villagers were all Catholics and worshipped in one place. The parishioners chose a site on what later became the lands of Nansidwell, towards the Carwinion side, near where St Edward's Church now stands. They began piling stones there for building, but during the night the pixies came and threw the stones into the Helford River. (If you know where to look, near Toll Point, you would see them there still.) After this happened several times, the villagers gave up and looked for a place that would not displease the pixies – which is why the old Parish Church was built at a particular site, at the bottom of Old Church Road.

Mass was celebrated there until the reign of Henry VIII. After the Reformation, Mass was not celebrated publicly in Mawnan until 1952, when Canon George Ford became the parish priest of Falmouth. Bishop Grimshaw gave him permission to say Mass on Sundays in the Mawnan Memorial Hall, provided that at least 20 people attended each week. The hall soon proved too small for comfort, especially when there were many summer visitors. After Canon Ford died, Canon Adrian Chapple came from Bournemouth to replace him. He first celebrated Mass at Mawnan in the summer holiday season of 1962.

St Edward's Catholic Church at Mawnan.

It was one of the days when 120 worshippers attended the Memorial Hall. Much encouraged by this experience, Canon Chapple remarked during the Mass that there ought to be a permanent church in the district. He was glad he had ventured the suggestion, for immediately after Mass Mrs Alice Rose Pilgrim, who lived at Nansidwell, offered him, as a memorial to her late husband (Edwin Albert Ezra Pilgrim), the very site the pixies had rejected many centuries before. Canon Chapple immediately set about obtaining the Bishop's permission, getting local planning permission, and collecting the necessary funds. Money came in with remarkable speed. The parish established a planned giving scheme and many gifts came from people all over the country who were grateful for being able to attend Mass in Mawnan during their summer holidays. Former parishioners who, like so many of the Cornish, had emigrated to distant places, also gave generously.

Canon Chapple knew about the pixies and their previous rejection of this site. Following an Irish custom, he threw a medal of Our Lady into the meadow, and this time the pixies gave no trouble. Building work began on Monday 27 April 1964. The church was designed by Waldo Maitland, a Catholic architect practising in Falmouth. He also went on to build the Catholic church at Helston and the chapel at Tremough Convent. The contractors were Gray Conoley and Co. Ltd, also of Falmouth. The church was finished by 8 December and the Bishop came to open it on 19 December. The total cost of construction was £14,200.

The roof is borne on six portal frames, which relieve the cavity-block walls of weight (although the east wall also bears the weight of the roof, allowing the possibility of extending the building in that direction). The narthex is divided from the nave by a glass screen. The original warm-air heating system, fuelled by an oil-fired boiler, was replaced in October 2000 by quieter and cleaner water-filled radiators and a paraffin-fired boiler.

Local workmanship and materials were used as far as possible. The Catholic Women's League of Falmouth presented the altar of Cornish granite in memory of Canon Ford. The blacksmith of Mawnan Smith, Dryden James, who was still at work in the village, shoeing the few remaining horses, made the altar rails. (He died in

1994.) However, the big stained-glass window of St Edward, given by Mrs Pilgrim in memory of her husband, was obtained from Harry Clarke Stained Glass Ltd of Dublin. As was then required by canon law, a handsome tester or baldacchino was suspended over the altar. The statue of our Lady Star of the Sea was given as a memorial to merchant seamen who were lost in the two world wars of the twentieth century. The font was provided for the baptism of Mark Pilgrim in 1965. The imposing white statue of the Sacred Heart that stands outside the church was re-dedicated by Canon Bede Davis on the feast of the Sacred Heart, 30 June 2000. It was given by the Daughters of the Cross when they closed their convent at Tremough, near Penryn. For many years it had stood in one of the Tremough meadows, a gift from Father Lynch, a chaplain in the US Navy, who enjoyed visiting the convent while his ship was in the River Fal during 1945.

St Edward's congregation has lost none of its vigour and plays a full part in the ecumenical and social life of Mawnan Smith. It is still common to have 120 or more worshippers at Mass in high summer, and at least half that number during the chilly damp of Cornish midwinter. The dedication of the church was suggested by Eddy Pilgrim's name (Edwin). St Edward the Confessor, King of England from 1042 to 1066, was the much-loved patron saint of England before King Richard I placed his crusading army under the protection of St George at the end of the twelfth century. Before the Norman Conquest of 1066, during a time of political strife and instability on the Atlantic seaboard of Europe, St Edward kept England at peace with her neighbours for 20 years. A tall bearded man with a ruddy complexion and fair hair, his generosity to the Church and to the poor was legendary. The people believed he had a gift of curing scrofula by the laying on of hands. A result of this was that the monarch of England continued to 'touch for the King's Evil' for nearly eight centuries. (Queen Anne was the last to perform the rite.) After his death pilgrims flocked to his tomb in Westminster Abbey, which he had virtually founded. His relics still lie there intact in a shrine behind the high altar.

THIS STATUE WAS GIVEN TO TREMOUGH CONVENT BY FATHER LYNCH U.S.N. 27th JULY 1945 WHEN THE CONVENT CLOSED IT WAS GIVEN BY THE SISTERS TO ST. EDWARD'S AND WAS BLESSED AND RE-DEDICATED ON THE FEAST OF THE SACRED HEART 30th JUNE 2000

Inset: *Statue of the Sacred Heart.*
Close up of the inscription on the plaque.

Mawnan Parish Church

A great deal of the information contained in this article was obtained from manuscript volumes compiled by Mr Charles G. Henderson, MA, late of Penmount and New College, Oxford. These volumes are now in the custody of the Royal Institution of Cornwall at their museum in Truro, and access to them was given by the curator, by whose courtesy certain material is here reproduced. Another source for which acknowledgement is due is an article on Mawnan by Mr Henderson, which appeared in the *Falmouth Packet* some years ago and by courtesy of the editor has been made available for use in this book. Other authorities consulted are *The Parochial History of Cornwall* founded on manuscript histories of Mr Hals and Mr Tonkin (1838), edited by Davies Gilbert, and *Lake's Parochial History of Cornwall* (1870). Considerable assistance has also been given by Major R.D. Baird.

The Parish Church of Mawnan was originally dedicated to St Mawnan, the latin form of whose name is St Maunanus, a saint of whom not a great deal is known. One theory is that he was a Breton monk who landed here in around AD520, another is that he was an Irish Bishop who with 27 disciples formed a peripatetic school.

In the fifteenth century the church was re-dedicated and given a second patron, St Stephanus. No reason for this re-dedication is known for certain, but it has been suggested that the Bishops of Exeter during that period, within whose diocese the parish was then included, had a poor opinion of celtic saints and preferred their churches to be dedicated to saints of a more established reputation. It is interesting to note that in a document of 1536 the parish is called 'St Stephen alias Mawnan'.

The church is situated within the confines of an ancient earthwork, which was in an excellent state of preservation until part of it was levelled when the churchyard was enlarged in or around 1920. This earthwork, crowning as it does a commanding eminence on the north side and near the mouth of the Helford River, must have been the rampart of an oval entrenchment. It is probable that primitive churches in celtic Britain were simply enclosures in which a cross was centrally placed.

During the thirteenth century a cruciform building appears to have been erected; there is a reference in 1231 to Eccesia Sancti Maunani. At a much later date the two transepts were

Above: *A view of Mawnan Parish Church from the churchyard.*

Left: *Lych-gate to Mawnan Parish Church.*

THE FOLLOWING POEM WAS COMPOSED ON 11 MAY 1889 BY THE NIECES OF THE REVD ROGERS, JANE, AGNES DENISE AND FRANCES JANE ROGERS, IN CELEBRATION OF THE DEDICATION OF THE CHURCH BELLS ON 24 APRIL OF THAT YEAR:

As we sat in the kitchen one evening in May,
It occurred to us that, Mother being away,
The occasion had come upon which to reveal
The events which took place when they tried the
first peal.

Now such a performance required a great thought,
And William was weary and much overwrought,
And to add to his weariness, wriggles and writhes
Came Tremayne the bounder to pay
up his tithes.

That this should upset the proceedings we need
Scarcely mention, but let us to details proceed.
The time had now come – it was half past three,
And the squash in the Vestry was
painful see –

To inveigle the people the Rector had got
A Canon from Truro, the pick of the lot
Called Woolledge, assisted by Mason and Rood
And game-legged Carnsew, who completed the squad.

The Clergy most solemnly paced up the church
Oh William! What is it you've left in the lurch?
The service most hitchingly scrambled along,
And though some things went right, they mostly
went wrong.

At length comes a pause – no one knowing the plan
Till born on the silence comes PINK A PANG PANG.
So tinny and feeble that no one could tell
They intended the sound for the chime
of the bell.

The service however is ended at last
And the sermon, thank goodness, a thing of the past.
The hymn is announced and the choir begin,
And the people all dive in their pockets for tin.

That something's gone wrong there's no room for doubt,
For Skewes and William seem finely put out.
Where's the bag? said the Rector Oh what shall I do?
I certainly thought I gave it to you.

I ain't 'ad no bag, Sir, Why what do you mean?
I reckon you're worried by Melchy Tremayne.
There's no time to fetch it; collect in you hands,
I expect they will amply fulfil the demands.

Oh no, said the Clerk – could never do that –
would rather go round and collect in my hat.
Having said this he then clattered back to his seat,
And seizing his hat made as tho' he'd retreat.

The sight which ensued no one there can forget,
It quite beats the record of blunders as yet,
Skewes clumped round the aisles hat in hand to receive
The offerings of those who had courage to give.

Convulsed were the people, the clergy in fact
Felt most nervous and did not quite know how to act,
For when all was collected and Skewes advanced,
They shied, almost giggled, retreated and pranced.

The Chef d'oeuvre of Skewes is about to take place,
For imminent now is the chance of disgrace,
But Skewes prevents it from coming to that
By himself on the Altar presenting the hat.

He retires; and our story is now at an end,
But just one more word if we do not offend,
The recessional hymn is now well under way
And they start for the Vestry in blushing array.

Uncle Bill leads the way; and now if we look
We may see that he's covered the hat with a book,
As clasped tight by his bosom he thinks it won't show;
And now we've concluded this bell-ringing show.

absorbed by aisles. The chancel is therefore the sole remaining portion of the cruciform church, but its masonry has been much ravaged by the nineteenth-century restorers.

In the south wall, however, are two interesting thirteenth-century objects: a single lancet window and a piscina. The lancet window is very plain, 40 inches high and 16 inches wide, with coloured glass of recent date. The piscina is trefoil headed and has a semi-circular dripstone terminating in carved heads. Other thirteenth-century relics include another carved head, now mounted at the west end of the north aisle; painting on the north wall which is surmounted by an ancient carved wall plate. This is matched on the south side of the same aisle by a similar wall plate.

In the fourteenth century the tower was built on the site, no doubt having been developed from an earlier structure. It is a picturesque granite building with crocketed pinnacles and a square newel projecting on the north side and extending only to the second stage. In it are hung three bells which it is said were originally dated 1675 and 1760. Two of them bear the words 'Recast by John Warner & Sons, London 1888' and in addition on one 'W. Rogers, Rector 1888' and on the other 'Laus Deo 1888'. The third bell bears the inscription 'May the Church of England Flourish' with the initials A.R. flanking the outline of the bell. The tower arch is quite plain.

Reverend Leverton and the choir of Mawnan Parish Church.

Reverend Leverton, Rector of Mawnan Parish Church, 1890–1934.

At one time there was a minstrel's gallery just to the east of the tower, but no trace of this now remains. It is, however, interesting to note that in a book containing the churchwardens' accounts, to which further reference is made later on, there are the following entries under the year 1803: 'Repairing the gallery doors ls.6d. and for painting the front of the gallery £1.3s.0d.' In the accounts for the year to Easter 1825 the following entry is to be found: 'Paid James Fox for painting the front of the gallery £2.8s.0d.'

In the fifteenth century the north aisle and part of the south aisle were added and the old fourteenth-century windows in the original north wall of the nave were moved to the north wall of the new aisle; the church was practically rebuilt.

Each of the three windows in the north wall is of two lights, the central and eastern windows being trefoil headed. The eastern window in the north wall and the window at the eastern end of the north aisle, the latter being of three lights, are very fine examples of cusping. The two arcades are of granite, the piers which are of the usual section, are eighty inches in height and fourteen inches wide. The octagonal granite font is of late-fifteenth century. Only part of the fifteenth-century screen has been preserved. Part of what remains shows Peter, Andrew, James and John.

At the west end of the north aisle there are two strips of wood bearing the inscriptions, 'Gilbertus Randall fecit' and 'Anno Dni 1684'. This refers to the roofs which were restored in that year.

A seventeenth-century alms box with iron lid and sides stands near the font on a wooden pillar bearing the inscription 'Remember the Poore'. Near the font is a thirteenth-century coffin slab bearing the remains of a floriated cross. It is set into the floor of the north aisle.

In the early days the floor of the church was constantly being disturbed by intramural burials.

This occurred to such an extent that in the 1678 it was found necessary to control the practice by imposing a fee of twenty shillings, which at that time must have been well-nigh prohibitive. It seems that this measure led the parishioners to adopt the practice of digging graves as near to the church as possible. In turn this led the rector John Rogers to give the following public notice on 26 July 1807:

Whereas the church has become damp from too great an accumulation of earth on the outside of the walls, and the foundations of the walls may be undermined by sinking graves too near the [walls], I hereby give notice that I shall not permit any graves to be dug for the future within three feet of the walls of the church. J. Rogers, Rector of Mawnan.

Even then, however, burials within the walls of the church were not unknown. The previously mentioned book containing the churchwardens' accounts records a payment of £1.0s.0d. for a Mr Peters to be interred in the church in 1804. Similarly, in 1811 a charge of £1 was made '... for breaking the ground in the church for Ly Nowell'. This was presumably the lady upon whom for a number of years the church rate had been levied in respect of Penwarne.

From a report of a rural dean it appears that between 1819 and 1826 the church was in a rotten condition; roofs falling and leaking, seats decaying, windows incapable of opening, and the earth outside the building rising to the windows, due apparently to the burials then recently prohibited by John Rogers. A decaying singing gallery blocked up the tower arch. Each seat bore the name of the estate in the parish to which it had been allotted, but many people refused or neglected to keep their seats in decent repair.

In around 1827–30 an ill-advised restoration led to many things of interest within the church being destroyed. The south porch was removed in order to extend the south aisle westwards. Part of the north aisle was also rebuilt and during the work the foundations of the old transept which it replaced in the fifteenth century were discovered. In 1880 the whole church was again restored, this time with more successful results.

Since the Second World War much has been done, at a cost of many hundreds of pounds, to ensure the preservation of the building. In particular the drainage system around the church, which was of a very primitive character, has been modernised and the walls have been re-pointed where necessary. In addition the west walls of both aisles, which were very damp, as well as the walls of the chancel and part of the east wall of the north aisle, have been stripped and re-plastered. In 1948 an electric lighting system was installed in the church and an electric blower was installed on the organ to replace the bellows.

At the back of the former rectory known as the Sanctuary, is the Holy Well. This is about 350–400 years old and was probably first used by the Revd Walter Quarme. It can be found at the end of a deep, narrow ravine, the sides of which are faced with clay slate. The well is at the deeper end of this ravine and is 12 feet below surface level. The archway is a very simple round-headed structure of clay slate or killas, which has been carefully restored. On the exterior above the key-stone is an ancient granite corbel head. The water is about seven feet deep and is remarkably cool and clear. The surplus is carried off by a gutter through the ravine. There is hardly any other well in Cornwall in such a remarkable situation. It was possibly dedicated to the Virgin Mary at one time; the adjoining enclosure still bears the name Lady's Field. The little granite corbel head is of great interest, as it contains three distinct faces – one frontal view and two profiles. This early representation of the Trinity is rarely seen in Cornwall.

It is said that there is also a secret passage leading from the kitchen floor down to the beach, most likely connected with the smuggling which was rife in the seventeenth century. The stables where the squire's horses were kept when he came to church can still be seen at the entrance to the Sanctuary.

Reverend and Mrs A.B. Gunstone. In 1936, after the retirement of Revd Hills through ill-health, the patron of the benefice of Mawnan, Capt. L.G. Rogers, offered the living to Revd Allan Bruce Gunstone, M.A. He was Scottish and had recently returned from South America, where for five years he had been Chaplain to the British community in Valparaiso and Chaplain to the Bishop of the Falkland Islands. Before being ordained, he served in France, then went to Caius College, Cambridge and later, to Westhill House, where he received his theological training. In 1937, the Bishop of Truro, Dr J.W. Hunkin, officiated at the marriage of Revd A.B. Gunstone and Mrs Kathleen Jackson, a widow from Trewince, Port Navas. Mrs Gunstone was a daughter of Mr and Mrs Robert Wilson Paton of Victoria, British Columbia. Revd and Mrs Gunstone had two children, Simon and Moonyeen, plus a housekeeper, known affectionately by everyone in the parish as 'Nanny' White.

Rectors of Mawnan

The following is a list of the rectors of Mawnan and, where known, the years during which they were instituted:

Sir Ralph Renewarde, before 1282
Sir Robert Flammanke, 1328
Sir John de Bodrugan, 1348
Master Roger de Bugworthy, 1348
Sir Ralph Henger, 1350
Sir Reginald Beauchampe, 1361
Sir John Cueffe, 1381
Sir Otho Treflumen
Sir Benedict Walesbreu, 1391
Sir Richard Gabriell, 1398
Thomas Pytyngton, 1405
Sir Richard Beauchamp, 1416
Sir Thomas Peryne, 1448
Sir John Oby, 1475
Master Richard Symons LLB, 1491
Sir Richard Merten (also known as Richard Vercayn), 1499
Master George Trevilian LLB, 1510
Sir John Jamys Alias Lord, 1526
Sir Matthew Selack, 1548
Christopher Trevylian, 1566
John Trevilian, 1586
Thomas Hunt, 1587
Walter Quarme, 1622
Joseph Trewinnard, 1663
William Peter, 1716
Samuel Thomas, 1750
William Peter, 1760
Philip Webber, 1799
John Rogers, 1807
Richard B. Kinsman, 1838
William Rogers, 1842
Henry L. Leverton, 1890
William G. Hills, 1934
Allan B. Gunstone, 1936
Malcolm Osborne, 1965
John Ruscoe, 1970
Patrick Connor, 1985
Nigel James Eva, 1990
David Wilcox, 1995
Harry Francis Jackson, 1996
Geoffrey Bennett, Priest in charge, 2001–

The name at the head of the list is that of the first rector of Mawnan of whom no record can be found and it would seem that at least some of the early rectors had scant qualifications for their office. This is shown in the diocesan records at Exeter, which then included the whole of Cornwall. It states that in 1281 'Ralph Renewarde appeared before the Bishop' and on 20 August 1281 obtained licence of non-residence for two years to study canon law and divinity at Oxford.

It also records Sir Robert Flammanke, whose is referred to as 'Rector, Sancti Maunani' on 17 September 1328, as being granted licence of non-residence for a year beginning 20 September 1337 in order to study. A third such record relates to Master John de Bodrugan who was instituted on 23 February 1348, and of whom it is recorded that on 4 April 1348 he had licence of non-residence for a year to study. Thomas Pytyngton was another of the rectors whose qualifications cannot have been beyond question; nor can his tenure of his office be regarded as creditable. On 7 July 1406 he was granted dispensation to study at Oxford for a year. Following this, on 27 August 1408, he was granted another dispensation for five years having previously suffered sequestration for non-residence and absence.

It should be noted that the use of the prefix 'Sir' cannot be regarded as indicating membership of the order of knighthood. It was merely a courtesy title applied to priests down to the middle of the sixteenth century.

One of the aforementioned rectors, Sir John Oby, who was instituted on 14 January 1475 to 'St Stephen in Mawnan in Kirrier infra Manerum de Treros', was a pluralist and a person of some importance. He was instituted as a Canon of Glasney College in Penryn in 1479 and in 1480 he received the living of St Gluvias at Penryn, as well as one other. In 1491 he resigned from the Mawnan living and was appointed Provost of Glasney College. In that capacity he was responsible for the collection of the tax brought in during January 1497, to meet the cost of the Scottish war waged by King Henry VII. His exactions appear to have been particularly severe and greatly resented by the Cornish of the western districts.

Following the failure of the Peasants' Revolt there came Perkin Warbeck's attempt to seize the throne in September 1497. Cornwall took a leading part in this uprising. However, after its failure and Perkin Warbeck's flight, it is recorded that 'the poor Cornishmen were amazed and disconsolate and very bitter.' It was in this mood that a band of several hundred sea-rovers, who had come to aid Perkin under the lead of one James, met with the unfortunate Provost of Glasney – Sir John Oby – whose exactions against them had been remembered. It was said that he had gathered more money than had come to the King's use. They seized him and brought him to Taunton and:

... there in the market place they slew him piteously, in such ways that he was dismembered and cut in many and sundry pieces. So he perished as example to too officious and eager tax collectors.

St Michael's Church

The church patronage was held by the Rogers family of Penrose, Helston, until the last decade. In 1874 the Rogers family of Carwinion built the church of St Michael, in the village of Mawnan Smith to serve the growing population and to reduce the lengthy journey to worship for a large proportion of the parishioners. This second church was dedicated to St Michael and consecrated on 15 July 1874.

Rising above a cluster of tall elms in the centre of the village, the spire of St Michael's gives passers-by a glimpse of the church's position. Approach it from the granite steps down to the roadway along the Grove Hill Road, or from the longer driveway opening on to the Carwinion Road, next to Trevanion Court. Built from granite, its design includes rectangular buttresses with a four-faceted altar facing east and a small porch jutting out from the far end. The gravel driveway acts as a shortcut for people by-passing the busier forked junction of the road outside the Red Lion.

At the entrance of the porch is the usual notice-board. The heavy oak door opens into the church. Simplicity is the keynote of this small church originally built as a chapel of ease but now used as a central place of worship for many services throughout the year. The oak beams overhead are set like the ribs of an upturned boat and curve down to the deep-set latticed windows. The single bell rope hangs by the end nave window.

The nave is one simple rectangle with its rows of dark oak pews, including hand-stitched kneelers. These were a special project started in 1962 by the Mawnan Church Needlework Guild that was formed especially for this work, as well as for the crafting of the altar frontal and the pulpit fall (and the chancel seats in the Parish Church). The pulpit is carved in a lighter oak. Upon the simple altar stands the rood cross flanked by candlesticks. On the right rests the Communion Bible. Two tapestry footstools depicting chalice patterns rest either side of the altar step. A small table covered with a white lace cloth, upon which is placed the decanter of communion wine, stands next to the altar.

The stained-glass eastern window marks the furthermost end of the church; its panes depict scenes of the crucifixion. Two other inset stained-glass windows either side of the altar window depict scenes of Jesus carrying the cross and the

Above Inset: *The green and gold pulpit fall worked by Mrs Gwen Ward in St Michael's Church.*

Right: *The Bishop's chair embroidered by Mrs Bayley for Mawnan Church in the 1960s.*

St Michael's Church.

The Nativity Play produced by Joan Martin in December 1966 for the Church Sunday School. The cast included five Christophers brothers; the Stevens, Lander, Martin and North sisters; as well as Peter Martin, Andrea Rogers, Gillian Cow-meadow, Andrew Foster, Bill Holliday, Janet Stone and Lorraine Wilkinson.

stone having been rolled away. Two more stained-glass windows, one on the side chancel wall, and one at the top right of the nave show scenes of the Ascension, and of St Peter and St Paul. The bishop's chair stands next to the flower pedestal to the left of the altar. The flower pedestal throughout the year is beautifully filled with a most varied selection of flower arrangements, due to the commitment of the Church Flower Guild. The altar rails are carved in light oak on a scroll design of gold painted wrought iron, worked by the local blacksmith

There are two rows of dark oak choir stalls. The choristers have cassocks of bright red. The organ was installed in 1905, the money being raised by fêtes and bazaars. On the lectern to the right of the chancel rest two bibles, one originally placed in the church some 100 years ago, the other a modern version. A print of an engraving of Leonardo da Vinci's Last Supper, has hung on the right wall of the nave since early in the century. The Mother's Union banner stands behind the font, and on the adjacent wall the Roll of Honour for those killed by war, 'I will go in the strength of the Lord'. A single bell is inscribed in Latin, the translation being, 'St Michael, pray for us'. In 1974 a clock mounted on the outer west wall was bequeathed by the late Cuthbert Fox.

Both churches are served by a loyal congregation and welcome visitors – both to attend services and to just look around. St Michael's participates in services with the children from the local church-aided primary school at Harvest Festival, as well as at Christingle service run by the Mother's Union and at the annual carol services.

Weddings, christenings and funeral services are traditionally held at the Parish Church, although they can be held at St Michael's if the occasion demands it.

Ringing in to the Twenty-First Century

In the middle of the last decade of the twentieth century considerable work was done to make the bells in Mawnan Parish Church ringable again. This included the installation of new bearings, new rope lead pulleys and new rope. At the point when work was completed there were no skilled ringers available in the village. In late 1998, Gail O'Dell and Lindsey Heslop started attending lessons in St Budock's to learn the skills of ringing.

In September 1999 two experienced ringers moved into the village. Nalda and Tony Grimmer had over 60 years' of ringing experience between them. As a result, the bells were rung for the midnight service on Christmas Eve 1999. They joined thousands of other towers to ring in the New Millennium at noon on the first day of the year 2000.

Soon regular sessions commenced; two new recruits, Hazel Stevens and Kay Dumont joined the team and from Easter Sunday 2000 the bells have been rung for every Sunday service in the church. In addition, the Mawnan ringers have celebrated weddings, and with half-muffled bells, funerals and Remembrance Day.

Mawnan is fortunate in having three bells and six capable ringers. It hopes to increase the number of bells to five or six and attract younger ringers to continue the tradition.

Mawnan Burial-Ground

Most sites of religious settlement by the Breton and Irish monks who arrived in Cornwall in the fifth and sixth centuries were secluded and safe, tucked well away in the landscape and not at all obvious from the sea, such as Mylor and St Clement, Lamorran and St Just-in-Roseland. In total contrast the Church of St Mawnan stands conspicuously on the cliff in a magnificent position overlooking Falmouth bay and the Helford estuary.

St Mawnan may well have settled first near the spring, now in the gardens of the old rectory, when he first arrived in Cornwall in the sixth century. However, he established his oratory and burial-ground on the higher drier ground of the clifftop within the confines of an ancient earthwork.

It was not uncommon for the early celtic Christians to settle on prehistoric sites and in the words of the Cornish historian, utilise pagan furniture for Christian purposes. The entrenchment on the cliff was typical of the small circular or oval enclosures known in Cornwall as 'rounds' which were built by the Celts (forebears of the Cornish) who came from the continent during the Iron Age. As warfare was one of the major occupations of Iron-Age society, these bellicose people built fortifications throughout the county, both on the coast and inland. The rounds were probably defended homesteads rather than forts. The other rounds in the Mawnan area lie a little inland but a celtic homestead where the church now stands would have had the added protection of the forts that guarded the estuary – the cliff castles that were on Rosemullion Head as well as Dinas Head, which was on the opposite side of the river. (The Celtic word 'din' implies a fortress or defensive site).

Until comparatively recent times the well-preserved earthbanks, which must have been the rampart of the original site settled by St Mawnan, formed the boundary of the churchyard. Parts of that earthwork still remain today. Describing it in 1916 Charles Henderson wrote that the bank which acted as the churchyard hedge for the western semi-circle of the round was in some places 15 feet in breadth and 7 feet in height and to the south and east a rise in the ground was still plainly visible although the original outline had been partially obliterated when the churchyard was enlarged.

The small enclosure with a diameter of around 150 feet sufficed as a burial-ground for the scattered community just over 100 years ago. Well-to-do parishioners were buried within the church rather than in the churchyard until 1678 when a fee of 20 shillings was levied for intramural burial. Burial within the building was considered a sign of respectability but the near-prohibitive cost forced almost everyone to bury their dead in the churchyard.

By the mid-nineteenth century it was becoming apparent that the old burial-ground could no longer accommodate the growing population of the parish. Whereas in earlier times bodies had been buried on top of existing graves, the ground was already up to four feet above the path in places and there was little room elsewhere for new graves. The steady rise in population during the century is shown in the census returns; in 1801 427 people lived in Mawnan, in 1821 there were 536 and by 1871 the figure had risen to 573. This increase in population was largely due to new estates being established in the area, providing work for both men and women in the large houses and gardens of Carwinion, Glendurgan, Trebah, Meudon Vean and later Bosloe, Nansidwell and Treworgan. The numbers were swollen by newcomers to the village, such as craftsmen (masons, carpenters, blacksmiths, dressmakers and laundresses, cooks, coachmen and shoe makers) as well as coastguards and miners, who worked at Bareppa and the Anna Maria mine at Penpoll. It was obvious that the growing community would need a larger burial-ground.

The administration of the parish was the responsibility of the Parish Vestry, a body of leading parishioners with the Rector as chairman, and in March 1863 it was proposed by Mr Pender of Budock Vean and seconded by Mr Pengilly that the churchyard should be extended. A committee was appointed to make the necessary arrangements and consisted of the churchwardens and others named

by the board. After the customary dinners that followed the meeting another decision was taken – that a fee of ten shillings should be charged for the burial of any non-parishioners in the future.

At a meeting of the committee on 4 May it was agreed that the proposed addition be fenced by a hedge and a proposal by Mr Freethy seconded by Mr Cheffers that the hedge should be let by tender was also carried. The churchwardens Mr Reginald Rogers of Carwinion and Mr Thomas Laity of Trerose were empowered to let it at their discretion. Mr James Treweek of Chatham Cottage proposed that the cost of enlarging the churchyard be defrayed by a church rate to be raised within 12 months of the completion of the work. This was seconded by Mr Hill.

The old book containing the Vestry minutes from March 1838 to September 1863, now held in the County Record Office, unfortunately gives no more information but the work was probably completed that year. Two headstones in this new section bear the date 1863, the earliest being the grave of 33-year-old John Ould. William Cheffers who was a member of the committee was buried there in June 1866. The new extension is clearly shown on the first Ordnance Survey of Mawnan made about 1878. The Tithe Map, drawn 38 years earlier, shows the original small oval bounded by earthbanks, whereas on the Ordnance Survey part of the bank to the east has been levelled and a portion of the adjoining field (glebe land named Church Meadow) added to the old burial-ground. A new hedge is shown running down to join the extended southern boundary and continuing to the cliff.

The churchwardens' accounts give no details of the cost of this work. However, in 1822 the Sexton William Pascoe received £1.16s.0d. for building the churchyard hedge. On that occasion the cost of the carriage of the stone was £2.0s.0d., a surprisingly large sum, particularly if the stone was obtained from the quarry near Trerose only a short distance from the church. After William Pascoe's death in 1847 the Vestry appointed his wife Mary as 'Sextoness'.

In 1794 a man was paid 4s.8d. to break the gravel and form the walk in the churchyard (four days' work). This presumably was the path from the main entrance into the churchyard where nearly 90 years later a lych-gate was built. The gate with a granite coffin rest was made in 1880 at the time of a further restoration of the church. Above the gate there is a Cornish inscription, 'Da thym ythyu nesse the Thu'. Translated this means 'It is good for me to draw nigh unto God'.

Digging on the site brought to light an ancient Celtic crosshead probably contemporary with St Mawnan (making it the oldest Christian relic in the vicinity) which was later built into the exterior of the western wall of the north aisle of the church. On the only visible side is a very irregular 'equal-limbed' cross in relief. Due to careless carving, the left arm is longer than the right and is tilted upwards. A granite cross base, also found at that time buried in the nearby hedge, is said to have been appropriated as a base for a memorial cross in the churchyard – most likely that of the Rogers family of Carwinion.

Above ground the earliest memorials are small, plain eighteenth-century headstones, bearing roughly-carved initials and dates. On the oldest stone, dated 1731, a crude representation of a head or skull with crossed lines beneath has given rise to the local legend that it records the burial of a pirate, a story which never fails to intrigue visitors to the church. Although pirates are known to have sheltered in the Helford River, a fact that probably helped to substantiate the strange tale, the most likely explanation for the skull is that it is a 'mementi mori' – a reminder that death must come to all men – rather than an indication of the deceased's disreputable profession. Morbid symbols of death are frequently shown on seventeenth or early-eighteenth century memorials. When Henry Spoute of Northill was buried in 1685, even the meat plates at the funeral were adorned with 'the death's head' and the words 'Mementi Mori'.

An entry for 1731 in the Mawnan Parish Register suggests that the initials RB which are carved on the alleged pirate's grave refer to Rich Barnicoat, yeoman of Bareppa, who was buried on 18 December 1731. The Register of Burials also gives clues to the initials on other eighteenth century headstones. 'AJ 1745' could refer to Anne Job who was buried on 22 December that year according to the register. Similarly 'CJ 1774' could be Charles Job, buried on 22 December 1774 and 'GP 1749', George Pollard, buried on 24 December 1749 and 'ES 1774' Elizabeth Stephens, buried in March 1774. Only two large eighteenth-century headstones survive; those of John Barnicoat dated 1784 and Nicholas Hill of Penpoll who died in 1799.

Many of the more detailed nineteenth-century headstones tell their own stories. Some are tragedies, such as the drowning of a coastguard, his three sons and a 13-year-old girl from Durgan who were returning from Falmouth in May 1845.

Another stone remembers Richard Rashleigh and his son 'Little Willie' who drowned off Rosemullion in 1882. There are memorials to Charles Wassell and Henry Pinfold whose bodies were found in the Helford River after the wreck of the SS *Mohegan* on the Manacle Rocks in October 1898. A total of 106 men, women and children were lost in this tragedy.

Other headstones tell happier stories; of faithful service to families and the community, and of gratitude and friendship. When Helen Horner died aged 86 a memorial from the Fox family of Trebah paid tribute to an esteemed and faithful servant for over 60 years. Over the grave of Mary Ann Vosper who died in 1857 a headstone erected by Mrs Pender of Budock Vean records 'A Dear Sister Esteemed Servant and Kind Friend. Sincerely regretted, her loss made many sorrow.' Mary Ann Vosper had lived with Mrs Pender for 37 years.

A headstone over the grave of John Peters tells us he was gardener at Glendurgan for 56 years from 1826 when Alfred Fox first began to establish his lovely gardens. Another headstone records James Skewes' 50 years of service as the parish clerk of Mawnan. The village schoolmistress for many years, Winifred James, is remembered simply as 'Miss' with the Cornish words 'Yn Cres', meaning 'At Peace'.

Some memorials include names of sons and daughters who went overseas and never returned: Nicholas Treweeke died in California, Lavinia Downing in Dehra Doon, India, and John Kempthorne, was murdered in the Maungoloigou mountains in New Zealand.

Graves dated 1894 or later lie in an area that was added during the 1890s. This section, originally part of Church Meadow, is shown with an extended and straightened southern boundary, on the second Ordnance Survey (1906). Yet more of Church Meadow was incorporated into the burial-ground in the 1920s and this sufficed until 1969 when the rest of the meadow was included. A beech hedge was then planted inside the western hedge to form a new footpath to the cliff.

The most recent addition was consecrated by the Bishop of Truro on 2 June 1970 following the induction of a new rector, the Revd John Ruscoe. In 1971 a Garden of Remembrance was designed and built in this part of the graveyard by Joe Paget, Mawnan's funeral director and undertaker. After his death in 1980 new lych-gates were made and presented to the church by the Paget family as a memorial to their father.

In recent years relations and friends have sometimes chosen to plant shrubs as memorials: camellias make a splash of brilliant colour in front of the church, and in the newest part of the burial-ground there is a cedar, a memorial to Mrs Mary Plumstead, musician and composer of *The Song of the Royal Duchy*, written and dedicated to the C.F.W.I. A Liquidamber Styracflua was planted by the Mawnan Flower Guild to commemorate the Queen's Silver Jubilee in 1977.

A pleasing innovation has been the placing of seats as memorials. Today parishioners and visitors alike can rest and admire the magnificent view across the estuary from this peaceful burial-ground where wild flowers grow throughout the year and birds sing and nest among the leafy trees and bushes.

Chapter 6

SCHOOL DAYS

Mawnan Voluntary Aided Church of England Primary School

Mawnan School was first established in 1833 on land provided by Revd John Rogers. Seven cottages were also built in the meadow and their rents used for the upkeep of the school and the teachers' salaries. Prior to this there were two 'Daily Schools'. One of these contained 56 males and ten females and was supported by subscription and small weekly payments from the children. The other (at which teaching began in 1823) taught 20 females at the expense of their parents. One of these schools was held in the house on the corner opposite the present Mawnan Post Office, and was run at one time by Miss Jane Nicholls.

Mawnan School was built to accommodate 120 children but it is unlikely it taught that many when it first opened. Children were expected to pay their school fee on a weekly basis and tallies of who had paid were shown on a board in the schoolroom.

The building itself was constructed of cob and local granite. The roof was made from slate-covered timbers, which were exposed inside. The wooden ceiling was varnished and the floor was made of brick. The two classrooms, which were each 12 feet high and 21 feet by 19 feet in area, were lit by a window at each end of the building and one in the middle of the south wall of each classroom. Open fireplaces burned wood and coal during cold weather. The lavatories were the usual primitive earth-closets – two for the girls and two for the boys – situated at the far end of the school yard. The playground was untreated ground, which became very muddy in wet weather. The entrance to the building was through the door in the south wall.

The earliest record of school business is the Admission Register of 1858. Children aged one year, three months, one year, seven months and two years, one month are shown to have been admitted – probably because their mothers had to go out to work or as a result of an emergency. Several of the infants lived two miles from the school.

The Revised Code of 1862 called for the compulsory keeping of a log-book and register. The earliest log-book for Mawnan National School

dates back to 1863. From 1860 Government Grants were available and the Revised Code stated that such grants were dependent on examination results obtained in the school. Her Majesty's Inspector visited the school each year and reported on the children, schoolmaster and other teachers, as well as the buildings and conditions in general. In his report of 1866, HMI wrote:

Register not made up, schedule incorrectly filled in, so that a child of seven years should be presented under the fourth standard – who must there have been wrongly entered for examination last year, etc... I can neither recommend the issue of the Head Teacher's certificate nor be surprised if the Managers see fit to appoint a new teacher.

A caretaker was employed to keep the premises clean, but the headmaster at this time made a punishment of sweeping the floor. The log-book entry of 6 July 1866 reads, 'Several home lessons repeated incorrectly, the children had to stop to sweep for a punishment.'

Three further discreditable annual HMI reports and further grant reductions resulted in the Master, Mr E. Wilkes, 'giving up charge of the school'. This seems to have been the worst period the school has suffered in its history. Reports improved steadily from that time.

The Revd William Rogers was rector of Mawnan from 1842–90 and during this period he took an active and essential role in the running of the school. Each week he would instruct the children in their scripture lessons and the Catechism. He acted as secretary and general supervisor, and led the opening service at the beginning of term and each Monday morning. School supplies were also obtained and distributed by him.

There was a Mistress in charge of the infants and she was responsible for teaching needlework to the older children. Monitors also helped.

The children in Mawnan School initially learnt to write on slates. A slate pencil was attached by string to a hole in the wooden frame. Only when they were proficient were they promoted to copybooks with pen and ink. Blackboards rested on easels for the teachers' use.

In 1867 the dangerous open fires were replaced by closed stoves, and HMI's report stressed the need to replace the brick floor with wood. He also recommended a gallery for the infant's room. This 'gallery' was a series of wide platforms, each a few inches higher than the one immediately in front of it, so that the children might more easily see the teacher – and vice versa. The gallery was erected nine months later. Although the recommendations were worded very politely – 'would be great improvements when the Managers can see their way to making them' – they were expected to be followed. The 1871 report states, 'A wooden floor should, at once, be provided for the main schoolroom or the Grant may be withheld under Article 17(c) New Code'. The new floor was completed within six months.

Mrs and Mrs Burge took charge in March 1872. The yearly reports steadily improved during their period in office. Attendance was still not compulsory but now the numbers on the Roll were increasing. In September 1872 the log-book notes 'increase in payments but it does not seem to keep the children away'. They now paid 2d. for a week or part of a week. The previous master had complained that parents did not send their children to school after an official holiday, Whit Monday and Tuesday for example, because 'they do not like to pay for only three days'.

There were other reasons why the children stayed away: Confirmation classes, potato planting, harvesting, a circus in Falmouth, a threshing machine in the village, threshing competitions, and Band of Hope Treats – although the children had an official half-day's holiday for this purpose, most stayed away in the morning too. There are many entries recorded of individual truancy or 'minching' as it is locally termed. Added to this, epidemics of diphtheria, scarlet fever and scarletina as well as the more common measles, whooping cough and mumps are named as reasons for the low attendance during many weeks. The weather often kept away those living in the furthest hamlets. Snowstorms could reduce the attendance by half.

From 1830, after Alfred Fox had built a house at Glendurgan, many other large houses were built overlooking the valleys which run down to the Helford River. The wealthy businessmen who owned these houses and estates employed many servants. The children of these employees swelled the numbers attending the school and in 1874 HMI's report states:

Great increases in number of scholars – desk accommodation barely sufficient. Should the

school continue to increase perhaps some enlargement will be found desirable or even necessary... The area of the schoolroom allows eight square feet per child for fifty children, which number the average attendance must not exceed.

The Reading Room in Mawnan had been built in 1866, and it was used in 1875 by the 'mixed' school-children when an additional 12 feet was added to the west end of the school. The infants were transferred to the 'mixed' schoolroom. By 27 September the walls of the school were up, the roof was on and the walls had received their first coat of whitewash, so the children returned to the schoolroom. All was not perfect, however; by October the weather was very wet and the new walls were running with water.

The numbers were now 60 boys and 58 girls. Mr and Mrs Burge gave up their charge in June 1876, and Mr and Mrs Hamley took over. Mr Hamley complained that the playground was far too small and that it was difficult to get the children's attention to call them into the school. He purchased a school bell for 18 shillings, which was loud enough for the most reluctant pupils to hear. This same bell has a special place in the entrance of the New School.

From 1873 the teaching of needlework gained importance. The older girls were busy with work which was to be exhibited at the Polytechnic in Falmouth. The monitor, M.A. Peters, won a prize for shirt-making at that exhibition. There were complaints of too much talking in the needlework class – especially as the work had to be finished for inspection by Mrs Rogers and subsequently sold at a bazaar in aid of the new church. The consecration of the new church of St Michael's built on land bordering the school ground was celebrated by a holiday on 13 July 1874.

In December 1874 a log-book entry reads, 'needlework well done, chiefly knitting as warm stockings seem to be in great demand', and in April 1875:

... the girls are generally bringing work for the examination and are trying to do it nicely. The great drawback to the neatness of some of the younger girls' work is the short time which they keep it clean.

The headmaster noted that the girls were not up to the boys' standard in arithmetic, perhaps, he added, because they were engaged in needlework in the afternoons.

Although the premises had been lengthened in 1875, the infant numbers were increasing so that by 1877 there were too few desks and some children had to hold their slates in their hands. As education had been made compulsory from 1876, all children had to attend school from the age of five. Many left when they were nine years old to take up employment locally – the girls to domestic service at the big houses, and the boys to help in the gardens or on the farms. There were a few apprenticeships to local tradesmen. The Education Acts of 1875 and 1880 raised the school leaving age to ten, but it did not significantly alter the pattern.

Mr Vickery was appointed Master in 1879, and Miss (or Mrs – both titles are used in the log-book) E.S. Vickery had charge of the infants. The first mention of a cricket match being played in Mawnan was made by Mr Vickery in his log-book entry in 1883. A number of boys stayed away that day; there are many such entries after that, with the same complaint of absenteeism. Mumps and diphtheria epidemics also caused many absences during Mr Vickery's period of office and his log-book entries show his concern when the children fell behind in their lessons.

Mr W. Borlase succeeded Mr Vickery in 1885 and during his headmastership science and nature study lessons occupied a large part of the timetable. HMI's report at this time included the observation that 'agriculture should be taught only to the boys, as the girls did not take to it so well.'

By this time there were three female teachers, one of whom was the part-time needlework teacher. The visits of the rector were becoming less frequent, limited to the opening service on Mondays and scripture lessons on Monday afternoons. When he died in 1890 the Reverend William Rogers was greatly missed. He had been the only Manager for 47 years. The Reverend H.L. Leverton, who became rector in his place, continued the scripture lessons at the school on Wednesdays.

In wet weather the schoolroom could smell very unpleasant with outdoor garments being hung all around to dry. Mr Borlase records that a lobby was added and that this was a great boon. Several bazaars were held where handicrafts made by the children were sold, to help towards the cost of equipping a new classroom which was built in 1894 on the north side of the larger classroom. With this addition, the school seems to have become large enough to successfully accommodate all its pupils.

This headmaster was the first to make a weekly record of the number of attendees and in 1899 he records 140 on the school roll. Attendances were better – probably due to the fact that in 1891 elementary education was made free and the children no longer had to bring their weekly pence.

Mr Borlase left the school in 1901 to be succeeded by Mr John Moore. There is no record as to when the harmonium was acquired for the school's use, but from 1874 onwards there are constant references by the Diocesan Inspectors in their annual reports to the beautiful singing. A log-book entry in 1875 states, 'the children are pleased to be taught a new school song, but they cannot believe that noisy singing is not the best.'

In the last decade of the nineteenth century the older children were taught geography, scripture and religious knowledge, science (including gardening for the boys), needlework for the girls, reading, writing with pen and ink on paper, arithmetic (including learning mathematical tables by rote), and drawing. The infants learnt to read from the board and from cards, they practised their letters and numbers on slates and worked their sums on slates also until they went up to the next standard, and were promoted to pen and paper.

Drawing deserves a special mention. The encouraging efforts of Mr Vickery in 1880 resulted in a special 'Science and Art Department' grant of £1.6s.5d. and the school received another grant of this kind in 1881. In 1899 this Science and Art Department merged with the Education Department and the Charities Commission to form a new Board of Education. The 1901 Education Act put all forms of national education under the administration of the County Council or County Borough Council and it became known as the Local Education Authority.

Transition

Mawnan National School was now, officially, Mawnan Public Elementary School and the first meeting of the new Managers was on 9 November 1903. They were: Revd H.L. Leverton, Miss Rachael Barclay, Mr John Coles, Mr H. Harvey, Mr Roberts and Mr W.W. Ward. The schoolmaster, Mr John Moore, was also in attendance. One of the first resolutions ratified was that there should be a half holiday once a month if the attendance for the previous month should be 90 or over.

Mawnan School was now to be considered a Non-Provided School. The shift of power made itself felt at once. The Endowment Fund which had brought in a steady, if decreasingly valuable, sum for the school during the previous 60 years, plus the rents of the houses, was now paid to a new account called The Mawnan School Managers Account at the Capital and Country Bank in Falmouth. An inventory of stock had to be sent to the District Clerk and requests for new furniture were to be made through the Managers and their Correspondent to the District Committee.

The rector now had to gain permission from the District Clerk for the use of the schoolroom for a children's concert and a charge of five shillings per night was levied. The Mawnan and District Gardening Association and the Village Brass Band and String Band were obliged to pay one shilling per night for use of the schoolroom. The band had previously paid only 15 shillings for the whole year for their weekly practise sessions and they resisted strongly – but their protestations were in vain.

The lessons provided by the visiting sewing mistress were dispensed with. Henceforth women teachers had to cope with all the subjects taught. The question of swimming lessons was broached but the Managers decided that it was not feasible except in the summer holidays – and the LEA made available a grant of £2 for this purpose. The LEA considered that a playing field was necessary but the headmaster argued that it would not be possible to spare time to play games in the field during school hours. The Managers agreed that the boys had sufficient outdoor exercise in their one and a half hours work in the garden each week, in the physical exercise at 11 o'clock and in their walk to and from school.

The garden produce which the boys had been allowed to take home was now to be accounted for. The District Clerk informed the Managers that since the LEA had provided seed then the sale of produce should bring in enough to repay the outlay. The Managers replied that the produce had no marketable value, but the directive from the Education District Committee ordered that in future sales of produce would have to be arranged.

In 1901 there had been a harsh report by HMI on the conditions of the buildings, etc. He mentioned broken window panes, rough walls and poor sanitary conditions. In 1903 the report suggested that:

... the old gallery in the infants' class should be removed and suitable desks provided and the seating of very young children on forms without backs is certainly objectionable.

Mawnan National School, 1907.
Left to right, back row: *Willie Thomas (Schoolmaster), H. Williams, J. Rashleigh, S. Courage, I. Gundry, A. Mann, A. Eddy, E. Sadler, Arthur Chinn;*
centre: *L. Eddy, J. Rowe, M. Rowe, H. Rowe, B. Ivey, E. Rashleigh, C. Lawry, W. Eddy;*
front: *J. Harvey, J. Williams, D. Mann, R. Lawry, W. Courage, J. Rowe, Alfred Chinn, L. Gundry, E. Ivey.*

In due course the school was improved – repairs effected and the privies re-modelled. Shelters were built in the playground so that the surveyor's report accompanying the School Plan of 1903 was generally approving, except for the criticisms that the playground should be levelled and the cloakroom was still not in accordance with the requirements of the Education Department. The playground was eventually levelled and the water drained off the surface, which flooded the blacksmith's shop next door. Alterations were soon made.

The Education Committee directed that any surplus of the Endowment income after expenses had been accounted for was to be paid to the LEA. The Managers replied that the whole of the income had been applied in repairs.

In 1908 the question of acquiring a piano was raised, but the Managers were not yet able to fulfil the LEA's conditions. More immediately a stove had to be replaced and a suitable cupboard obtained to house the library of 60 books. It took some years, but gradually matters were smoothed out between the LEA and the Managers. The LEA was responsible for the school finances, but the Managers co-operated with the Education Committee to buy a piano in 1924. They also co-operated to buy 67 new library books in 1932, but the Managers presented the school with a sewing machine from their own funds.

The increase in motor traffic had long been a cause of anxiety. Motor signs had been put in suitable places and there were notes of reminders to the children of the care needed on the road. The old hedge in the boys playground adjoining the road was removed, to be replaced by a wall and railings. The road was widened by three feet as a result of the alteration.

Mr John Moore, headmaster from 1901 until his death in 1911, is remembered by one of his pupils as being always fair. Mr Edgar Ivey of Falmouth was a pupil at Mawnan School from 1905 to 1914 and he recalls the paper chases and 'Hunt the Fox' on fine afternoons. Edgar remembered when the headmaster – who had been away from school due to illness for some weeks and had been back at school a few days – collapsed and died in the classroom. The 11-year-old Edgar jumped through the window and ran the 100 yards to his home, to enlist the help of his mother.

The school's first inter-school cricket match was played in 1903 against Falmouth Grammar School and Mawnan won.

Mr Smith of Carlidnack found the head of a Roman Standard when ploughing near the ancient camp. This was brought to the school and caused a great deal of interest.

Miss Winifred Chinn, later Mrs Knowles of Seworgan, was 11 years old in 1908 and recalls:

When I was 11 the master told me that I could try the examination for a special place at Falmouth High School if my parents agreed. They did, and I sat the examination on the following Saturday. On Monday the master told me I had passed, and on the Tuesday I started at the High School. During term time I walked to and from Falmouth every day for seven years – and I was never put off by the weather. I stayed at school until I was 18, and then I came back to Mawnan School as a student teacher to do my year's training (1915) but almost at once I had to go to Constantine because the teacher there had been called up. I was in sole charge of 54 children. I stayed there for a year and then returned to Mawnan. I taught at Mawnan for seven years and then I left to get married.

Mrs Knowles' sister, Mrs Tabb, is three years older, and she remembered the awe with which she peered round the classroom door when a new teacher was in class. She also remembered being made to stand in the corner holding a slate in each hand above her head as a punishment for talking. There was a sewing mistress who would rap the children's hands with a ruler if the work was carelessly done. The children who lived near enough went home at midday for lunch. Those who had to walk to Bareppa managed the mile-and-a-half there and back (and a hot dinner) before the bell rang for afternoon classes. Children who lived in Trenarth brought a packed lunch to school and often took their food to the warm houses of their friends and shared their table. The children from Durgan went as far as the crossroads and were met by some of the mothers carrying their hot pasty dinners.

Mr Stephen Harvey was appointed head-master in 1912. He was a keen gardener and encouraged the boys in the cultivation of the school plots. Dr J. Blamey, who was the Schools Medical Officer for many years, gave prizes for the best-kept plots in the Mawnan Garden Shows and in 1914 Mr J. Downing and Mr W. Eddy adjudicated. Part of their report which was copied into the log-book states:

We were again struck by the cleanliness and neatness which prevailed, and we consider the fact that the boys have been working without supervision for the past four weeks with such excellent results as highly creditable to them as well as to their Master.

The garden plots, each about 16 feet by 12 feet, occupied the land where the bungalow 'Hilbre' stands.

Mawnan School, 1928. Left to right, back row: *Leslie Tallack, Hartley Peters, Stanley Ruberry, George Willmet, Douglas Lewarne, Ivor Rashleigh;* centre: *Mary Benney, May Chinn, Florence Eddy, Audrey Benney, Alice Tresise, Dorothy Eddy, Nellie Thomas, Mr Harvey (Headmaster);* front: *Mary Tresise, Myrtle Simmons, Mary Rickard, Naomi Ould, Kathleen Stevens, Percy Randlesome, George Benney, Gordon Peters, Maurice Simpson.*

Mawnan School, 1935. Left to right, back row: *Warren Richards, Clifton Williams, Stella Mann, Winifred Chinn, Dorothy Chinn, Joan Bray, Ivan Spike, Frank Ruberry;* centre: *Phyllis Playle, May Williams, ? Knowles, Pearl Treneer, Veeny Ruberry, Sylvia Treneer, Mary Mitchell, Reggie Eddy;* front: *John Christophers, Solomon Andrew, Alan Bailey, Cecil Eddy, John Browne, John Rickard, Bernard Badger.*

War

War was declared in 1914 during the summer holidays. Soldiers were quartered in the schoolroom at the beginning of August and this had delayed the work of removing the fixed partition between the main and infants' classrooms, and the erection of a movable glass partition in its place. As a result, the school opened a week later than usual.

In 1916 arrangements were made for children who lived a far distance away to have their dinner at school in comfort. The teachers laid on hot cocoa, and a new stove with an oven was provided in place of one of the older stoves. This was also used for cookery lessons.

The headmaster was called to active service in 1916. He was welcomed back in 1919 to resume his duties, but during his absence Miss W. Harris took charge of the school. During the war the children collected eggs and vegetables to send to the Forces. They were also allowed half holidays for the the purpose of potato planting and harvesting. In the autumn of 1918 children helped at Lower Penpoll, Lower Tregarne, Bosveal and Nansidwell farms with the potato harvesting. By this time there was a Rural Adviser to the County and he came to instruct the boys on manure, lime, insects, etc.

Armistice Day, 1918, was celebrated with a half holiday. In 1920 Mrs R.N. Rogers visited the school on 11 November to address the children. She spoke of the unveiling of the Cenotaph at Whitehall, London, and the burial of the Unknown Soldier at Westminster Abbey.

Secondary Education

The Fisher Education Act of 1918 stated that more money should be spent by the LEA's on secondary education. As a result, more places were available for the brighter children – if the parents were able to take advantage of the opportunity. The preliminary examinations were held at the school, supervised by two of the Managers. The first were held in 1924. The 1918 Act had raised the school leaving age and children who did not gain minor scholarships stayed on at Mawnan until they were 14 years old.

Classes suitable for these older children were arranged. Butter-making classes were held in Boskensoe Farm dairy in 1921, and in 1929 weekly dairy classes were held at Constantine School. The Reading Room in the village was used for domestic science classes, in which the senior girls were taught cookery and laundry. The boys continued their good work in the garden plots and Mawnan School garden was 'Best in the District' in 1921 and again in 1923, when it earned a first prize of £1.0s.0d. and the silver 'Reginald Rogers Cup'.

Special Events

The children did their share of preparing handicrafts and produce for various bazaars and fund-raising efforts to raise money for the new Memorial Hall which was opened on 19 July 1923. They had a half holiday to celebrate its opening.

On the occasion of HRH the Duke of York's wedding in April 1923 the children had a whole holiday and were given a tea party by Mawnan WI.

In 1924 Miss Courage, the infants' teacher, took two of the senior girls from Mawnan School and two from Mabe School to the British Empire Exhibition at Wembley with a party of Cornish elementary schoolchildren.

In 1928 the first Parents' Day was held. The rector, the Revd H.L. Leverton, presided and Mrs Hext JP presented the prizes. The exhibition included handwriting, maps, drawings in pencil and crayon, cardboard modelling and needlework. The County Council presented the playing field for the use of the children; the headmaster was asked by the District Clerk to 'make use of the field as you think fit'. This was the small field south of the council houses in Field Place.

For many years Mrs Hext brought Father Christmas (her gardener) to the school to give presents to each child and member of staff. Another welcome visitor was the Diocesan Inspector, the Revd (later Canon) E.F. Taylor – familiarly known as Tommy Taylor. He was a great favourite of the children and they took delight in bringing flowers to school for his visit. They were examined in the scriptures and then sang hymns and the Te Deum. When he left he took with him the flowers for the Falmouth and Budock hospitals.

Miss James, who taught at the school from 1919 remembered 1933 as the year when she took 16 children to Messrs Fry's Chocolate Factory at Somerdale in Bristol. Also in this year there was a Boy Scouts Rally at Glendurgan and 12 boys from Mawnan School attended.

By the 1930s, the issue of the children's health was receiving more attention. 'Military Drill' had given way to Physical Training with a visiting County PT Organiser. The children who wanted milk could now be supplied with their daily cupful at school.

The senior girls and boys were now able to attend handicraft and cookery classes at the Penryn Centre.

The punishment book records that on 4 May 1936 two boys were guilty of leaving Mr Banfil's bus by the emergency exit against Mr Banfil's wishes, for which dire crime they received the cane once on each hand.

Mr Harvey resigned in 1937 and M. Kingsley-Wood was appointed. He notes that there were 78 children on the registers at that time.

War Again

Part of the preparation for wartime emergency in 1939 was the breaking-up of part of the playground for use as extra garden space. The autumn term was due to start on 4 September but was delayed until the 11th – 'war having been declared and air-raid arrangements to be made'. Several evacuees from the Latymer School in Edmonton, London, arrived during the next few days. They were eventually accommodated in the Village Hall which became a wartime school.

During the summer holidays water had been plumbed into the school and hand basins had been fitted in the porch. The headmaster disagreed with the Managers because they persisted with the earth system for the privies, and there was still no provision for a teachers' lavatory. Flushing toilets were not installed until 1954.

In common with other reception schools Mawnan School was kept open during the usual summer holidays, but attendance was very low. The District Nurse visited once a month instead of once each term. Vigilant notice was taken of any scabies infection. In 1941 the children were given their first inoculation against diphtheria.

The children helped in the war effort by bringing National Savings, collecting waste paper for re-processing, and knitting scarves, helmets, socks, mittens, gloves and pullovers at home using wool provided by the Managers.

Mr Dunn was appointed headmaster in 1940. In July he recorded an air-raid drill, followed two days later by a surprise air-raid and another the following day. The children sheltered in the lobbies until the all-clear sounded at 3.50pm.

Mawnan was bombed on 8 May 1941 and the headmaster made the following entry in the log-book:

May 9th on arrival this morning I found considerable damage had been done to the school by the explosion of two German land mines or very heavy bombs during the night. The lobby roof on the south side was badly damaged and damage was also done to the main roof. One window frame was displaced and a number of panes of glass broken in various windows. The glass in the door between the main room and the infants classroom on the north side was shattered.

The following day saw the arrival of about 100 evacuees from Bristol. They were accompanied by three teachers and some helpers. The Methodist church schoolroom was put into use and the schools, Mawnan and Bristol, merged. The village co-operated well in all ways. When the matriculation candidates from Latymer Secondary School (Edmonton) required the use of the Methodist schoolroom, the juniors' class was given permission to use the Bowling Club Pavilion for a few days. Durgan school was also used for a short period, but was closed in November, and the children returned to Mawnan. Some of the Bristol evacuees went home during the summer holidays and did not come back.

Five pupils were awarded scholarships to the Falmouth Art School in 1943. Forms had to be completed showing numbers of children suitable for 'New Modern School, Grammar Schools and Junior Technical Schools'.

In 1943 the LEA directed that 11 October would mark the beginning of an Agriculture Week. Children over the age of 12 were allowed to assist farmers in lifting potatoes. A comparison with the First World War is interesting – the 15 October 1943 log-book entry reads 'Attendance 93.6% – only one boy absent to lift potatoes.'

In July 1943, 118 children were evacuated to Mawnan from the badly bombed Bromley area in Kent. No teachers arrived with them and since no records were received it took a week to organise the classes. The Methodist schoolroom was officially rented as a schoolroom and was occupied by the infants in the charge of Miss James. Miss Lisle taught the juniors in the east classroom and the headmaster taught the pupils that were over 12 years old in the main room. The north classroom was set aside for the Secondary and Technical Schools evacuees. Two teachers from Bromley eventually arrived.

In January 1945 it was recorded that as only

27 Bromley children were still attending Mawnan School, the tenancy of the Methodist schoolroom was terminated.

Victory in Europe was celebrated in May 1945 with three days' holiday. In September the number of pupils on the roll was 57. Miss Lisle retired leaving a staff consisting of only the headmaster and Miss James. When Miss James was ill, Mr Dunn was left with 30 children in the infants and lower division and 24 in the seniors. The shortage of teachers was acute and Mrs Courage was called in to help for a short time. Mr Dunn left in December 1946 and Mr F.B. Maunder took office on 1 January 1947.

The Growth of the School: 1960s

The Mawnan branch of the Parents and Teachers Association was formed and Mr Maunder explained to the interested parents the plans for secondary education in the Secondary Grammar, Modern and Technical Schools, and the importance of getting the child into the type of school which would be most beneficial.

The acquisition of the large village playing field was welcomed and a local committee was formed for its administration. This committee consisted of two representatives from the school Managers, two from the PTA as well as the headmaster.

The County Library delivered 40 juvenile books in 1974, which was the first of many deliveries. These were placed in the charge of the headmaster to form the school library.

The school had had a flagpole in the yard since Edwardian times. In 1948 the Union Jack was flown and the ceremony of saluting and singing patriotic songs was held on the following occasions:

21 April for Princess Elizabeth's birthday.
26 April for the King and Queen's Silver
Wedding Day.
24 May for Empire Day (in 1948 it was
renamed 'Commonwealth Day').
26 May for Queen Mary, the Queen
Mother's birthday.
10 June for the King's official birthday.

The school held a sports event in 1948, which has since become a regular occurrence. The Coronation of Queen Elizabeth II on 2 June 1952 was celebrated by a week's holiday and Coronation Day Sports were arranged by the staff, followed by tea and the children's carnival.

Mr Maunder was absent from his duties for many weeks during 1954, and during the Christmas holidays he died, a comparatively young man. A county supply teacher filled in until Mr Godwin was appointed headmaster in April 1955.

Folk Dancing Group, 1948. Photograph taken in Miss Arpin's garden at 'Castelnau', Carwinian Road. Miss Arpin had been a pupil of Gustav Holst and made a significant contribution to the musical life of the village. Left to right, back row: *Marlene Warren, Yvonne Snell, Dorothy Curnow, Beryl Musto;* front: *Heather Sandford, Amelia Eddy, Betty Williams, Anne Bray, Margaret Badger, Sylvia King.*

Further Change

The surface of the playground had been macadamised in 1950 – paid for by the Managers. This treatment had the unfortunate effect of causing water, which had previously drained away, to penetrate the wall of the main room at floor level. Over the years the floor of the fireplace in the main room had become burned, as a result of placing buckets of hot ash on the wood. The wood was eventually replaced by fire bricks. A regular fire drill was established, and the necessity for a separate door exit for the north classroom was noted. The new exit was built onto the north wall in 1956.

Extra office work required the services of a school secretary. Mrs Farrell, the first secretary to be appointed, remembered that she was mainly involved with the school meals accounts, plus a small amount of typed correspondence, and stencils which had to be cut and duplicated. This often resulted in almost as much ink on the operator as on the resulting sheets of paper! She was also conveniently on the premises when her son was sent in to tell her he had gained a scholarship to Falmouth Grammar School.

By this time the selection tests for the three different secondary schools were usually called the ten and eleven plus. In July 1957, 47 scholars left the school – 39 went to the Quarry School in Falmouth, three to Falmouth Grammar School, one to Helston Grammar School, one to Camborne Technical College and two to seek employment. The new term started with 56 juniors and infants on the roll.

Mr Godwin left to take up an appointment in Coventry and Mr H.G. Stone succeeded him in March 1958. His ten years as headmaster are notable for the expansion of the school's interests. A school uniform and badge were agreed upon, the PTA being actively concerned. The badge, a cross on a blue background, represents the strong link between the church and school. The black blazer and grey skirt or trousers were chosen with an eye to the future, they accorded with the uniform of the Penryn and Falmouth secondary schools.

With the help of the PTA's fund-raising activities various costly items of equipment were acquired, including a record player, tape recorder, a new duplicator and a 35mm film strip projector. The county authorities helped towards the cost of providing radio and television sets; the school was as well-equipped with such aid as any in the district.

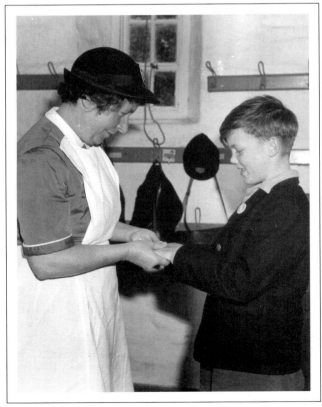

Nurse May, the District Nurse, with Andrew Christophers doing the termly health inspection.

School dinners cooked at central kitchens in Falmouth (opposite the Fire Station) and brought out to the chapel schoolroom to be served by Olive Rowe and Betty Meneer, 1960s.

The influence of the Health Authorities gradually increased. The Schools Medical Officer visited to give oral vaccination against polio and inoculation against diphtheria, tetanus and whooping cough. Vision and hearing tests were made and school dentists attended the school regularly. The dental clinic was available for treatment in Falmouth.

The County Music Adviser came to hear the children's musical efforts on their percussion instruments and recorders. He condemned the piano, which had been so strenuously fought for in 1924, and a new one was delivered.

The school had a maypole, and country dancing displays were highlights of the annual prize days. Such events were held outdoors whenever possible. One of the prizes presented annually is the Latymer Prize. This was a gift from the governors of the Latymer School, Edmonton, to commemorate the hospitality shown to the evacuees by Mawnan people during the Second World War.

The children who were able to swim were tested at Helford Passage by the visiting PE Organiser. A swimming pool was constructed in the school playground in 1963 and in July that year 15 children gained their Elementary Swimming Certificate and one passed the Intermediate Test. By 1965 most of the juniors could swim and several were successful at the Cornwall Schools Swimming Association Area Trials.

A rabbit-hutch, which was home to a rabbit and a guinea pig, was installed in the playground. The infants took it in turns to care for the pets. A wendy-house became part of the infant classroom equipment, and a pile of dressing-up clothes went with it.

In 1967 the Methodist church schoolroom was leased as an infants' classroom. Also, for a period from the 1950s to the 1970s, the Sunday school room was leased as a dining hall. The front door to the school was never the same after the bombs hit the school in 1941. A new door was installed in 1967. The possibility of building a new classroom was considered for a while, but this notion was eventually dropped. By this time the register included 100 names.

Television programmes and films, besides the long-established radio programmes for schools became regular features in the school's timetables. Mrs Benham, a part-time teacher, had a story read on the 'Listen with Mother' radio programme which the infants heard.

The Christmas carol service held in church before term ended in December 1967 was accompanied by the children's percussion and recorders. In July 1968 the school entered its recorder players into the County Music Festival, and they won joint first place. Mr Stone left in 1968 and was succeeded by Mr D.J. Manley. In October he noted that:

Class I moves into the large room, Class II into ex-classroom I, part-time class into room III and the infants into the dining hall (the Methodist schoolroom).

The infants formed a crocodile to walk the 30 yards from their annexe to the safety of the school playground. A barrier had been erected at the door of the Methodist schoolroom for safety (the road is very narrow here) but it was a matter of anxiety to the teachers.

Recording pupils' deaths in the log-books had been very infrequent since 1884, when a diphtheria outbreak had killed four children, three of which were from the same family. Although the log-books record pupils' absences due to their attendance at funerals, deaths of children were unusual after the 1930s. In January 1969, however, a very popular little six-year-old girl died and the occasion was marked by a special service led by the headmaster.

The School in the 1970s

Mr Manley's period in office is marked by the involvement of the children in the school's extra-mural activities. The school sale, an annual event, was held in the Memorial Hall, and the stalls were run by the children. Some of the girls made jam at the headmaster's house, supervised by Mrs Manley.

History lessons became more 'hands-on'. Primed with pertinent questions, the children went to see for themselves such places of historical interest as Mawnan Parish Church, Pendennis, Maenporth Beach, the round field, etc. Truro Museum was visited, followed by a trip down river to Falmouth which returned by coach. In 1970 a trip to Plymouth combined a visit to the Mayflower Exhibition and an educational boat trip to the Brunel Bridge. The children also enjoyed the swimming pool and the zoo.

Local farms were visited and studied; the farmers answered the children's questions on such topics as: growing pedigree see-wheat, rearing calves, the decline of sheep-rearing, winter feeding, breeding sheep to eliminate horns, milking, rearing pigs, annual farming activities, grinding wheat in the mill, birds in the farmyard, etc. Those farmers deserved some praise!

Through the previous 20 years the school roof had given cause for concern and the various inspections by government surveyors and diocesan authorities resulted in the decision to build a new school in Mawnan. The work began in 1971.

The PTA was still very active. Two of the mothers came in for afternoon sessions to supervise craft groups. The craft sale held before Christmas raised money to finance the Christmas party at the Memorial Hall. This was preceded by the school play which became an annual event during Mr Manley's headship.

When the new school's equipment began to arrive the small room was emptied of library books, which were then housed in the porch, so that some storage room might be available for the vast amount of new furniture. It must have been a relief for the teachers of classes I and II to leave all this behind when they accompanied the children on their visit to RNAS Culdrose and the Lizard Lighthouse.

The final entry in the log-book dated 25 July 1972 reads, 'Mawnan school, opened 1834, closed the doors of the original building for the last time as a school after an end of term service in the church'.

The school re-opened in its newly-built premises on Grove Hill in September 1972. For some months the old building remained empty, awaiting the decision as to its ultimate fate, and in 1976 work began on its demolition. A stone bearing the words 'National School 1833' is to be seen in the boundary wall of the new flats, Trevanion Court, which stand on the old site.

MAWNAN SCHOOL PUNISHMENT BOOK: EXCERPTS 1920–1936

NB: *The punishment usually meant a caning.*

DATE	NAME	MISDEMEANOR
22 April 1920	Wesley Christophers	Idleness.
28 April 1920	Tom Peters, Arthur Hurst	Bullying a new boy.
14 December 1920	Hellyar Tremaine, Roddy Thomas	Burning floor and form with hot poker.
4 July 1921	Roddy Thomas	Stone throwing in playground.
27 July 1921	Arthur Hurst	Punching a girl's leg in school.
14 June 1922	Harold Chinn, Teddy Sanderson & William Eddy	Throwing stones in playground.
20 December 1922	Hellyar Tremaine	Indolence during a lesson.
11 January 1923	William Benney, Eric Folkhard	Idiotic giggling for no apparent reason.
	William Eddy, James Cornish & Roddy Thomas	This silly habit of catching each other's eye and smiling for no apparent reason has always been a peculiarity of this school.
27 March 1923	Arthur Webster	Making unnecessary noises with a ruler.
22 October 1923	Colin Hurst	Struggling with his teacher, Miss James.
18 January 1924	Harold Chinn, Ivor Rashleigh	Throwing stones at the church bell.
11 March 1924	Arthur Hurst	Came to school late and said his mother told him to say he should always come late if kept in on a previous day. On telling him that I should give him a black mark, he muttered that I could give him two if I liked.
3 April 1924	Arthur Christophers, Harold Chinn	Interfering with Helen Muir, by throwing stones at her watering-can.
28 September 1925	Harold Chinn	Exhibiting an indecent picture.
13 April 1927	Hartley Peters	Going to the cupboard immediately after being forbidden to do so.
20 May 1927	George Benney, Hartley Peters	Imitating a boy who had been sick.
30 June 1927	Hartley Peters	Using obscene words.

26 July 1927	Leslie Tallack	Disobedient and impudent. Stole out of school after being punished and stayed away all day, his parents not being at home. The following day his father sent a verbal message to the effect that he was going to send his boy to another school.
12 October 1927	William Rashleigh	Sulkily refusing to read or to answer a question.
25 October 1927	Hartley Peters	Taking iron from the blacksmith's shop.
31 May 1929	George Benney	Was told to stay after school but did not do so.
30 September 1929	George Benney, Douglas Lewarne & Gordon Peters	Placing hot nails across the road to puncture tyres.
18 November 1930	Gordon Peters	Cruelty to a cat.
18 November 1930	George Willmett, William Rashleigh, Frances Hodge, George Pascoe Richard Ruberry, Kenneth Tabb & Gordon Peters	Creating a disturbance outside Memorial Hall while a Girl's Friendly Society class was being held.
17 April 1931	Freddie Williams	Striking notes on the piano.
March 1933	Reggie Randlesome, Francis Hodge, Albert Bray Dick Cocking	Writing obscenities on a scrap of paper and passing it around the class.
March 1934	Dick Cocking, Reggie Randlesome & Ernest Lewarne	Squirting water from a water pistol over strangers passing the school.
March 1935	Freddie Williams, Kenneth Symons Charles Mann	Taking pens out of school pen-holders and making darts of them.
4 May 1936	Albert Bray, William Eddy	On returning from Penryn Handicraft class, leaving Mr. Benfil's bus by the emergency exit against his wishes.
19 October 1936	Ivan Spike	Throwing turf at another boy.

The New School in Grove Hill

Mawnan School moved from its original homely, but overcrowded premises to its new campus on Grove Hill in 1972. At this new site a wider variety of interests could be catered for in a modern and spacious setting. The original bell is still rung, but nowadays it hangs from a frame outside the main entrance. In the reception area is another memento from the old building, the sports shield which was made for the 1948 sports meeting. Captains of that first winning team were Eric Pascoe and Betty Williams.

In 1983, a guide to Mawnan was produced by the pupils. It included the following:

Visit Britain's largest Military Vehicle Museum at Lamanva Cross! Nearly 100 British, American and German vehicles are on display, including armoured cars, ambulances, staff cars and even tanks. OPEN DAILY.

Martin Gardner.

There are two banks in Mawnan, Lloyds and Barclays. Barclays is open on Tuesday and Friday. Lloyds is open from June to September on Monday, Wednesday and Friday and October to May on Tuesday and Friday. Both are situated in the centre of the village

Simon Minter.

When the old school was built, it had no gates, so the children went down to the village to play. The headmaster got a bell and put it on the roof and rang it at the end of playtime. This did not work. The children continued to go off and didn't bother to come back in time. So the school had to get some railings and gates to keep them in the school grounds at playtime.

James Laurie.

In 1999, a group of children at the school were involved in writing a song to celebrate the millennium as part of a national competition. It got through to the second round of the Voices of Promise project. Written by Jemimah Gosney, Stephanie Curtis and Katie Pinch, it was performed by Emma Smyth on saxophone, Leah Taylor on keyboard, Joseph Gosney on drums, plus Jennie Gutmanis and Amy Smith on vocals.

The school band plays at many local events and the annual folk dancing at Trebah Gardens on Daffy Down Dilly Day is a colourful sight. The proceeds of the Harvest Auction are used to sponsor Ellensdale School in Zambia. Letters from the African children to their benefactors are eagerly awaited. One recent note revealed that Mawnan's contribution enabled footballs to be purchased, which meant that plastic bags stuffed with paper were objects of the past!

Today, the headmaster Randall Brook and his staff, deliver the National Curriculum, effectively backed by many attractive facilities, including playing field, netball court, gymnasium, kiln, audio and visual aids, two well-stocked libraries and a computer suite. The Parent Teacher Association funded the adventure play area, with the pièce de résistance being a decommissioned Newlyn fishing boat, The *Hollena*. Environmental education resources include a botanical pond and garden plots, as well as the nature reserve in nearby Carwinion woods. School clubs cater for a variety of sporting, artistic and musical interests.

It is hoped that in this new century, the school will continue to be one of the focal points of the community.

HEADMASTERS OF MAWNAN SCHOOL

1863: Mr E. Hallett.
1864: Mr Wilkes.
1871: Mr Potter.
1872: Mr Burge.
1876: Mr Hamley.
1879: Mr Vickery.
1885: Mr Borlase.
1901: Mr J. Moore.
1911: Mr Ireland.
1912: Mr S. Harvey.
1916-19: Miss W. Harris (Headmistress).
1937: Mr Kingsly Wood.
1940: Mr R. Dunn.
1947: Mr F.B. Maunder.
1955: Mr Godwin.
1958: Mr H.G. Stone.
1968: Mr D.J. Manley.

HEADTEACHERS SINCE 1968

Len Truran
John Hoban
Len Truran
John Vipond
Pam Griffey
John Newman
Randall Brook

In 1999, over 120 pupils, staff, parents and friends took to public footpaths, leafy lanes, woodland trails and foreshore paths from Budock Vean to Calamansack to raise money for the £14,000 computer suite. Enjoying well-earned refreshments at Calamansack are: Left to right: Liz Shaw, Angela and Andrew Christophers, Tony and Kally Hutchings.

Mawnan Playgroup. In 1975 Pat Tremaine formed a playgroup for 3–5 year olds in the Chapel Schoolroom. Liz Shaw and Rosemary Curtis continue the task of educating the under fives in the Methodist Church Hall. Rosemary, Liz, Helen and children are photographed at Trerose House in 1997 after a walk across the fields to Parsons Beach.

Chapter 7

THE RED LION

The Red Lion has been offering hospitality to local people and visitors since the seventeenth century. It is situated at the meeting of two ancient trackways, one leading to the Parish Church of St Maunanus on the cliff, the other to the ferry at Helford Passage. Along with the smithy, it was the focal point around which the village of Mawnan Smith grew. It is believed that the smithy gave the village of Mawnan Smith its name. It is known to have existed in 1645 and the inn may well have been standing at the crossroads then. What better than a tankard of ale while waiting for your horse to be shod?

Undoubtedly one of the oldest buildings in Mawnan, it was in existence long before Walter Lory, innkeeper, made his will on 27 September 1717. He died in 1718. Married to Hannah Pollard, he is the first landlord we know by name.

The Red Lion, the heraldic emblem of the Scottish kings, became a popular inn name early in the seventeenth century after James VI of Scotland became King of England. It seems very likely that Walter Lory was responsible for enlarging and improving the original inn; the part facing the cobbles outside the original building would certainly not have had a great chamber. As detailed in Lory's will, it was probably just two rooms divided by a cross passage, the hale (living room) and the kitchen with a hearth at each end, and perhaps two small rooms tucked in beneath the thatch, in the roof.

Walter's son (from a previous marriage) was also called Walter and may have become the landlord after the death of his father, but nothing more is known of the inn or its occupants until early in the next century.

In 1803 there were references to the Red Lion at Mawnan and to the landlord John Hender in the newspapers, the *Sherborne Mercury* and the *Royal Cornwall Gazette*. A similar advert in 1809 names Grace Downing as the landlady of 'the house known by the sign of the Red Lion'. Richard Shore, a widower of Penryn who married Grace in 1813, is named as the landlord in 1830.

When the inn was offered for sale in 1834 it was probably bought by George Trenwith of Redruth; he was named as landlord in 1838. He was involved in the affairs of the parish in the 1830s and '40s and was a member of the Vestry which dealt with the administration of the parish of Mawnan, assessing the rates and appointing officers, churchwardens, constables, waywardens (people responsible for the roads and paths), the parish clerk, sexton and overseers of the poor.

The account-books of the overseers bear witness to the benevolence of the Mawnan Vestry, not only to the poor of the parish but also to those who passed through. In the eighteenth and early-nineteenth centuries there are a number of entries of payments, usually one or two shillings, to wounded soldiers or seamen. A payment of five shillings was for some 'poor distressed travellers who came from Turkey, and others being taken by a pirate coming from New England.' Did these distressed travellers receive a meal and lodgings at the Red Lion? Vestry meetings, which usually preceeded a meal, were often held in the inn.

The parish had been growing steadily throughout the nineteenth century; its inhabitants rose from 397 in 1811 to 573 in 1871. Newcomers to the parish included craftsmen if the 1851 census is to be believed; there were 11 shoemakers in Mawnan at that time! There is, however, no doubt that the parish was prospering, as was the Red Lion and its landlords. When George Trenwith made his will in 1849 his property included three cottages adjoining the inn. One was unoccupied, one was rented by Charles Chinn and the other by Rachael Downing, who had opened a grocers shop in her cottage.

After the death of George Trenwith in 1852, William Hill became the landlord. In turn, he was followed by Mrs Rashleigh. In 1862 the licence was transferred to John Boswarrick of Truro and, on his death in 1869, to his widow Sophia Boswarrick. When the census was taken in 1871 Sophia was living at the Red Lion with her daughter Matilda and her son-in-law John Chappel, a coachman who later became the landlord. Soon after this the inn became the property of Carnes, brewers of Redruth. It was later bought by the Devonish Brewery.

In 1894, John Peter Sadler an ex-coachman, like John Chappel his predecessor, became the new landlord. A Durham man, John Peter Sadler had come to Mawnan with the Backhouse family when they came to live at Trebah and he married a local girl, Ellen Skewes. In 1927 Russell Sadler became landlord in place of his father and so began the Sadlers' long association with The Red Lion. Their eldest son, a flight engineer in the Royal Air Force, was one of five young men from Mawnan killed in the Second World War. When the Sadlers left the inn, they held a free party for the village, in appreciation of the support given to them over the years.

Stanley and Stella Jackson took over from the Sadlers in 1971. They had previously run The Castle Inn at St Ives. The Jacksons soon became very much part of the Mawnan community. Whilst making alterations to the inn, they dug out of the beer cellar an old Cornish range which was then installed in the pub.

One of the bedrooms was believed to be haunted – the one with the trap door through which coffins were lowered to the ground floor (a practice widely used where staircases were too narrow for coffins). A wardrobe once fell to the lower floor through this trap door (which is no longer used). Fortunately nobody was injured.

In case of emergency, Stanley and Stella established a hospital car service for the village people; 31 volunteers were recruited, which meant their services would be called upon only once a month. A raffle was organised to raise money to help pay for petrol if required. The couple also encouraged the playing of dominoes and the old Cornish card game, Euchre. After retirement they lived in the village until their death.

From 1979 until 1987 Frank and Mavis Welch were the landlords, during which time further alterations were made. Philip and Cherida Regan took over from between 1987 and 1990, followed by the Richard's family until 1994. With Richard and Elizabeth Dearsly in charge, the social side of the pub was encouraged – they held quiz nights, bridge nights and specialty food nights as well as live music. It was very much promoted as a family-friendly local pub.

During recent years there have been temporary landlords but during 2000 Mr and Mrs Cotterill took over, and further improvements have been made – most notably the re-thatching and tiling of the roof. It is interesting to note that the breweries have also changed; from Devonish to Greenalls, before becoming Scottish and Newcastle. It was and still is the most photographed and painted building in Mawnan Smith.

Left: *The Red Lion, Mawnan, early twentieth century.*

Below: *The Red Lion, Mawnan, 2001.*

Chapter 8

IN TIMES OF WAR

The First World War, 1914–1918

In the early days of the First World War, after the proclamation, it was volunteers who answered the call. In Mawnan, seven ex-Scouts, plus their Scout Master, six members of the Cricket Club and several men from the United Methodist Church at Carlidnack joined the Army.

The following comes from an issue of the *Falmouth Packet* of July 1915:

> The DCLI recruiting detachment commenced their sixth route march on Tuesday. The first halt, yesterday, was at Port Navas. At 12.30 in

Mawnan the officers and men were met by Mr W.W. Ward JP, Mr R.N. Rogers and members of the local committee. A luncheon was held in the Wesleyan Sunday school, kindly decorated by Mesdames James, Chinn, Rowe, Cheffers, Bray and Rashleigh.

After the lunch, Mr R.N. Rogers presided over a meeting in the Square. Major Pike said that Mrs Hall had four sons, four grandsons, a son-in-law and another descendant serving in the King's forces. That lady had set a fine example to the parish in which 62 eligibles were still left.

Some of the Mawnan Servicemen photographed in the village school playground on their return from the First World War. Left to right, back row: *Mr Rowe, (gardener at Trebah), Edward Sadler, Edward Eddy, Fred Evans, Albert Robins, Reginald Courage, Russell Sadler, Leonard Courage, George Pascoe, George Houghton, William Christophers, Caleb Knowles, Jack Stevens;* standing: *Charles Evans, Alec Pascoe, Alfred Chinn, Arthur Chinn, Walter Hurst, F. Tresidder, Stephen Harvey, Clifton Pascoe, Arthur Eddy, Arthur Mitchell, Edward Trenear, George Lowry, Mr Jenkin;* sitting: *Edgar Ivey, Joe Chinn, Ernest Trevarthen, Charles Rendle, Sidney Pascoe, Alarick Horton, William Toy, Thomas Hall, Charles Tallack, Herbert Trevarthen, Jack Sara;* front: *Harry Tresize, Phillip Tippet, John Henry Christophers, Philip Playle, W. Sanders, Edwin Webster, Cecil Thomas. (The two nurses and two men on left and right of front row have not been named.)*

When the appeal was not responded to in sufficient numbers to satisfy the demands of the fighting forces, conscription was introduced. Local newspapers printed regular news of the men, several of whom received honours and commendations:

Mr E. Ivey, RN., Sapper C. Pascoe and Privates E. Pascoe, E. Sadler and A. Pascoe have been home on leave. Sapper G. Houghton is home on leave from France, after 14 months strenuous duties there.

On Empire Day 12s.6d. was sent from Mawnan School to the Overseas Club, for tobacco and chocolates for soldiers at the Front. The school received the following reply:

France 28 July 1915

Dear Young People

In a wood in France there is living a fellow who has been in the trenches and is waiting his turn to go in again. He spent a holiday visiting his brother in Falmouth, and during that visit, he had a very happy day in Mawnan, and on the Helford River. He little thought, that day, when he stood outside your school, that the time would come when he would be away from dear old England, and the children inside would send him a nice parcel of tobacco and chocolates. He hopes to come to Mawnan one day to thank you all.

When the war finally ended, the news was met with great joy and relief.

The Armistice

The news that the Armistice had been signed reached Mawnan about 9.30am, on Monday through a telephone message at the Post Office. The church bells were rung at once and all available flags were hung in the village. The schoolchildren, after singing the National Anthem and loudly cheering, were dismissed in great excitement. They immediately secured all manner of pots, pans, bells, etc. and with flags waving, paraded the village and every extremity of the parish.

In the evening, a remarkably well-attended Thanksgiving Service was held at St Michael's Church.

Falmouth Packet, November 1918

Peace celebrations continued in 1919, culminating in a Peace Day extravaganza, which included a church service, tea, sports, carnival and bonfire. The stars of the carnival were the nurse and her 16 stone baby. 'If the management of Drury Lane are short of comic men, we in Mawnan are prepared to strongly recommend the combination of James and Jose.'

The Second World War, 1939–1945

At Durgan on 3 September 1939, at a little after 11am, Charles and Winifred Rendle; their 19-year-old daughter, Barbara; their friend, Jack Hall; and next-door neighbour, Edward Downing, were all squeezed into their tiny kitchen overlooking the Helford River, when the announcement came over the radio: '... This country is at war with Germany'. During matins at the Parish Church, Mrs Gunstone, the rector's wife, conveyed the news to her husband, who informed the congregation.

Village life changed considerably. Food, fuel, clothing and household goods were severely rationed. A rigid blackout was enforced. Signposts were removed. While both men and women were working in the Services all over the world, others at home joined the Home Guard, ARP (Air Raid Precautions), Red Cross, Women's Land Army, or worked in the coal mines as 'Bevin Boys'. The Mawnan Working Party met every Wednesday afternoon at Carwinion to knit socks and gloves, etc. for the troops and air-raid victims. Members of the St John's Nursing

Division practised every week in the Methodist Sunday school room. At the annual meeting of the Cricket Club, presided over by Mr R.P. Shakespear, the secretary, Mr W. Pascoe said in his report:

... A few of us are meeting for the second time with the country at war. Several familiar faces are missing tonight and let us hope they will soon be with us again... I hope the time will soon come when the club can resume its normal activities. What could be more cheering than to hear the village ringing with that well-known cry of 'Up Mawnan'?

In spite of the outbreak of war, work continued on the construction of Argal Dam. Gravel Hill became submerged and was replaced by a wider, less-inclined road, in front of the dam. The pupils of Mawnan School were not so fortunate! Their school managers (now governors) decreed that plans for flushing toilets should be shelved until after the war.

ROLL OF HONOUR: BOTH WORLD WARS

William Cowling	A naval pensioner who lost his life at sea in Nov 1917. Lived at Helford Passage.
Norman Downing	Durgan. Born 1896 D.C.L.I. Posted missing on the Somme, October 1916.
Peter Eddy	Durgan. Born 1879 10th Battalion. London Infantry Regiment. Died of wounds on 24 August 1918. Buried in Bagneux Military C.
Hugh Adair Finch	1899–1918. Second Lieutenant Grenadier Guards.
Philip Gerard Finch	1898–1918. Lieutenant Northumberland Fusiliers.
Nevil Fox	1894–1917. Welsh Regiment. Killed in action 31 July 1917.
Ivor Mann	1895–1917. Devon Yeomanry. Died of wounds in France, 13 October 1917.
Francis Matzen	1888–1917. R.E. Motorcycle accident in Esher, Surrey.
Sampson Pascoe	1895–1917. Second Battalion Royal Warwickshire Regiment. Killed 9 October 1917. Name inscribed on the Tyne Cot Memorial to the Missing, north of Ypres.
Hugh Passey	Joined the Navy in 1915. Drowned on a mine-sweeper in the English Channel, 24 June 1917.
Reginal Rogers	1882–1916. Rifle Brigade. Fell on the Somme.
Walter Sara	1891–1916. Died in France, 18 August 1916.
James Stockton	1895–1917. Captain Ox, Bucks Light Infantry. Killed on the Somme.
Edward Thomas	1890–1918. Died of wounds received in action 10 April 1918.
Francis Ward	1887–1917. City of Bristol Regiment. Killed in action near Poel-Cappelle in Flanders, 9 October 1917.
Edward Eddy	1922–1944. Naval Commandoes. Killed in action at Anzio, February 1944.
Francis Hodge	1919–1945. Coldstream Guards. Killed in action on the Western Front, 15 February 1945.
John Sadler	1922–1944. Flight Engineer shot down over Germany, 6 December 1944 and is buried in Hanover War Cemetery.
Anthony Terry	1910–1942. RN Sailed from Singapore and disappeared.
George Willmet	1923–1943. Killed in accident in North Africa.
Ernest Lewarne	1924–1945. RN Telegraphist. Died on HMS *Cornwall*.

Mawnan LDV & Home Guard

As with most villages, a group of volunteers in Mawnan decided to patrol the parish. A wooden hut was placed on the grass verge close to what is now Mrs Lugg's shop. Armed with shotguns and the occasional .22 rifle, they kept guard from dusk to dawn. Later it became a national force with Canadian Ross rifles, uniforms and an Army-based order of privates, NCOs and COs. The hut was dispensed with and headquarters were established in a house called Green Acres on the Mawnan/Carlidnack road. It was from here that a more disciplined, uniformed and better-armed force patrolled the parish, liaising with Falmouth Home Guard based near Nansidwell Beach.

Rosemullion Head became the training area for Mawnan and neighbouring parishes. They had at their disposal Lewis guns, Blacker bombards, rifles, Northover projectors, Mills grenades and other weapons, some of which had been discarded by the Army.

Green Acres was eventually vacated and Lloyds Bank in the village became the patrol point, whilst a bungalow was acquired almost opposite the entry to St Michael's Church to serve as the Home Guard's headquarters.

Once the threat of invasion was lifted, the day came when equipment had to be handed in. Confusion reigned; the battalion quartermaster was in a state of collapse. Most men kept their great-coats but other bits and pieces did not match what he was supposed to collect. Mystery surrounded the Comforts Fund and the electric kettle vanished, together with the teapot and mugs. No doubt Mawnan was no different from the rest of the country – the greatest danger came from within!

Home Guard outside the Memorial Hall, Mawnan Smith: Back row: *J. Woodgate, G. Benney, H. Pascoe, F. Rowe, ? Dolbey, E. Pascoe;* front: *F. Williams, T. Pascoe, W. Pascoe, W.H. Rowe, L. Woodgate.*

Mawnan Home Guard as Gunners

At the beginning of the Second World War the regular Army decided to put gun emplacements on Toll Point. This enabled them to cover an area at the mouth of the Helford River that was out of the range of the protective guns at Pendennis Castle. They were all under command of the colonel based at Pendennis.

Two French 75mm guns were put in separate emplacements, while another was mounted on wheels and was towed by a half-ton truck. For air cover there was a Bofors gun.

To aid night attack, two searchlights were placed with generators at tide level, inside a perimeter fence. All was controlled from the Battery Observation Post (BOP) constructed in thick concrete, topped by a massive roof. It was dug deep into the ground. The viewing window was at ground level, so that when the operators were standing inside only their heads were exposed. A stove warmed the men in winter and heated the cocoa, in which a spoon would stand.

Mawnan and Budock Home Guard supplied men to be trained as gunners and BOP staff in case of an emergency. The discipline was strict but fair. Gun practise was gained by firing at a towed target steaming from Rosemullion to the Manacles.

When river training took place, Bren guns were attached to the 75s. With the order to fire, only a 303 bullet would be aimed at the target as it proceeded upriver. On one occasion, when the men were training at night, the launch grounded on the Gedges. The Army boys suggested it was deliberate when the crew were informed that the Home Guard were in control that night!

The men's quarters were placed around the church, in the field leading down to Parsons Beach. Training huts and stores were connected to Toll Point by a metalled road. The training huts were mainly to train BOP staff to correctly identify enemy ships. It was very successful; one Home Guard team equalled the regular gunners, as on the Home Guard gun floor were two men who were gunners in France during the First World War.

Every June the Battalion met at Falmouth Recreation Ground and marched around the track as a band played. Toll Point sent a selected group to be involved in these activities and the sergeant major asked some members of the BOP who were the right height to join the training, which he believed they needed. They were duly trained and performed well on the day. The general public were there and many amusing remarks were made about their local heroes.

MEMORIES OF THE HELFORD RIVER IN WARTIME
by Robert (Bob) Still

The Special Forces, as it was then known (it is now called the Special Boat Service), was being run by Lt. Cdr Nigel Warrington Smythe and his brother, from a base on the Helford River. The mother ship was the Sunbeam, a three-masted steel sailing ship, owned by Lord Runciman.

My father, Chief ERA A.A. Still, was chief engineer and was involved in a variety of maintenance work on visiting small ships that came into the Helford River. When they went on operations to France or Southern Ireland he went along. Many of these missions, which were carried out at night, were to bring home escaping prisoners and pilots who had been shot down over occupied France. On one such job, a German had infiltrated the group, and in order to protect himself from being shot as a spy, he allowed himself to be brought back to the Helford along with the rest.

One day whilst the skipper was ashore, my father took my brother Terry and myself on a small boat to the Sunbeam. We went aboard and met people of many nationalities as well as the British crew. Having people who spoke many different languages was vital for the type of work that was conducted by the Special Forces.

Towards the mouth of the river, a landing stage was put into position. It was square, with a tower on each corner, with guns on the towers for anti-aircraft purposes, as well as guns facing the sea in case of attack from the water. It was really a floating fort, and was manned by American troops.

One day as we were coming home from school in Constantine, we saw four Navy chaps dashing across the fields carrying a rubber boat with them; they looked very tired. They stopped at the cattle trough at Treneers Farm and drank a lot of water before staggering on with their mission; it was obviously a hard training exercise. A lot of this kind of thing went on around the Helford prior to D-Day.

One evening just before dark, on a rising tide, a Motor Torpedo Boat, obviously damaged, was towed into Porth Navas creek by several rowing boats acting as tugs. It tied up at Porth Navas pier. The next morning it was gone.

The Shipwrights pub at Helford was the Naval Special Forces pub; they all belonged to what was known as 'The Chocker Club'. As a sign of recognition they all had a small piece of red cloth inside their caps, and this was shown on entry. Those without the red cloth were viewed with great suspicion!

In the fields below Constantine, a large group of Italian prisoners was put to work. They were quite happy about this as they were mostly farm-workers at home. They kept their tools in a cave, by the junction of the Porth Navas road.

Boys from Ponjaraveh Boys Academy were allowed to work, lifting potatoes, if they were 12 years old. A green card was issued to them; they had to be paid 6d. an hour. This was recorded on the green card, which was a sign it was official.

One evening, a lot of the men from the Sunbeam decided to go for a drink at a small pub close to Gweek, on the right as you go up the river. It had a small stone jetty. My father had to row a heavy boat, but many of the sailors had made canvas canoes and one had an Indian-style canoe. Using his brains, my father started early with four of us in the boat, but the rest caught up pretty quickly. We had just gone through the narrows by Calamansack, and one called 'Which way, Gus?'. My father directed them up Frenchman's Creek. When they found that he had lied to them they soon caught up with us. I cannot repeat here what they called him! When it was time to leave, the tide had gone down a lot, and the chap with the Indian-style canoe thought he would jump down into his boat. His foot went straight through the bottom – alcohol had clouded his judgement somewhat!

On the way back it was very dark on the river, and the tide was going out fast. My father gave me a wide-bladed canoe paddle and said, 'Stick it over the stern and steer. Get us on the mud and you'll be in real trouble!' (Remember I was just under 11 years old, but people grow up quickly in a war!) As we neared the Helford River basin (where the oyster beds were) we heard the sound of an engine. A powerful searchlight shone on us, and a voice shouted, 'Get off the river quick or we will blast you off.' My poor father started rowing like a man possessed. When we got ashore at Calamansack he held on to a tree and was violently sick; it was really very frightening, especially for two young boys.

One day after school my brother and I were playing in the woods along Porth Navas creek, when we saw many aluminium boats stacked upside down among the trees. It transpired that they were designed by Nigel Smythe. They were light and pointed at both ends, so that you could hit the beach and go out again without turning round. These were later used for the D-Day invasion.

Being a child at the time, I knew very little about what was going on, until early one morning we awoke to the distant sound of heavy guns. My mother came and sat on my bed and put her arms around me and my brother. It was 0600 hrs on 6 June 1944: D-Day!

A professional rabbit trapper used to work on the whole of Calamansack. I used to see a five-bar gate, with rows of rabbits hanging the full length of every bar. It must have been a great help to the village as fresh meat was not easy to obtain, because of rationing.

I used to take a small milk container to the farm each morning, on the way to school, and collect it on my way home in the afternoon. My brother and I used to walk to Treneers Farm each morning. We would get a lift with the horse and cart that was carrying the milk to the road. The churns were put on a wooden platform, and we

would wait for the milk lorry, which gave us a lift to the Ponjeravah Boys Academy, at the bottom of Constantine Hill.

At lunch we used to sit on the huge rock in front of the school and wait for the 'Pasty Man' (Renfrees Bakery Van). Then the teacher used to make cocoa in a bucket on the pot-bellied stove in the classroom. Boys that brought their own home-made pasties used to warm them by the fire. After school we used to walk home.

AN EXCITING ADVENTURE

An account by Margaret Stevenson, of Form IV, Latymer, at Mawnan, 1941.

It happened on 10 May at 3.20 in the morning. I was fast asleep in bed when suddenly I was rudely awakened by a terrific crash. I opened my eyes and sat up just as a large piece of plaster missed my head. Startled, I looked around and saw that my room was a total wreck. The ceiling had come down, the plaster was off the walls, the door blown off and debris was every-where. It was a brilliant moonlit night and all this was plainly visible. I heard the sound of running water and in my dazed condition my first thought was that there had been a burst pipe. I got out of bed and dug out my slippers and found my slacks, which I pulled on over my pyjamas. I could just open my cupboard door a few inches and I pulled out a coat and slipped it on. Violet, who was sleeping in the next room, came into mine and pulled on a few clothes. The villagers were in the house by this time trying to get my

'foster father' out of his blocked room. A kind lady put Violet and me up for the night. Mr and Mrs Beck were not hurt and they went to stay with some friends. The next morning we went round to have a look at the wreckage. We found that a land mine had fallen 20 yards in front of the house, making it a total wreck. We certainly had a lucky escape. Mr Blackwell and Mr Edwards had not known what had happened and they were very sorry to hear of our unfortunate mishap. In all 15 children were affected and fresh billets had to be found.

Everybody has settled down again now and the houses that were damaged have been repaired but 'Loenter' (pictured), my former home, is being pulled down and will be put up again after the war. I am sorry to say that Mr and Mrs Beck lost practically everything, but we consider ourselves lucky to be alive.

ELDERLY PEOPLE'S COURAGE WHEN UNDER ATTACK: 'KEEP SMILING' SAYS ONE

Mawnan's reaction to the nocturnal bombing activities of the German Air Force was remarkable. The bombs shattered the moonlit stillness with explosions that woke people in villages many miles away. A couple of high explosives killed two people and destroyed the homes of many others. Although there was extensive damage in the small village, the casualties were extraordinarily small, considering the size of the bombs.

Most of the villagers, apart from the civil-defence patrols, were in bed at the time. The blasts from the bombs battered many houses, and only a few in the whole village escaped damage of some sort. Several buildings were smashed beyond repair.

One of the missiles made a direct hit on a recently-built bungalow, occupied by Mr A.E. Cutter, a chauffeur, and his wife, both of whom were killed. The dwelling was completely obliterated, concrete

Above: *Air Training Corps marching through Mawnan square.*

Right: *Air Training Corps at the rear of the Memorial Hall, Mawnan Smith. Left to right: Eric Chatfield, Peter Butler, Dick Morley, Reg Wheatley.*

blocks were strewn far and wide, and furnishings and clothing was blown far into a neighbouring copse. The bodies of Mr and Mrs Cutter were found under rubble near a hedge in the garden. Apparently, they had been asleep in bed at the time. Fortunately the two evacuee children, who had been staying with the couple for some time, were away on holiday.

A private house and one cottages close by were completely wrecked. From the house, Mr and Mrs Culley, and Jean Streeter, a London evacuee, escaped without injury, even though ceilings and part of the roofing had fallen into their bedrooms. They escaped through a broken wall. Some of the cottagers sustained cuts and bruises, and their homes were very badly smashed. They were Mr and Mrs Benny, Mr and Mrs Randlesome and family, and Mr and Mrs Williams. Some went to hospital for treatment. The scene of many local fêtes and social events in peace-time, a fine old house standing in its own grounds took the much of the force of the blast. However, 80-year-old Mrs Rogers, veteran public worker and leader of many of the village charitable and social activities, was quickly out of bed and helping the other distressed villagers and her cottage tenants. She set a splendid example by the energy and courage she displayed as she cheered up her friends and employees by telling them to 'keep smiling'.

The other bomb fell between two private houses standing in their own gardens, and both properties looked as though a tornado had swept through the grounds. In one, Mr J. Gundry, who was over 70, and his wife were sleeping. Mr Gundry refused to be perturbed, and remained in the wrecked premises until the morning had advanced, commenting, 'the excitement is all over – we can do nothing until daylight comes, so we will sit up and have a cup of tea.'

In the other house were Mr and Mrs Beck and two evacuees. The front of this house was blown away to reveal the interior as though for the purposes of sectional demonstration, but all the occupants escaped unhurt. Damage extended right through the small collection of homes, and for some distance windows and doors were blown in, while many people's ceilings fell down on them as they lay in bed.

Despite all this, morning found the village folk undaunted. Everybody had turned a willing hand to help where possible, and good work was being done by the civil-defence services. Typical of this spirit of village co-operation were the impromptu canteens set up by the blacksmith, Mr James, and by a neighbour, Mrs Webster. Many cups of tea were provided for the workers and villagers who had been made temporarily homeless.

Taken on 3 June 1944, three days before D-Day, this photograph shows soldiers of the United States 29th Infantry Division (as noted from their shoulder patches) turning off the road leading down to Helford Passage onto the new road that was built to give tank and vehicle access to Trebah Beach. The 29th was involved in the invasion of the Normandy beach, which earned the soubriet 'Bloody Omaha'.

American troops passing through Mawnan Smith on their way to board LSTs (Landing Ship Tanks) at Trebah Beach prior to the D-Day landings. Just above the rear wheel of the 'Bofors' and set into the wall is one of the village water 'stand pipes' for residents without water on tap.

PRISONER OF WAR: *Percy Randlesome's Story*

Percy Arthur Randlesome was born in Norfolk. His father served on mine-sweepers during the First World War and after the war ended he worked in drifters out of Lowestoft until the fishing industry went into decline. It was at this point, when Percy was eight or nine months old, that the family moved to Durgan in Cornwall. This is where Percy and his brother Reginald grew up. Percy attended Mawnan school and then worked for a time at Glendurgan before going into the building trade. He initially worked for Charlie Pascoe of Maenporth, before working for E.H. Moss, then Williams of St Austell. He helped to build the Odeon Cinema in Falmouth. After that he went to Nansidwell, where he helped the Pilgrim family convert the house into a hotel. He also worked on a house at Penryn which was built for, but never lived in by, Dr Blamey.

In October 1939 Percy was conscripted into the Devon and Cornwall Light Infantry before being transferred to the Seventh Royal Sussex Regiment just before they went to France. He was caught up in the retreat before Dunkirk and was taken prisoner by the Germans near Amiens on 20 May 1940. He and his comrades were first taken to the Luxembourg border and then to Trier. After that they were taken on a three-day trip in cattle trucks to Shubin in Poland, near the Vistula River. It was a terrible camp and Percy recalled seeing 'men throw themselves into a big soup container in a frantic attempt to get food.'

Percy worked on the land for a time, digging irrigation ditches, but after catching scabies he was moved to the river to help excavate a pool for a fish farm. He was also put to work for a time in a factory; he conducted experiments to test the effectiveness of cleansing Norwegian wood pulp with caustic soda. Later on he was moved again, this time to a big camp at Shildberg. This was also a hospital camp, and he was appointed Camp Mason. He was once caught smuggling bread into the camp under his great-coat and was sentenced to ten days in solitary confinement. Percy and a carpenter also smuggled parts of a radio into the camp, which was assembled and kept in a jam tin that stood on a table in their barracks. At 9 o'clock every night a man wearing earphones would listen for the sound of Big Ben on the radio and then dictate the BBC news to a shorthand writer, who would take it down and pass it around the camp.

In August 1944 Percy and his comrades were moved to Gliwice. As the Russians were getting closer, the prisoners were made to march across Europe, over the mountains and into Czechoslovakia. They ended up near Munich, where they were liberated by American troops. During the march, the weather was bitterly cold and some of the prisoners collapsed with frostbite. On one occasion they were forced to march for 95 hours, pausing just once in a field. They marched mainly by day and slept in barns

at night. Their rations were two portions of bread per week and three boiled potatoes every day. They were given soup on two occasions.

Once at a crossroads in a small town they got mixed up with inmates from Auschwitz, who were being hit with rifle butts and kicked by their guards. Percy said that he never forgot 'the moans of those poor devils in their striped uniforms'.

On another occasion when they were in a barn for the night Percy managed to catch a pigeon and the prisoners boiled it in a tin and had a feast.

Percy was at the rear of the marching column one day. He was utterly exhausted, and the guard started hitting him on the back with his rifle butt, so Percy grabbed the rifle. He had no option but to hand it back and said he was lucky that there hadn't been another guard around or he would probably have been shot. Another time he saw a column of marchers in striped clothes ahead of them in a forest. They were being escorted by SS guards. He watched as eight people in the column were shot and a smiling guard told his comrade that he had used 150 rounds of ammunition.

As the prisoners moved further west they began to see the US Air Force. They all cheered when one day eight Mustangs did a victory roll in the sky over their heads.

Men were dying through lack of food and cold and once, when they were in a narrow street in a town, Percy looked through the open door of a house to see a loaf of bread lying on a table. He rushed and grabbed it before the people inside the room could recover from their surprise.

A Red Cross lorry finally appeared and each prisoner received a parcel. The first thing they did was make tea! Later Percy and a friend crawled down an embankment into a cellar when the guards weren't looking and found some pickled eggs. When they returned they found the column had gone on without them, so they went to a nearby town and asked a waitress in a hotel for bread and she gave them half a loaf. They found a farmhouse, but when the farmer let them in they saw three German Air Force officers inside. The Germans had been shot down and told Percy and his friend that the war was almost over. They stayed at the farm for four days and were well fed and rested by the time the farmer's daughters told them the Americans had arrived. Percy and his friend were taken to a US camp and boarded a Dakota to Rheims. They returned to England in a Lancaster.

Percy ends his fascinating story with the words:

At Falmouth Railway Station I caught a bus to Carwinion Lane. Mr Jim Vague, head gardener at Carwinion, made me a 'welcome home' in flowers. I received a welcome from the village and a party in the Memorial Hall which I shall never forget.

Evacuees

With the advent of war, children from big cities were sent to safer, rural areas. On 17 June 1940, 90 children from Latymer School, in Edmonton, London, arrived at Mawnan School. Local families were ordered to go to the school and choose a child to take home.

Tina Ahn was one of the 30 younger brothers and sisters who accompanied the Latymer pupils. She attended Mawnan school, where she was taught by 'a large, forceful but kind' teacher, Miss James. After two very unhappy billets, she was transferred to Budock Vean Cottage, to live with Mr and Mrs Johnson. Tina enjoyed playing croquet on the lawn and driving to Falmouth in an open-topped car with her foster parents. The Johnson's cook/housekeeper, Miss Ethel Peters, proved to be an indulgent companion. This is her own account:

My brother and I were taken to a big house, but after a few weeks we were sent to a very small cottage. Mr H. was kind to us but his wife was rather sharp and gave us bread and scrape for our meals. Our mother came to see us and we were dirty and hungry, so she insisted we went to live somewhere else. She had to go back to work in an aircraft factory. Peter and I went to different places. I went to live with the Johnsons, who had a large cottage and a lovely garden. They were quite rich and were very kind to me.

To mark their pleasant war-time association with Mawnan school, the Latymer school authorities gave a sum of money for the Latymer Prize, to be awarded each year to the scholar making the best general progress. At the 60th anniversary of their arrival in Mawnan, a plaque was unveiled in the Memorial Hall in memory of the evacuees and of the families who took them in. This was organised by Mr Desmond Dyer and Mrs Sylvia Rickard (née Withey), with assistance from other former pupils who have remained in the area.

Re-union of Latymer School Evacuees in the Memorial Hall, 17 June 2000. The ladies with flowers are foster mothers who welcomed the evacuees into their homes in 1940. Left to right: Naomi Richards, Audrey Martin, Dot Hurst, Ethel Wright, Marjorie Tremaine.

THE BEST YEARS OF MY LIFE: 1940–42

by Marion Arpin, 'Castelnau', Carwinion Road. Adapted from the Mawnan Magazine, 1973.

17 JUNE 1940
Our boys and girls from Latymer School, Edmonton, arrived at the old village school, where prospective foster parents selected their children. I did not go, but when one of their teachers, probably Miss Cobby, brought children up the Carwinion Road to find homes for them, two 13-year-old boys were fixed up with me. I had the nicest boys in the school! There were 90 children, including their little brothers and sisters who were sent from Latymer to Mawnan School. The Memorial Hall and the Chapel Sunday school room were adapted for the older ones. After a month I took in a friend of the boys, whose foster parents were leaving the district.

RATIONS
The menu was very restricted, owing to rationing and the weekly allowance for each child was

11s.0d. Bread was not rationed, so the boys consumed mountains of bread and margarine, with just a speck of jam.

SUNDAYS
During that glorious, sunny summer of 1940, Alan, Peter, Robin and I often visited my cousin Mrs Paine at Treloe, Bar Road. Her 14-year-old son, Geoffrey, had a boat and often took us for trips up the Helford River.

LATYMER SCHOOL ACTIVITIES
The school often organised swimming evenings at Grebe or Maenporth. It also arranged for the pupils to go on long rambles with Miss Brown. (Miss Brown married a local builder, Mr Wilfred Pascoe, and settled in Mawnan.) Other activities included visits from the Air Training Corps., as well as involving the pupils in amateur dramatics, cricket and football.

Above left: *Outside the Kidley Wink Cottage, Bareppa. Back row, left to right: Olive Aubrey, Edwina Moore, Jean Kerr, Doreen Moore, Iris Martin; front: Philip Aubrey and Heather Kerr.*

Above: *The drinkers, outside Pascoe's. Left to right: Alan Cooper, Brian Rabin, Leslie Robinson, Reg Wheatley, Eric Chatfield, Dick Morley, Peter Butler.*

Left: *During the Second World War, the Memorial Hall was used as a schoolroom for the evacuee children. The chairs and tables had to be put away daily for functions in the hall in the evenings.*

Headmaster, V.S.E. Davies visited Grebe Beach in 1940. Included are: Eric Chatfield, Jack Hinkley, Doreen Moore, Olive Aubrey with Eileen Manley in front of her, Mrs Davies, V.S.E. Davies, Mrs Edwards, Mrs Blackwell, Miss Cobby, Grenville Downe, Daphne Palmer, Reg Calvert, Geoffrey Ball, Derek Elliott, Donena Bundy, Alan Lewis, Margaret Nickson, Joyce May, Lilian Terrell, Mavis Birkitt, Gwen Smith, Joan Morgan, Mr Blackwell, Margaret French.

LAND MINES, MAY 1941

The night the bombs were dropped on Mawnan, a 71lb lump of the bungalow on Carwinion Lane, in which Mr and Mrs Cutter were killed, came hurtling through the roof into the boys' room. I heard Alan shout out cheerily: 'Oh, I say, we can see the stars.' Another large piece of the bungalow was found at the top of the garden.

17 JUNE 1942

When the time came for the children to leave, I threw a farewell party in my garden. The children entertained us with songs and recitations. It was during double summer time (the clocks were put forward two hours), so when the last guests departed at 11.30pm it was still light.

Once a month the boys were measured on my kitchen wall. How I hated obliterating those marks when the kitchen was re-decorated after the war. The kindness of the evacuees and their parents is written (to adapt Chronicles 11) on the tablets of the Book of Memory of a grateful foster mother, Marion Arpin.

AFTER THE WAR: MANY YEARS LATER, PETER, ONE OF THESE BOYS WROTE:

Alan and I were almost the last evacuees to be 'claimed' by the villagers of Mawnan Smith. Our spinster foster mother, Marion Arpin, had requested two girls, but she felt sorry for us and took us for the night, intending to arrange an exchange in the morning. But she changed her mind and soon after, Leslie Robinson (Robin) joined us. We all developed an appreciation of and great affection for Marion Arpin and the people of Mawnan.

THE STORY OF AN EVACUEE FROM BRISTOL
(Dedicated to Mrs Carter, 'A Most Wonderful Foster Mother')

It was Tuesday 20 May 1941 (my mother's 43rd birthday) when we arrived as evacuees in the village hall of Mawnan Smith, where we were greeted with tea, lemonade and buns. It was a time of concern as we sat around and waited to be collected by our prospective foster parents. We didn't know how things would turn out.

My name is Mervyn and I was 12 years old at the time; carrying the responsibility of making sure that my younger brother, Terry (aged eight) and my sister Audrey (aged seven) were billeted in their new foster homes. So, full of apprehension, we sat there waiting for someone to collect us. A Mr and Mrs Cheffers of The Rosary, Carlidnick Lane, announced that they were looking for a boy and I pushed Terry forward. I watched him going off to God knows where. Audrey and myself then waited patiently for our turn, for what seemed like an age, then a Mr and Mrs Carter of Rosewarren Cottage collected us and took us to their home. We were greeted by the wailing of the air-raid sirens, which was a good start. (Little did I know then that the friendship that developed between us would still be going strong 60 years later, by way of Mrs Carter's daughter Julie.)

I cannot tell you anything about the other Bristol children, as I didn't see much of them beyond school. For some unknown reason I was adopted by the village boys, such as Dick ('Spinner') Rowe, (whose daughter Beatrice I still visit to this day), Tommy ('Broccoli') Bray, Jim ('Pickles') Mitchell, Bernard James, Ronnie Bray, John ('Wuffles') Chinn, John Badger, Cecil Spike and many others. The first six mentioned became my best mates during my stay at Mawnan.

I also knew the girls, including Rosemary Spike, Edwina Moore, Lucy Parry, Sheila Smith, May Gay and Audrey Hatton. Being a bit shy with girls at the time, I didn't have much to do with them. Although I still have a letter written by Rosemary, some 58 years ago.

Mrs Carter gave me the freedom to go out and about with Dick, Tommy, Jim, Ronnie and Bernard, all of whom she knew by name. Many a good time we had going into the woods and down to the beaches. We indulged in a fair amount of mischief (innocent mischief I might add!). Twice a week, Tommy and I used to weed the garden for Mr Dunn the headmaster (nicknamed Dick). He paid us 1s.0d. (5p) for our efforts each time.

I used to go up to Mr Benny's farm at Trerose to help Eustace and two of the boys from Bristol, Billy and David, who were billeted with Mr and Mrs Benny. Some evenings I would go along to the Headland at Rosemullion to watch Mr James (Bernard's dad) fishing and more than once he gave me a fish to take home.

Sometimes I would take a message to Nansidwell Hotel for Mrs Carter, where I would speak to the waiters in their evening dress. I had never seen anything like that before – except in films! It was magic! I also collected the milk from Mrs Tremaine at the nearby farm. She had a son called John who was about six years old at the time.

I recall the day that I collected the bicycle that my father sent me. Having come out of the station, I went cycling the wrong way along Market Street, waving to Dick as I passed, only to be stopped by a policeman. Out came his notebook to take down my name and address, when Dick came up and told him I was an evacuee from Bristol, upon which he replaced his notebook, gave me a smile and let me off, 'Phew!'. Every Saturday after that I cycled into Falmouth, to go to the cinema, with the half crown (12½p) Mrs Carter used to give me every week.

I remember Mr Christophers who used to cut my hair every two weeks (I don't have much to cut these days), Mr Eddy the village cobbler, Mr Rashleigh (Mrs Carter's gardener) and his daughter Joyce (I secretly fancied her), Mr Gunstone the rector, Miss Cochrane's sweet shop (which was always overrun by the Latymer boys and girls), Mr Pascoe who kept the filling station, Mr Craft who always sported a straw hat and Mr James the village blacksmith and his son Dryden; we often watched them shoeing the horses, through the playground railings. Dryden was a giant of a man to me.

There was the time I cycled over to Porth Navas, to take a letter of thanks to Mrs Scily (Mrs Carter's mother) for the Christmas present she had sent me and I believe she must have told Mrs Carter on the phone that I had been over with the letter. In turn, Mrs Carter told cook who was pleased as punch to think I had taken the trouble to hand-deliver the letter. That really was a feather in my cap, as cook was a stickler for good manners. Cook (Mary Brougham) was a lovely lady but if she was upset it was a case of 'beware the wrath of a woman scorned'. Even Mrs Carter kept clear of the kitchen, never mind the rest of us!

There was the day Stewart Berryman and I were given the job of pumping the church organ at Mawnan church for Mr Dunn but things did not go according to plan. Taking an interest in something on the opposite side of the room, we forgot to keep pumping, causing the music to fade away to nothing. Needless to say Mr Dunn was most displeased but he forgave us eventually – he was a nice man.

One time we cycled over to Constantine, taking it in turns to ride or run, as there were 12 of us but only seven bikes between us. We played football with some children in Constantine; I can't remember the score but I know we had a good time, returning home by the same method.

I only knew one boy from the Latymer school, and that was Alan Kerr. It was Alan who took me down to The Rosary to find my brother and introduce me to Mrs Cheffers. Alan also had a sister, called Helen, although I never really knew her.

I remember introducing the old game of 'Five Stones' to the boys in the playground; they had never heard of it, although the older people, such as Mr and Mrs Albert Peters who lived in the Square, had seen it before.

I recall a trip on the ferry across to Flushing (the fare was two pence in old currency), which was quite an adventure to me. I also remember shooting a goldfish in the pond at Rosewarren Cottage, with a bow and arrow I had made. Believe me, I was absolutely terrified. I related this story to Julie a few years ago and she laughed her head off. But as a 12-year-old boy it was quite a traumatic experience. In fact it was just like an episode from a Just William story. Come to think of it, my whole time at Mawnan was like a Just William adventure, particularly splashing away in the altogether down on the beach, below Mawnan church. We lived in a world of innocent mischief, with no inhibitions over anything like that – although I wouldn't do it now! We used to spend time in the old cricket hut, on the sports field, talking about the war and getting up to all sorts of things. The old hut is gone now and has been replaced with a posh pavilion.

There were times when Tommy took me down to Maenporth to cut tennis balls from the floats on the edge of the water. I felt like a traitor, convinced that I was helping the enemy to land but Tommy assured me that would not happen. Tommy was always the one who reassured me, especially when we were doing things we shouldn't be doing. But with all of the boys, I grew to trust and rely on them and they never let me down...

When the time came for me to go back to Bristol, I was very sad, for I really loved Mawnan and its people, grown-ups and children alike. It was the most wonderful period of my life. I have visited the place time and time again. Even after all these years I can't help seeing the place as my second home. Most of the grown-ups are gone now and a fair number of the lads. Whenever I come down to stay, I always pay them a visit up at Mawnan churchyard and quietly spend some time recalling the happy times we shared. It's nice to have the friendship of Dick's daughter and her family as well as that of Dot Rowe (Dick's wife), to keep in touch with such wonderful memories. If they awarded medals for villages that took on children during the war, Mawnan should be top of the list.

Inset: *Mrs Carter's evacuee, Mervyn Hale (back) and his family after he arrived in Mawnan in 1941.* Seated, left to right: *Mrs Hale, Terry and Audry Hale, Mr Hale.*

Mawnan Smith Evacuees: 60th Anniversary Reunion

The organising committee for the 60th anniversary reunion of the evacuated children was led by Sylvia Rickard (née Withey 1939) and Des Dyer (1939). Held on 17 June 2000, it was a testament to the strength of feeling both for Mawnan Smith itself and those kind residents who acted as host families that so many former evacuees made the journey back that day. In all, 30 former evacuees returned to Mawnan. A few, such as Sylvia and Des, were living in Mawnan but most had travelled from much further afield. Each wore traditional luggage labels stating his/her name and inside the hall was a wonderful display of old photographs and memorabilia from that time. The stories people exchanged were fascinating. It was remarkable that having only spent a couple of years of their lives in this community, these Latymerians felt compelled to return to Mawnan so many years later.

There was an added air of excitement with the arrival of Carlton TV who had sent their reporter, John Doyle, and a cameraman to record a piece for their In Focus programme. A number of evacuees were personally interested and there was particular interest in film footage showing young evacuees getting to grips with rural life. After lunch, a meal was provided by the catering team under the direction of Sylvia. The villagers started arriving including six of the former foster mothers. Finally it was time for the plaque to be unveiled. Sylvia and Des had invited Mary Cockeram (née Pascoe) daughter of the former schoolteacher Miss Brown to do the honours.

Inevitably perhaps, came the traditional meeting at Mawnan's Red Lion pub, where a few stalwarts who were staying locally gathered to chat until closing time.

Inset: *Plaque unveiled in the Memorial Hall on 17 June 2000 by Mary, daughter of one of the Latymer (Edmonton) teachers who married the local builder, Wilfred Pascoe and remained in the village.*

1940 - 1942

DURING THE SECOND WORLD WAR, PART OF THE LATYMER SCHOOL EDMONTON NORTH LONDON WAS EVACUATED TO MAWNAN SMITH.

THE 89 PUPILS, 7 TEACHERS AND 21 YOUNGER BROTHERS AND SISTERS WERE WELCOMED HERE ON 17th JUNE 1940. THIS HALL BECAME THEIR SCHOOL AND THIS VILLAGE THEIR HOME FOR TWO YEARS.

SIXTY YEARS LATER THEIR TIME HERE IS STILL REMEMBERED WITH AFFECTION AND GRATITUDE.

17th June 2000

Subscribed by Latymer Old Students Association

VE Day

Prior to 8 May 1945, VE Day (Victory in Europe), Miss James at Mawnan School had been rehearsing patriotic songs with the pupils, so, like children all over the country, when the time came, they lined up in the playground to hoist the Union Jack and sing There'll always be an England; Land of Hope and Glory; Rule Britannia, and God save the King. In November 1943, they had been informed that Pilot Officer Ted Sanderson had been to Buckingham Palace with his parents, Mr and Mrs George Sanderson of Glendurgan Cottage, to receive the DFM from the King. Teenagers and young people too celebrated on VE-Day; they cycled to the Model Farm Barn at Lamanva to join 300 other people at a dance, where the winners of various competitions went home with a dozen eggs each!

It was a bitter-sweet time for the Cricket Club. At the first game of the season, Mr Pascoe welcomed Percy Randlesome, after his five years spent in German prison camps. He then referred to the great loss the club had sustained during the war through the death of such sportsmen and cricketers as Edward Eddy, killed with the Naval Commandos in Italy; Frank Hodge, Coldstream Guards; John Sadler, killed on his first operational flight over Germany; and the previous year's captain, Ted Cornwall, killed in a cycle accident on Maenporth Hill. Mr Pascoe also mentioned George Willmet, DSM, who had been apprenticed to local builder Wilfred Pascoe before the war, and Lieut. Com. Anthony Terry, DSC, presumed to have drowned off Singapore.

In August the Pendennis Motor Cycle Club, with Bill Barbary and Joe Paget, staged a motorcycle gymkhana in front of an enthusiastic crowd, with the proceeds going towards the Mawnan Welcome Home Fund. Thanksgiving Week in October closed with a grand carnival, dance, bonfire and fireworks. Although there was much rejoicing, there were also solemn moments of reflection, gratitude to those returning home, and hope for a better future.

Chapter 9

GROUPS & ORGANISATIONS

The Bowls Club

Lord and Lady Rendlesham formed Mawnan Bowls Club on 29 July 1924 when they presented the club with two sets of bowls, and agreed that they could play on the front lawn of Bosloe Estate. The subscription was 2s.6d. With help and advice from the Falmouth Bowling Club they carried on meeting at Bosloe until 1927 when a decision was made to construct a bowling green in Mawnan Smith.

The club was built on part of a field and the bowling green had a tennis court at one end. In this field a bungalow was also built for the Nursing Association, and Mrs Hodgkin of Treworgan donated the remainder of the land as a playing field. Lord and Lady Rendlesham also gave £100 towards the construction of the green, along with monies from 15 other vice presidents (patrons). Club members volunteered to carry out the necessary work and the large estates gave their workmen/ gardeners to the club for a week at no cost to enable them to do this. Mr Ruse of Falmouth constructed the actual green once a level surface had been obtained but unfortunately the length of the green was incorrect, and a further account of £46 was charged by Mr Ruse to lengthen the green to 120 feet. Lord Rendlesham gave a further donation of £50.

Lord Rendlesham gave the ground 'in trust' to Mawnan Bowling Club, including the tennis courts. The first trustees were Mr J. Gundry, JP, and Mr R. H. Tremaine. The club opened as the Mawnan Bowling Club on 10 June 1929 at 6.30pm, with a friendly match against Falmouth. The wooden clubhouse was lit by tilly lamps and heated with paraffin heaters until electricity was installed in 1949. Water was obtained by means of a well and windmill; mains water was not plumbed in until 1970.

In about 1936 Mr Philip Charles Pascoe, green adviser to Cornwall County Bowling Association, invented a solid-punch roller turf cutter, grass-levelling and aerating machine that revolutionised the way the turf was kept in order. The club purchased one of Mr Pascoe's turfing machines.

The club continued, but with the Second World War, membership dropped off and by 1945 membership was down to seven playing members and only one rink in use.

In 1948 the club produced the county singles champion, Mr Alec Pascoe, the son of Philip. Well known for his bowling prowess, he played little in club matches, but got his practice at home on a private green which was kept in perfect condition by his father. His delivery was unorthodox, but the shots were never far from the jack.

After the war, membership began to pick up again and on 19 April 1949 Mr Arthur Rowe joined the club. He is still a club member and holds the post of Club President. Mawnan Bowling Club has always had a member of the Rowe family in their club, taking an active part in the running of affairs, and often raising money for the charity SCOPE. In about 1955 Harry Rowe, Arthur Rowe (Harry's son), plus David and Michael Rowe (Harry's grandsons) played as a rink together for Mawnan Bowling Club against Carnon Downs. In 1957 Mr Philip Pascoe and his son Alec, at their own personal expense, constructed the new top green.

In 1984 the membership had risen to a sufficient level to justify the replacement of the old wooden clubhouse. Fund-raising events, interest-free loans from some members, donations and council grants enabled a new clubhouse to be built. A sponsored walk by Mr Jim Spiers raised in excess of £700 when he walked to each bowling club in the area – a total of approximately 29 miles. The new clubhouse was completed and opened on the 24 July 1987.

Inset: *Badge of Mawnan Bowling Club.*

The Mawnan Bowling Club has grown in membership with both male and female members totalling about 70. An indoors short mat has proved successful. The club runs internal competitions, as well as fund-raising events. There are two men's teams and two ladies' teams, and a very popular stroller's team. The club plays in excess of 120 matches as well as club competitions.

The success of the club has only been possible because there has been an army of volunteers over the last 75 years. There are many social functions held during the year by the club members, and the annual 'Bowling Tour' is especially popular. For the 75th anniversary, the National Trust granted permission for the club to hold their celebration of this event at Bosloe Estate, where the bowls club began. In May 2000, the club's contribution to the local millennium celebrations was to stage a 'Rendlesham Day' at Bosloe, along similar lines to the garden fêtes that were held there in the 1920s and '30s. The Local History Group held a mini photographic exhibition depicting the history of the club and of Lord and Lady Rendlesham's involvement in village life.

Left: *Some of the first members of Mawnan Bowling Club, early 1930s.* Left to right: *Mr Chinn, Mr Rashleigh, ?, Mr Gundry, Mr Culley, Mr Cutter.* Bowling: *Mr Albert Bray.*

Below: *Mawnan Bowling Club, 1927 season.* Left to right, back row: *Mr J. Roberts, Mrs Harvey, Mrs J. Vague, Miss I. Chinn, ?, Mr B. Chinn, Mr H. Wilson;* centre: *Mr J. Culley, Mr F. Cornwall, Mr J. Gundry, Mr G. Sanderson, Mr W. Tremayne, Mr Day, (Secretary);* front: *Mr J. Harvey, Mr J. Vague, Mr Cutter (Treasurer), Mr J. Chinn.*

Cricket

Mawnan Cricket Club was formed in 1879. Games were first played on Boskensoe Downs and then, following the First World War, at Penwarne. In 1920, the club moved to Bosveal, where they played every year until 1935. The last move was to Carwinion for the 1935 season and they still play at these grounds.

Cricket in the early years was not taken very seriously as the leagues did not exist at that point; but to play, and even to watch, was quite an event and much anticipated. There were not so many matches played either, because of transport problems. Before 1900 there were no cars, so people tended to get to their destinations by pony and trap or on foot.

As the years passed, village life and cricket were disrupted by the First World War. After the war, however, the club grew steadily stronger. Local leagues were formed and in 1929 the club joined the Cornwall Cricket League, Junior Division I, which is still running. The Second World War temporarily put an end to League cricket, but in 1946 the players became the Junior Division I Champions and winners of the Western Morning News Cup. In 1947 the club won the Vinter Cup – the first junior club to do so. In 1949 a new League was created – the Senior Division II, West of the County – in which there were ten clubs. At that time, there were 11 clubs in the league, but Constantine, Leedstown and Mawnan were the only clubs to have played since its inception. In 1950, Mawnan's cricketers became champions of the Division and won the Lanisley Cup.

They won this cup again in 1970 and were again in the Vinter Cup final, although they lost to Troon. In 1972 they again won the Lanisley Cup, Senior Division II West, and the Jewell Cup. They were in the Vinter Cup final again in 1974 but this time lost to Truro.

There has always been a Second XI to keep the First XI strong. Many members started in the Second XI and have been taught and encouraged to play the game which, as they progressed to the First XI, has made them worthy members of the senior team.

Over the years, many names are repeated, mainly because the love for the game has been passed from father to son; in some cases the whole family has been involved in working for the good of the club.

Although the club had been running for 100 years, there was no record of a club badge. It was felt by the committee that centenary year, 1979, was an ideal opportunity to produce a badge for general club use. The task of designing a badge was given to the children of Mawnan Primary School with the permission of the headmaster, Mr John Vipond. Children from the age of five produced a variety of very good designs which were examined and discussed in detail by the committee. The badge was born from one of these ideas.

The club competes in various cup competitions during each season and there are several individual club trophies to be won each year.

Mawnan Cricket Team, 1995. Standing left to right: *D. Mason, C. Mason, M. Hoban, W. Barbary, D. Pascoe, Scorer D. Rickard;* sitting: *I. Barnes, S. Penrose, R. Pascoe, D. Penrose, Captain G. Andrew, E. Benney.*

CRICKET FACTS

1953: F. Williams won both the batting and bowling in the Second XI.

1954: F.G. Meneer won both the batting and bowling in the Second XI.

1974: M. Mace won both the batting and bowling in the Under 16s.

1975: R. Pascoe won both the batting and bowling in the Under 16s. (This has never happened in the First XI. The nearest to it was in 1964 when Cecil Eddy won the bowling, and in 1965 when he won the batting.)

In 1973 Peter Smith won the bowling and in 1974 won the batting.

In 1951 Harry Pascoe won the batting, whilst younger brother Eric won the bowling.

Peter Rickard won the Second XI batting in 1955 and the bowling in 1956.

John Hodge won the Second XI bowling in 1957 and the batting in 1958.
H. Pascoe won the First XI batting cup nine times. The highest average on this cup was achieved by P.R. James with 39.6 in 1975. The next best was Cecil Eddy with 36.6 in 1959.

G. Curtis won the First XI bowling cup nine times. The best average on this cup was achieved by T. Hodge, with 4.8 in 1946. The next best was W.H. Williams with 6.1 in 1958.

Arthur Christophers won the Second XI batting cup seven times. The highest average on this cup was achieved by R. Trewella with 31.7 in 1973. The next best was H. Pascoe with 30.7 in 1933.

W.H. Williams won the Second XI Bowling Shield six times. The best average on this shield was achieved by W.H. Williams with 4.6 in 1960. The next best was F.G. Meneer with 5.5 in 1958.

In 1981 Martin Churchouse scored the quickest century versus Beacon at Mawnan in 29 deliveries, including 4 fours and 13 sixes.

In 1996 Chris Mason made the highest individual score, 195 not out.

In 1999 the highest batting partnership of 284 runs was made by Chris Mason, 132 not out and G. Andrew 123, not out.

In 1999 Chris Mason made the most runs in a season, 970 and the highest average in a season of 53.89.

In 2001 versus Mullion the highest team score was made, 366 for 4, including a partnership of 264 between David Penrose 131 and D. Griffiths 145.

In 1964 at the age of 50 years, W.H. Williams took 104 wickets (League and Friendlies).

G. Curtis has won The Sportsman of the Year Cup five times.

Soccer

Mawnan Association Football Club began life playing friendly matches in the 1936/37 season. They joined the Falmouth District League the following season. In the 1939/40 season the team reached the Lockhart Cup Final, but was defeated by a Royal Artillery team from Pendennis Castle. The war years then intervened.

The club's first playing field was at Nansidwell Cross. From there it moved to Goldmartin before finally settling in the village National Playing Field. Just before the war the club played a team from the German Battleship *Schleswig-Holstein*, on a visit to Falmouth. Incidentally, this was the first German ship to go into action in the war.

When organised football was restarted after the war it took the club a few years to win its first trophy – the Wheatly Cobb Cup in the 1953/54 season. The club's President at the time of writing, Mr Ben Spike, scored two of the goals in that final and the side included Mr Gordon Meneer and life member, Mr Cecil Eddy.

The history books show that Mawnan Association Football Club became one of the mainstays of junior football in the district and whilst some clubs come and go as rapidly as the seasons, this club has fashioned a well-deserved reputation for reliability and continuity.

During the 1957/58 season the club dropped to the junior league and fostered the policy of developing the skills of youngsters. This proved most successful; the team won the Goldman Cup at the first attempt.

In the 1959/60 season, two teams were again fielded; the First Team reverted to their original status and were successful in winning the Junior

Cup Group (Festival Cup) but were beaten by Chacewater in the next round.

The golden period for the club, until the 2000 season, was in 1970/71 and 1971/2 when it achieved the League and Cup double in the Falmouth-Helston League. It was in the latter season that the club reached the Western Section final of the Cornwall Junior Cup – the only time they reached that stage until the 2000 season, when they were beaten 2-1 after extra time by Truro Hendra at Falmouth Town's Bickland Parc.

Since those heady days the club has enjoyed some success, but during its diamond jubilee season both teams won trophies: the Lockhart Cup and the Wheatly Cobb Cup.

The club has had one or two big names associated with it, including 2002 Barnsley goalkeeper Kevin Miller. He joined Crystal Palace for £1.2 million and has also played for Exeter City, Birmingham City and Watford. There is also England youth international, Matthew Etherington, one of England's brightest prospects who is with Tottenham Hotspur at the time of writing. He was a member of Mawnan's youth teams.

The club has always attracted loyal support through its players and officials and the 2002 chairman, secretary and treasurer have been in office for over 20 years with several other committee members also enjoying long service. This loyalty to the club is embodied in its ability to field a veteran's side, which has become part and parcel of club life at Mawnan. Such is the magnet of veterans' football that even Graham Kelly, the former high-profile Football Association chief executive, can boast that he's played against the club at Carwinion Road.

The club's success has continued into the 2000/2001 season, with the First XI winning the Falmouth-Helston League Division One Championship. The Second XI were runners-up in Division Two and the First XI reached the Cornwall Junior Cup (West) Final again, (which they won, although they lost the Cornwall Junior Cup Final 1–0 to Biscovey).

The club's current officers are: Mr Ben Spike (President), Mr David Rickard (Chairman), Mr Colin Bate (Vice Chairman), Mr Leon Prynn (Hon Secretary) and Mr Barry Christophers (Treasurer).

Mawnan AFC 1953–54. Wheatly Cobb Cup Winners (First trophy won by Mawnan AFC)
Left to right, back row: *Ned Young, Ivor Rashleigh (Chairman), Brian Martin, Ivor Young, George Benney, John Christophers, John Hodge, G. Glover (Team Secretary)*; front row: *Walter Trevenna, W. Campbell, Cecil Eddy, Cecil (Ben) Spike, Gordon Meneer and Arthur Rowe (Falmouth)*

Friendship Club

In 1984 it was realised that there was a need in Mawnan Smith for a club to enable the senior citizens to get together for a weekly meeting and chat over a cup of tea. Mrs M. Tytherleigh and Miss V. Chegwidden met to see if a club could be provided for this. The sum of £200 was given to the club, which was raised as a result of a Harvest Festival Auction held at the Red Lion. The Friendship Club was then formed on 3 October 1984, since which time it has proved to be very successful indeed.

When the club started there were 20 members but 17 years on there are more than double that figure (with 42 members). Each week speakers or entertainers come to the club, outings are arranged and lunches supplied. The highlight of the year is the Christmas lunch. Flowers are provided by the club for members' birthdays.

After the club was formed, a local charity generously helped by paying the yearly rent of the Memorial Hall where the members meet. Only once in 17 years has the price of tea been raised – from 20p to 30p – which caused a great outcry!

Mrs D. Deakins is still looking after the tea ladies and Miss J. Ould is responsible for organising speakers and entertainment.

Friendship Club, 1998. Left to right, back row: *Beryl Ennis, Di Lambert, Dot Christophers, Harold Rondeau, Dorothy Deakins, Edith ?, Ivy Gardner;* third row: *Florence Rashleigh, Audrey Martin, Doreen Rondeau, Phyllis Barker, Veronica Chegwidden, Phyllis Benney, Dora Budd;* second row: *Phyllis Christophers, Joan Simpson, Edith Martin, Estella Barrymaine, Kath Dyer, Margaret Moyle, Marjorie Tremaine, Pat Tunley, Mrs Hobart, June Ould;* front: *Dorothy Barker, Mrs Siers, Naomi Richards, Joan Forward, Lilian Lord, Joyce Combellack, Mrs Ottoway.*

Mawnan Wives

The millennium year was a double celebration for the wives as it was their 30th anniversary in October 2000. The organisation started out as the 'Young Wives Association' back in 1970 – a small group of young Methodist mothers and their children, meeting at each other's houses every Tuesday afternoon for a weekly sub of one shilling. Although named the Young Wives, as part of the ground rules, age limit was discussed and it was decided that anyone who was young at heart, regardless of years, would be welcome and this philosophy still remains today. As time progressed the numbers increased and by 1975 a larger venue had to be found; for the next 15 years the chapel schoolroom became the meeting-place.

The group then started meeting regularly in the evenings, on the first and third Friday of every month. The group was very much allied to the chapel; it served teas after the Sunday-morning service, and supported the NCH (National Children's Homes) by holding coffee mornings and by members keeping Light of Life collection boxes at home. It is still involved in such activities today.

At one time, the number of members dropped to an all-time low of just six people. The possibility of folding the club was discussed, but numbers started to rise again with new members coming from the new Shute Hill Estate. By 1977 the Young Wives had become 'Mawnan Wives', dropping the 'Young' as some members felt that they were now only 'young at heart'! For several years the group put on a variety show (including South Pacific and Seven Brides for Seven Brothers) in the Memorial Hall. All members took part; most quaking in their shoes. Mawnan Wives, along with many others, miss the Mawnan Carnival, as the group always entered a float and won the Carnival Cup many times. Weeks were spent deciding on a theme, of which the 'Roly Polys' and 'Gnomes and Gardens' were two of the best and funniest. The trailer was always decorated under a veil of great secrecy at Richard Matthews' farm. Through jumble sales, fairs, coffee mornings and many other fund-raising events – all hard work but fun – the group has contributed a great deal to charities and good causes both close to home and further afield; from the village Methodist Church Fund, the sports field, the Memorial Hall Fund and Cornwall Air Ambulance to aiding flood relief in Pakistan, as well as the plight of people in Cambodia to name but a few.

In 1990 the Wives of Mawnan moved to the Memorial Hall Committee Room and by 1996 had made their way into the main hall. The programme of events has always been varied – both light-hearted and those of a serious nature – with speakers on all topics from local and maritime history and charities, to talks on wine-making and flower-arranging. There have been many outings through the years, such as trips to the theatre, walks in the vicinity, boat trips, demonstrations and games evenings.

The group has clocked up 170 members since October 1970. In 2002 it is thriving and is an important part of the village community. It is still a lot of fun, although it is more structured nowadays due to increased numbers. The group averages 25 members at meetings but sometimes up to 40 people attend. Early members such as Margaret Moyle and Jane Roberts still belong to the Mawnan Wives. Margaret Lugg, a founder member, was secretary for many years and is still very active within the group. The group feels that it has a bright future and is looking forward with enthusiasm.

Mawnan Wives Group, 1998. Standing left to right: *Jill Glover, Sally White, Lorraine Bannister, Bridget Trout, Pat Mandy, Diane Leopard, Barbara Smith, Jackie Neville, Liz Goddard, Joan Sherratt, Pam Standring, Margaret Gardner;* kneeling: *Barbara Himms, Sue Pitman, Jill Brock, Ann Allen, Pauline Allday, Barbara Pascoe, Paula Fox, June Fox;* front: *Sally Davies.*

Mawnan WI

When the Cornwall Federation of WIs (CFWI) came into existence in 1919, the County Chairman was Mrs Harcourt-Williams of Pencalenick, Truro. In 1931, after being widowed, she married Lord Rendlesham, thus adopting the formal title of Dolores, Lady Rendlesham. She was a staunch supporter of Mawnan WI as was her predecessor, Lilian, Lady Rendlesham.

In February 1920, Mrs Susan Dunstan of Budock Vean Farm (now the hotel) drove around the parish in her pony and trap, encouraging the women of Mawnan to join this novel organisation, run by women for women. Being greeted with considerable interest, she held a meeting in the chapel schoolroom, where Mawnan WI was formed with 30 founder members.

The first communal project was raising money for the proposed Village Hall. Fund-raising events included whist drives in the chapel schoolroom, with the organisers scouring the village for tables and chairs. Large iron nuts lent by Mr W. James, the blacksmith, became useful candle holders. The War Memorial Hall opened in 1923, with the WI holding meetings on the first and third Thursday of each month. By 1930, there were 130 members, who walked to the meetings from as far afield as Estray Park and Helford Passage. This confounded the menfolk, who had predicted a quick demise to this new group!

After 1937, meetings were held once a month. In the early years, the WI started a library and a tennis club and arranged parties, picnics, concerts, etc. Outings, too, were the source of much pleasure. When Penzance was visited in 1924, the return fare for the 'Red Cars' bus was 4s.6d. (22p).

Members of the Men's Club were invited to join a WI choral class to form a choir, under the conductorship of Mr E. Spargo of Mabe. The choir was re-formed in 1951 by Miss M. Arpin, who led parties of carol singers around the area every Christmas.

From 1939 to 1945 the war effort had top priority. Members made jam, collected salvage, organised a National Savings Group, sent parcels to POWs (prisoners of war) and merchant seamen, welcomed evacuees and established a canteen for servicemen. The group even experienced a bomb falling in the field behind the hall, just as a meeting was about to start in 1941.

Arranging and serving teas at community gatherings has long been a WI privilege. On

Coronation Day 1952, members were busy all day, in spite of the fact that those fortunate households with a television set could have been at home watching the crowning of Queen Elizabeth II. During the morning, a marquee was erected in the playing field, tables were decorated, and new dustbins, fitted most ingeniously with taps, were set up for dispensing tea. Sports, teas and the presentation of coronation mugs to the children took place in the afternoon. At the carnival later in the day, the WI won much acclaim for its entry, 'A Pageant of Women', in which members portrayed women through the ages. Prizes were presented by the WI president, Mrs Fawell, who had chosen to celebrate Coronation Day in Mawnan, rather than in London with her family.

The Drama Group is proud of its long reputation for providing first-class entertainment, both for local and county audiences. The commanding, charismatic, pipe-smoking Mrs Doris Wernhard, JP, was responsible for some excellent productions between 1954 and 1959. Three one-act plays were presented at the Memorial Hall in 1955. The plays chosen: *The Six Wives of Calais* (an historical drama), *One Hour Alone* (with Queen Victoria as its subject), and *Closed Windows* (tackling conflict within a family) gripped the audience, whose attention never wavered. A year later, the programme included four sketches by member's children, with the following husbands working tirelessly back stage: Steve Wernhard, Bob Roberts, Gordon Meneer and Ken Minter. In 1959, when *George Comes Home* was performed at the Cornwall Drama Festival, Mrs Frances Hodge was judged to have given the best performance in the county. Other producers included Mesdames Allerton, Bayley, Farrell, Nash and Woodbridge.

The skills learnt at WI courses and classes have enabled members to achieve considerable success in shows and competitions. Both Mrs Mabel Sadler of Norways Farm and Mrs Rita Tremayne of Windyridge Dairy became cookery demonstrators. Mrs Sadler gave four demonstrations at the Ideal Home Exhibition in Olympia. As a result of the publicity, she was invited to appear in 'Westward Diary', on Westward TV in Plymouth on which occasion she made ginger fairings. Added to this, for several years up until 1987, the monthly WI spot on Radio Cornwall was presented by Mrs Frances Hodge (President of Mawnan WI, 1975–1979). Her deep-throated chuckle and sparkling personality came over the air waves exceptionally well.

In recent times WI members have supported Treliske Hospital's Mermaid, Joey and Sunrise appeals. They have also responded to environmental concerns by co-operating with Mr Tony Lugg, the North Helford National Trust Warden, in an annual 'Beach Spring Clean'. Members participate in an ever-increasing choice of activities organised by the county and national federations, such as advanced driving, computing, surfing and hot-air ballooning and four Mawnan members are on county sub-committees.

Every year there are two or three resolutions to debate and vote on at national level, which may eventually have an effect on Government legislation. Interests and commitments may have changed since 1920, but the Institute's popularity remains. It continues to play a central role in village life, contributes to community initiatives, offers a variety of activities to women of all ages, and gives a warm welcome to visitors and newcomers.

The Mother's Union

The Mothers' Union is 125 years old, and was founded in 1876 by Mary Sumner, the wife of the Revd George Sumner, Vicar of Old Alresford, near Winchester. He was the youngest son of the Revd Charles Sumner, Bishop of Winchester. They enjoyed 61 years of married life. Mary came from a wealthy, cultured home, and was a gifted musician. For 30 years she devoted her life to bringing up her family and supporting her husband's ministry. However, by 1878 she had come to the conclusion that women of every class needed to understand that motherhood was a profession. She believed that women's execution of daily household chores, as well as caring for one's children, contributed to the creation of a

loving, happy home in which the family could develop along the lines of Christian thought. So she gathered together all the mothers of homes in Alresford for the first Mothers' Union meeting at the Vicarage in 1878.

The Union is now an international organisation teaching the love and faith of the Christian family. Every branch throughout the world, however small, works towards and contributes to this ideal. It is believed that parishes that have a supportive Mothers' Union are blessed.

It is not absolutely clear when the Mothers' Union was started in Mawnan Smith. It might have existed before 1908, but it was certainly in existence after that date. Mr and Mrs Horton

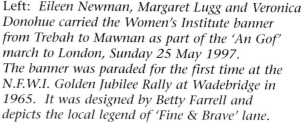

Left: *Eileen Newman, Margaret Lugg and Veronica Donohue carried the Women's Institute banner from Trebah to Mawnan as part of the 'An Gof' march to London, Sunday 25 May 1997.*
The banner was paraded for the first time at the N.F.W.I. Golden Jubilee Rally at Wadebridge in 1965. It was designed by Betty Farrell and depicts the local legend of 'Fine & Brave' lane.

Below: *Old Tyme Music Hall, 1971.*
Left to right: *Irene Jack and Jean Christophers on 'A Bicycle Made For Two'.*

Above: *W.I. 50th Anniversary Dinner,*
Budock Vean Hotel, Monday 16 February 1970.
Among those present were the following members:
back row, left to right: *Joan Pitts, Mrs Mumford, Dorothy Christophers, Betty Manley, Phyllis Roberts, Pearl Roberts;* middle row: *Phyllis Barker, Mabel Smallwood, Rita Tremayne, Frances Hodge;*
front row seated: *Mrs Nash, Priscilla Stephens, Mrs Woodbridge.*

Women's Institute picnic on Maenporth Beach, 1931.
Mothers, left to right: *Mrs Cheffers, Mrs Berryman, Mrs Pascoe and Mrs Eddy.*
Children, left to right: *Phyllis Playle, Jean Critchlow, Joan Wernhard, Billy Eddy, Ada Pearce, Marjorie Pascoe, Blanche Eddy, Rosslyn Cheffers, Sheila Smith, Mary Hodge.*

retired from Godalming to Mawnan Smith in 1908 and lived at Trehunsey Vean and took great interest in local activities. By 1911 Mr Horton was the church organist and Mrs Horton a Sunday school teacher, and no doubt the enrolling member of the Mothers' Union as well. Their meetings were held at Trehunsey Vean until 1924 when the Memorial Hall was opened.

Those early days were very active. A garden fête was held at the Rectory in 1913, where many stall-holders were stalwart Mothers' Union members, parents and secondary-school teachers. Mrs Horton was also responsible for the annual Nativity Play until the Second World War.

In 1919 Mrs Horton's daughter-in-law Dorothy (née Willink) was enrolled as a Mothers' Union member at Mawnan Parish Church. In 1921 a garden fête was held in the grounds of Treworgan near Mawnan Smith, arranged by Mrs Hodgkin and Mesdames Horton and RN Rogers, in order to raise funds for the Church Missionary Society's work in Uganda, and to augment the funds of the local Mothers' Union branch and the Girls' Friendly Society. This was opened by Mrs Warman, wife of the Bishop of Truro.

The branch and a large number of the village community took part in the Diocesan Pageant at St Agnes in 1924. A huge cast from Mawnan was transported by charabanc. Dorothy Horton, who had a beautiful voice, took the part of St Endelion (who, by legend, only lived on cow's milk!), and had to appear leading a docile cow. Dorothy, being town bred, was not too happy about this and neither was the cow, which bolted as the brass band began to play. The cow was captured, and banished to the shrubbery, where it demolished all the greenery within reach! The parishioners taking part in the pageant were Ethel Eland, Lucy, Enid, Eleanor and Dorothy Horton and Mrs Rogers.

During the years of the Second World War life in the village was very much disrupted. Canon and Mrs Hope retired to Mawnan Smith in the early 1940s and meetings were continued under Mrs Hope's leadership. Mrs Moyle moved to Meudon Farm in 1944, and remembers supplying milk for the meetings. These were still held in the Memorial Hall, and were opened by the rector with a prayer. A hymn was then sung. In the winter, members sat in a circle around a warm fire. Mrs Hope would take the meeting, with a talk followed by tea. The young children had their corner with games to amuse them, and were joined by their elder brothers and sisters after school.

St Agnes Diocesan Pagent, 1924. On left: *Ethel Eland, Lucy Horton, Mrs Rogers, Mr Rogers, Enid Horton, Eleanor Horton.* On right: *Dorothy Horton in flowing white robes as St Endelion, others unknown.*

*Mawnan
Mothers Union
Banner.*

Above: *Mothers Union Centenary
Eucharist at Truro Cathedral 3 June
1989. The Mawnan Banner is
shown second from left, carried by
Mrs Margaret Gardner.*

Right: *A tea party in company with
the Kenyan representative of the
Mother's Union, 14 August 1997.
Left to right: Dorothy Wickett, a
teacher from Kenya, Josephine
Mwaniki, Margaret Gardner
and Nookie Capon.*

Left: *All Saints festival 1984.
Members showing their
certificates of service in the
Mother's Union. Back row,
left to right: Sylvia Weatherhead,
Mrs Sainsbury, Mrs Syrett,
Mrs Meneer; front row: Maud
Rickard, Joan Stevens,
Naomi Richards.*

There was always a Christmas party for members and children. Coffee mornings and tea parties were arranged each year to augment the funds of the Mothers' Union and the church. The annual Diocesan Services at Truro Cathedral were always attended.

Mesdames Joan Stevens, Naomi Richards, Maud Rickard and Betty Meneer were enrolled in 1949. They have been members for over 50 years.

The Annual General Meeting of 1967 is the earliest written record of the branch. Mrs Phyllis Benny was the enrolling member who arranged many interesting programmes during her time in office.

In 1968 Mrs Benny retired, and as nobody came forward for election, the Revd Osborne agreed to take the Chair with a small working committee including Mrs Howard (Secretary), Mrs Meneer (Treasurer) and Mrs Farell to run the branch. During this period a sewing guild that met each month was formed to facilitate the making of articles for charitable purposes. Corporate communion was also held on the first Wednesday of the month at St Michael's Church.

The Revd Osborne resigned in 1969, and the Revd John Ruscoe became rector. His wife, Mrs Beth Ruscoe, followed as the enrolling member. She inherited an efficient and well-run branch.

The group agreed to clean the brass in St Michael's Church, and hold a stall at the Christmas bazaar. Members also arranged flowers in the Parish Church on Mothering Sundays.

By 1972 the Union had a banner. Miss Eland, from the staff of Falmouth Girls School, left a legacy in her will for one to be made for the Mawnan Smith Mothers' Union. It was designed and made by the Sisters of the Epiphany at their convent in Truro. Sister Cecilia and Miss Kathleen Gauntlett embroidered the banner and Mr Cecil Lowrey framed it and made the carrying pole. It was first carried at the Penweris Deanery Festival by Mrs Alcock, Mrs Wright and Mrs Mannering and has been taken to all Diocesan and Deanery Festivals through the years. In 1972 Mrs Manning, Mrs Birch and Mrs Clark were enrolled.

By 1983 the Revd John and Mrs Ruscoe had retired, and the organisation lost two much-loved and respected people who had done a great deal to make the Union a strong working and a spiritual presence in the parish. Mrs Anne Peck and Mrs Karen Bray were enrolled, and Mrs Fox, Mrs Wickett and Mrs Anne Palmer were welcomed to the branch. The Mothers' Union now faced many challenges in a changing world. During this period, the leadership was in the hands of Mrs Anne Palmer, Mrs Dorothy Wickett and Mrs Nookie Capon, assisted by Secretary Mrs Sylvia Weatherhead, and Treasurer Mrs Margaret Gardner, as well as other loyal, friendly and hard-working members. The Union's new rector was the Revd Patrick Connor, followed by the Revd Nigel Eva and the Revd Jackson, who all gave the group a great deal of help. Mrs Liz Goddard was enrolled during this time, as was Mrs Joan Sherratt.

Mr and Mrs Hird kindly opened their lovely garden with swimming pool for a strawberry tea and a swim, as part of the celebration of Truro's centenary year.

Divorced women are now allowed to become members, and are given support when it is needed. Additionally, more work is focussed on developing the Union's overseas commitments. Locally, young families are helped and support is given to the Mothers' Hostel in Truro. The organisation has sent food parcels to AWFI ('Away From It All') who give holidays to families who need a rest. A little bit of knitting is still done; the organisation keeps the premature babies' clinics well supplied with warm woollies.

At Christmas 1989 the group gave their first Christingle service jointly with the Methodist Church and the Girl Guides, who helped to make the Christingle oranges. It is a lovely service held at St Michael's and is a time to remember all those children in the world that are not able to celebrate and have fun at Christmas. The service serves as a joyous act of family worship; the local children present the money they have raised, and in return are given a Christingle orange and candle. They proceed to their seats, the church lights are extinguished and carols are sung by candlelight. Their parents fill the church and make the happiest start to the Christmas season in Mawnan.

In 1997 the Union was visited by Mrs Josephine Mwaniki and friend from Nairobi, Kenya. They are Teacher Guiders and Mothers' Union members. They had been to the Scout and Guide jamboree in Cornwall, and wanted to meet some Mothers' Union members before they left England. A tea party was arranged for them at Dorothy Wickett's house, and a wonderful afternoon was had, comparing family lives and charitable works in the UK and Kenya; a true sign that the Union's overseas commitments are so worthwhile.

The Union's work goes forward into the 21st century. Mrs Beryl Balchin, Miss Sylvia King, Mrs Elizabeth West and Mrs Christine Grint are all now among our members. Thanks must go to all the mothers for their loyalty and faith.

The Helford River Gig Club: The Story So Far

by Martin Wills

The tranquil waters of the Helford River with its secluded creeks have inspired local people since the beginning of time. Those of us who love to see traditional racing boats on the river have long imagined a Cornish pilot gig, a six-oared, clinker-built 32-footer slipping quietly up Port Navas creek or carving its way through the famous easterly seaway off Mawnan Shear.

The pilot gig which is now used for racing is in fact a working boat designed for a life on the open sea. Historically, such gigs were used all around the Cornish coast, primarily for putting a pilot aboard an approaching trading ship. However, the speed and seaworthiness of these vessels made them very popular for smuggling.

In the summer of 1994 the dream became reality when the Helford River Gig Club was formed. Its aim was to attain enjoyment of the sea by proficiency in the skills of watermanship, seamanship and oarsmanship – and most of all to win the numerous races against other racing gigs, which are held all around our magnificent Cornish coastline and on the Isles of Scilly.

There was obviously huge enthusiasm around the river, but there was no gig. Ralph Bird, pilot-gig builder from Devoran, was duly instructed to lay the oak keel and after the elm had been steeped in Devoran sea water the vessel gradually took shape. The pilot gigs of Cornwall were probably never designed, but were the result of centuries of evolution. More recently, standards have had to be set for competitive racing gigs.

The pilot gig, *Helford*, was launched at Gweek in August 1995. Her maiden voyage included

Right: *The pilot gig* Golden Gear *with Mens B crew including Simon Walker, Alex Grant, Simon Hill, Tim Pinfield, Simon Tregonning, John Welch, Martin Wills (coxwain).*

The pilot gig Helford *on her maiden voyage from St Anthony-in-Meneage to Helford.* Crew (from bow): *Tom Wills, Jo Trout, Martin Wills, Ann Muller, Rob Jeffery, Fergus Miller, Roger Rosier (coxwain).*

navigating around the Dennis Head, in a dramatic easterly sea. By now blood was running high to join the competition and enter her in the World Pilot Gig Championships in the Scillies in the spring of the following year.

The club entered an enthusiastic crew who had trained hard to be among 50 other gigs from around Cornwall, Holland and the USA in the two-mile race from St Agnes to St Mary's. The adrenaline rush paid off as they coasted home after a mid-field finish.

This was only the start of things to come. By 1997 the club had six racing crews, and each training session ended at the Ferry Boat Inn for an analysis of technique, timing and fitness. Even the gig fittings came under scrutiny. How could one win without breaking the rules? An exciting

season of events around the coast followed, with a steady improvement in results, and people were beginning to sit up and take notice of the Helford River Gig Club.

By 1998 membership had increased to 170 and the second gig, the *Golden Gear*, had been launched. The club's men's crew had achieved an outstanding fifth position in the County Championships at Newquay.

Rowing on Sunday mornings continues, and all visitors are welcome. The gig has now become an integral part of the Helford River and the parishes that surround it. She offers young and old an opportunity to get out on the water, keep fit and most of all have fun.

One thing is for sure... the best is yet to come!

Guides & Scouts

The first company of Guides, First Durgan Company, was registered on 3 November 1932 and met at the school room at Durgan. The Captain was Mrs G.R. Fox and the Lieutenant was Miss Lorna Croft (now Mrs Black), who later became Captain for some years.

The company moved to Mawnan and eventually changed its name to First Mawnan Smith Guides, and was registered on 6 November 1944. It subsequently closed in 1948, but re-opened in 1950 with the Captain Mrs A.L. Goodman and Lieutenant Miss M.A. Richards. It then appeared to close again on 22 November 1954. Details of the organisation's activities during the 1960s are rather hazy.

Mrs Yvonne Moore became the Guide Leader in the 1970s when her three daughters became involved in Brownies and Guides, but the company closed again in 1978.

It was opened under Miss Doreen Burtt, who was the Guide Guider between 1979 and 1984. She started a strong camping tradition for the unit.

Mrs Christine Grint took over from Miss Burtt in 1984, having moved from running the Brownie Pack, and is still the present Guider. Miss Wendy Griffith has also been Young Leader and Assistant Guider from 1994 to the time of writing.

The First Mawnan Guides

At the time of writing the Guide Company has 19 girls aged between 10 and 14 years. There is usually a group from the top class at Mawnan school, as well as from the various schools in the area; thus Guides provides a chance to keep up with old friendships in the village. Since 1984 the

Guide Leader has been Chris Grint, who says that time flies when you are enjoying yourself.

The normal programme is discussed and agreed with the girls, and the aim is to have a varied and balanced programme over the year with a mixture of arts and crafts, outdoor activities, service projects, international aspects, health and safety (such as first aid and fire fighting), homecraft skills and of course fun and games. Sometimes the activities are all carried out together and at other times the Guides plan and enjoy activities in their smaller groups or 'patrols', which encourages team work and leadership skills. Any activities connected with food are especially popular. The group recently raised money for the Joey Hospital Appeal, taking part in a joint Gang Show with the other uniformed groups in the village – which was great fun but exhausting!

Guides can also work for a very wide selection of interest badges. The highest award is the Baden Powell Trefoil which requires a lot of commitment to complete. The group were delighted that Hannah Rae completed this award last year and was presented with the badge by the District Commissioner. She abseiled half way down the cliff at Goodygrane Quarry, watched by her fellow Guides. Four other Guides also gained this award and were presented with their badge at the Cornwall Scout/Guide Jamboree in 1993.

The Guides were very fortunate that Guide Leader Doreen Burtt made a huge effort to establish the unit with tents and camping equipment during the early 1980s. The Guides have camped every year since then. They mainly camp in Cornwall, but have also been to Foxlease in Hampshire and Chigwell (outside London). The Guides have even been on a trip to Switzerland,

Above: *The First Mawnan Company was formed in 1950, with Guide Captain Mrs Sam Goodman and Assistant Leader Mrs M. Richards. It continued for four–five years. Sam and Sally Goodman of Carlidnack gave much time, effort and financial assistance to the Guide Company and later to Mawnan Youth Club. First Church Parade of newly formed Girl Guides, December 1950. Left to right: Marlene Warren, Irene Nancholas, Sylvia King, Pat Penrose, Jean Paget, Amelia Eddy, Dora Sale, Margaret Badger, Susan Male, Yvonne Snell, Heather Sandford, Ann Christophers, Ann Bray.*

The First Durgan Guides outside Durgan schoolroom, 1932.

Guides and Scouts, 1968. Left to right, back row: Robin Nichols, Gary Sams, Debbie Spike, Caroline Gundry, Jayne Briars, Stephen Phillpot, Anthony Hutchinson, Hugh Clark, Andrew Christophers; front: Suzanne Gendall, Susan Gundry, Vicky Lander, Janet Stone, Becky Briars, Jackie Rickard, Fay Rickard, Nicola Hutchinson, Susan Clark, Marcia Spike, Jenny Coombes.

where they visited 'Our Chalet' – one of the four World Centres which belong to the Guide Association. Guides still have the opportunity to practise some of the traditional camping activities, especially cooking on their own wood fires!

They have taken part in the three Scout/Guide Jamborees held in Cornwall. The last one was held in 1997, and the Guides hosted a group of Kenyan Guides during camp and for the following week, which was a wonderful experience.

Guiding offers great opportunities for leaders as well. Wendy Griffiths, as their Young Leader at that time, and Chris Grint took part in a Sail Training Trip four years ago, which was also a remarkable experience.

Mawnan has had a Guide Company in the village for a very long time. During 2001 the *Falmouth Packet* reported a reunion of former Guides who were at Durgan in the 1930s.

To sum up, Guides mostly enjoy coming along to be with their friends, but hopefully they will learn some life skills and care for others and the environment along the way. As Baden Powell said, 'If it is not fun it is not Guiding.'

Chris Grint would like to convey her thanks to all her helpers over the years and to the parents who, especially during 2000/01 have been a tower of strength, helping on a rota while seeking another regular helper. Thanks also go to the Chapel Hall where the Guides have met for a long time.

It is amazing how being involved with Guiding means having friends all over the world. Guides, Young Leaders and Guiders have found it is very helpful when applying for colleges and jobs to say they have been involved in Guiding in some capacity. As a Guide, all sorts of challenges come your way, but there are also lots of small ways in which help can be given. Chris Grint would recommend Guiding to anyone – it can be an amazingly challenging hobby and it is never too late to start!

Mawnan Brownies

Brownies were first established in 1914, when they were called 'Rosebuds'. Mawnan Brownies, however, have been running for over 25 years. Brownies have come a long way since 1914. The uniform has changed a lot, and so have the badges the girls wear. Brownies are able to choose interesting things to do from eight different

Bishop's Forum Activity Centre, Goodygrane Quarry, summer 1999. Photograph shows a mixture of First Mawnan and First St. Budock Guides, Leaders and sport centre staff. Leaders: Chris Grint and Jill Rae; guides: Hannah Saw, Emily Druce, Hannah Christophers, Lucy Rae, Ruth Hodges, Zoe Treen, Hannah Bray, Stephanie Curtis, Katie Pinch, Elizabeth Hill, Leila Heppel, Benyna Richards, Claire Lawson, Susie Gutmanis, Hannah Rae and Kate Parsons.

challenges on three journeys: footpath, road and highway.

The eight challenges are Wide Awake, Keep Fit, Do Your Best, Make Things, Be Friendly, Lend A Hand, Help At Home and Fun Out Of Doors. At the end of each Journey (which takes about a year to complete) the Brownie is awarded a badge.

The girls can also earn interest badges. There are 69 in total, some of which are staged. For the older Brownie there is the Go Challenge badge. Working towards this badge teaches the Brownie to think for herself.

A Brownie Pack is run by an Adult Guider (an unpaid volunteer). The Guide Association trains all Guiders.

The Mawnan Brownie Pack (for girls aged seven–ten years old) meets every Thursday, at the Methodist Hall from 5–6.30pm.

First Durgan Troop, 1932–1944
by Eric Chinn

In 1932, Lord Rendlesham of Bosloe persuaded all the local landowners to help him form The First Durgan Troop, with the headquarters in the school room. The gardener and butler at Bosloe, Alfie Smith and George Walton, became the Scout leaders, with Lord Rendlesham being the very generous benefactor. At the annual meeting of the Falmouth and District Scouts in 1932, the District Scoutmaster remarked that at Durgan there was a keen, enthusiastic, well-led troop – a really brilliant example of what a village troop can be.

During the next few years the boys played host to other troops, arranged fund-raising bazaars, spent a holiday in London and took an extremely active part in all community events. Weekly meetings had been well-attended, considering that the boys from Mawnan and outlying farms had to walk an average of two miles to their headquarters. The troop consisted of Scouts Francis Eddy, Ron and Ted Smith, Percy and Reggie Randlesome, Joe Rashleigh, Maurice Simpson, Jim and Brian Stevens, Ken Tabb, George Pascoe and Douglas and Philip Bailey.

These boys were of the right age to be in the Armed Services for most of the Second World War: Francis Eddy had a successful career as a Naval Officer, Douglas Bailey, DFC, became a Squadron Leader in the RAF, Percy Randlesome was in the Army and a POW for most of the war.

From 1936 onwards the country was struggling to get out of depression and quite a number of Scout troops came to Mawnan for summer camps: from Chalfont St Giles, Epping Forest, Hampton and Richmond, Middlesex and Sheffield. They often challenged the local troop to various sports, such as swimming and cricket.

Around this time troop leader Douglas Bailey was to become Assistant Scoutmaster as Alfie Smith was semi-retired. Four Bailey brothers from Bosanath were in the troop: Douglas, Philip (later with the paratroops at Arnhem), Alan and Peter.

In 1939/40 Douglas joined the RAF and Troop Leader Eric Chinn took over, later to become ASM, followed by John Browne in 1943. When John was conscripted in 1944 the troop disbanded.

Residing in the parish in the pre-war period was Brigadier General Billy Croft, the Scouts County Commissioner who kept the troop 'on its toes'. His daughters, Lorna and Angela, ran the local Girl Guides.

At the time of writing, Douglas is living in retirement at Grampound. Eric kept in touch with the village over the years and returned to live here in 1998. John, a retired Police Sergeant in Bristol, came back on retirement, but was tragically killed in a cliff fall at St Agnes whilst fishing.

In the summer months from 1930 until disbandment, the troop met at Durgan school room and generally had a great time around the cliffs and woods. Weekly meetings in winter were held at Mawnan school, Dryden James' Reading Room and a room at Cocksclose at the foot of Shute Hill. Mr Hewitt from Helford Passsage taught knot-tying.

Many well-attended whist drives were held in the Memorial Hall and the Scouts' trek cart was seen around the village collecting old newspapers for the war effort. Durgan schoolroom was often several feet high in newspapers, and the troop remembers the dust when cleaning up after the papers were collected.

There was a successful camp in August 1939 in the field opposite Bosloe Lodge, with visiting troops joining in campfire sing-songs and games on Grebe Beach. Another camp was held in 1941/42 at Bosanath, when evacuated boys from Latymer School, London, had joined the troop.

As well as attending village functions the troop also attended the annual St George's Day Parade at Falmouth Church.

A typical cost of the Scout uniform in 1940/41 was:

First Durgan Strip	2d.
Woggle	3d.
Pair of stockings	3/11d.
Pair of garters	8d.
Purple scarf	1s.8d.
One shirt	5s.8d.
One belt	2s.9d.
Pair of khaki shorts	6s.0d.
Corduroy shorts	9s.0d.
One hat (superior)	4s.9d.

Everyone wanted a hat superior, on which the brim had to be stiff and straight.

As well as those mentioned above, Scout personnel before and during the Second World War (who were members of the Seagulls, Otter, Fox and Woodpigeon patrols) included:

Local Boys

Doug Bailey	Cyril Curnow
Alan Bailey	John Christophers
Peter Bailey	Bernard Rowe
Eric Chinn	Cyril Playle
John Chinn	Bernard Badger
Ivan Spike	Joe Gundry
Cecil (Ben) Spike	Stewart Berriman
Reg Eddy	Arnold Toy
Cecil Eddy	Arthur Blishen
John Browne	Geoff Paine
Tommy Bray	P. Newton
Herbert Curnow	

Latymer boys (Edmonton, London)

Alan Pearce	Reg Wheatley
Ronald Gascoine	David Bolam
Geoff Poole	Alan Lewis
Dennis Boost	Robert Marley
Reg Calvert	Gordon McLeod
Brian Rabin	John Brooks
Robert Manning	Eric Smith
Grenville Downe	James Smith
Lawrence Morgan	Ken Morris
John Francis	

Between 1940–45 life was very full for many of the Scouts who were also in the Home Guard and Air Training Corp. This probably contributed to the disbandment of the troop.

The Helford River Children's Sailing Trust

'Confidence through Competence' is the purpose of the Helford River Children's Sailing Trust. This imaginative charity aims to give 8–9-year-old local children confidence for life, by enabling them to learn to sail single-handed and then to pass on their skills. Since its foundation in 1997, the Trust has provided instruction for more than 700 children and has enjoyed support from all quarters – volunteers, schools, neighbours in the sailing community, the RYA, donors, funding bodies and trustees. Success is due to the proven dedication of all involved: from the volunteer boatswain, who visits every day, to the 70 volunteer instructors, who each give a minimum of five sessions in the season.

Each group of volunteers is based on a particular local school, fostering a sense of ownership within each team. A grant has been secured from Sport England to provide for an RYA Senior Instructor to be out with every outing. With the business sponsorship the plan for 2002 provides a ferry and towed dinghy-mother ship for 12 dinghies enabling multi-site embarkation, saving travel time and vehicle miles, wider choice of sailing area, more effective sailing time, a multi-level activity, doubling rate of learning and value added by every volunteer's hour.

In 2004 the Trust plans to more than double the fleet, and make many other improvements including facilities for the disabled. The Trust will then be offering 'Sailing for All' to all primary schools in the Helford catchment and on the Lizard, including those affected by economic, social and amenity deprivation.

Of perhaps more than 300 sailors, 150 new young children each year will have opportunity, not only to acquire a skill appropriate to their locality, but to gain confidence in themselves and their ability to achieve and to help others.

Friends of Mawnan Smith Surgery

The Friends of Mawnan Smith Surgery was formed in September 2000 when it was announced that the Penryn Group Practice of Doctors were purchasing the Barclays Bank building in the centre of the village to convert into a much-needed, one-storey surgery, replacing the old one in the square.

The aim of the 'Friends' is to provide equipment and a comfortable environment for the benefit of the patients of Mawnan surgery. Since the organisation's formation the members have been overwhelmed with the kindness, interest and help shown by the supporters of the fund-raising events.

The committee of eight persons, chaired by Gill Glover, works well but the group would not exist without its willing band of volunteers and the generosity of its supporters.

Chapter 10

LOCAL BUSINESSES & FACILITIES

Commercial Directories

By the 1830s directories were being published not just for cities and towns, but also for smaller towns and villages.

The following is a list of the chief inhabitants of Mawnan, 1910, taken from Kelly's Directory of that year:

PRIVATE RESIDENTS:

Miss Bulmore, Bareppa
Charles Francis Cole, Meudon Vean
John Cole M.A., J.P., Treworgan &
United University Club, London
Harold Coode, Trerose
George Harcourt, Penwartha
Revd George Theodosius B. Kyngdom,
MA, Trehunsey Vean
Revd Henry Lewis Leverton, BA (rector),
The Sanctuary
Thomas Case Morris, Rosewarren
Henry Rashleigh, Trevean
Mrs Rashleigh, Laden Vean
Reginald Nankiville Rogers, Carwinion
Sidney A. T. Rowlatt, Nansidwell
Rupert Valentine, Carwinion Cottage
William Welsford Ward, JP, Bosloe &
United University Club, London

COMMERCIAL RESIDENTS:

James Bray, dairyman, Bareppa
Richard Cheffers, market gardener, Carlidnack
Charles Choak, farmer, Penpoll
Charles Cock, farmer, Rosemullion
Edwin Charles Courage, farmer and overseer
Arthur Hall, shoemaker
Humphrey Harvey, farmer, Bosveal
Thomas Harvey, miller (water), Tregarne
Thomas Hodge, farmer, Nansidwell
William Houghton, carpenter and sub-
postmaster, Post Office
William James, blacksmith

Alfred Jenkin, dairyman, Penpoll
John Wesley Julian, Meudon
Thomas Lawry, farmer, Tregarne
Humphrey Mann, farmer, Penwarne
William Manuel, builder
William Orchard & Son, farmers,
Chenall Farm
John Ould, farmer, Carlidnack
Henry Pascoe, shopkeeper, Durgan
John William Pascoe, shoemaker
James Phillips, carpenter
Henry Rashleigh, builder,
contractor and undertaker
Reading Room & Library (John Moore,
secretary)
Reading Room & Library (William
Retallack, secretary), Durgan
Charles Roberts, farmer, Higher Tregarne
John Roberts, farmer, Boskensoe
John Peter Sadler, Red Lion Inn
Edward Skewes, farmer
William John Toy, farmer, Bosveal
William Tremayne, farmer, Glebe Farm
Peter Wilmet, butcher, Carlidnack

The businesses operating within the parish in the year 2001 included:

Alanco – garage/shop
Post Office and Spar store
Feathers – ladies' wear
Japonica Lingerie/Arts
Jans – hairstylist
Giuseppe's Ristorante Italiano
Hammer 'n' Hoe – iron-mongery/gifts
Bradford & Bingley – estate agent
Berry & Co. – estate agent
Red Lion Inn – public house

N.L. Medlyn – butcher/delicatessen
MS Electrical
Sadler TV Service
Beechwood Tree Services
Victor Stevens – landscapes
Keith Penrose – funeral director
Riverside Flowers
Meudon Country House Hotel
Trelawne Hotel
Budock Vean Golf & Country
House Hotel
The Ferry Boat Inn
Helford River Boats
Trebah Gardens
Glendurgan Gardens
Carwinion Gardens

FARMS

Mr Benney – Trerose Farm
Mr Benney – Rosemullion Farm
Mr Roger Williams – Meudon Farm
Mr Rex Sadler – Norways Farm
Mr Kessell – Trebah Farm
Mr Percy Lawry – Tregarne Farm
Mr Richard Matthews – Boskensoe Farm
Mr Edward Benny – Penpoll Farm
Mr Paul mann – Penwarne

The village is also very ably served by dairyman Colin Sweet and a doctors' surgery. Over the years the village has lost, due to closure, the Dairy, café/shop, two general stores as well as Lloyds and Barclays bank branch offices.

Berry & Co

Berry & Co, surveyors and estate agents, occupy Goldmartin House, which is the most southerly property in Goldmartin Square. It was previously occupied for many years by the Plater family who ran it as a general store. Berry & Co was established in 1988 and specialises in commercial agency and development work. During the 1990s the firm became increasingly involved in the acquisition of some of the larger residencies in Cornwall, and it was a natural progression for them to open a residential agency in Mawnan Smith in 1998. This office specialises in the niche market of the North Helford Conservation area. The Principal, Peter Berry, began working in property in the late 1960s. He moved to Cornwall in 1983, where his family had been associated with the village of Mawnan Smith since 1937.

Bradford & Bingley

Originally the village estate agency was located adjacent to the Red Lion Inn, bearing the name of Stockton & Plumstead. This was a rural estate agency dealing with properties in the local area. There have been several changes of name over the years, including Stockton Plumstead & Barns and Stockton & Blackford, which incorporated Adriana Antiques.

Then there was a change of location to the present site in Goldmartin Square and another name change to Stockton & Mutton. The name subsequently changed again, to R.E. Prior & Co., then Pass Barton, followed by Black Horse Agencies, and finally to its present name – Bradford & Bingley Stratton Creber. The prices of properties have also altered dramatically.

In terms of the day-to-day running of the business, equipment such as typewriters, cameras and photostat machines have changed for the better following the introduction of computers, digital cameras and colour photocopiers.

There has also been huge changes in the way in which prospective purchasers make contact with the agents, as they now use faxes, email and, of course, the internet.

Although the equipment and the names may have changed, the professional service that the company offers has remained the same. Bradford & Bingley Stratton Creber prides itself on its continued success in selling all types of property in and around the North Helford area. It offers a personal service providing clients with accompanied viewings whenever required.

The company has 'moved with the times' and is pleased to be able to offer vendors and purchasers alike selling and buying advice, with the backing of retail branches, together with national advertising and colour property publications.

Feathers

Mrs Bethel-Gibson, has lived in the village since 1979 and took over the shop in August 1989. It was previously a haberdashery and gift shop, selling jumpers, skirts and many wellies! Both the interior and exterior were completely renovated and refurbished to accommodate the sale of classics, casuals, separates, underwear and accessories. The clientele includes a high percentage of visitors, who revisit the area throughout the year, and of course locals from a large catchment area.

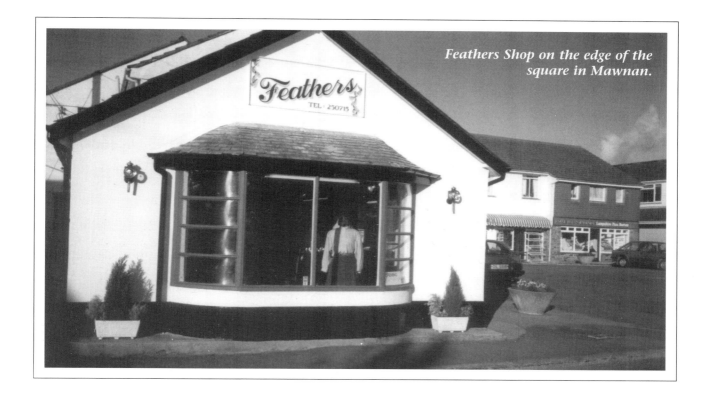

Feathers Shop on the edge of the square in Mawnan.

The Hammer 'n' Hoe
by Gill and Ivan

It is now over ten years since we became owners of the Hammer 'n' Hoe. The shop is situated at the rear of the Square, which is in the centre of the village, opposite the Red Lion Inn. The store originally sold hardware and gardening products and although it still sells similar equipment, the emphasis is now much more on being a village shop and general store.

The success of the business comes from stocking a wide range of goods, and the shop now sells just about anything that we consider to be useful and an asset to the local community. In doing so we have introduced a wide selection of gift items, whilst always endeavouring to promote products made in Cornwall. We have also increased our greeting-card selection into a comprehensive range, including many cards depicting local scenes.

Probably the most enjoyable aspect of running a village shop is the overview one gets of village life – seeing people move in and move away, getting to know some lovely customers, watching the children growing up and hearing all the news of births, deaths and marriages... and some more interesting things!

Having taken over the shop as complete novices, we can now say we know a modesty block when we see one, and can provide items as diverse as a walking stick ferrule and a tooth-fairy box, to a cafetiere cover and a cabin hook.

We also derive much satisfaction and sense of accomplishment when visitors say 'what a nice shop you have – we wish we had a similar one where we live.'

Mawnan Memorial Hall

This was initially known as Mawnan War Memorial Hall, because very soon after the end of the First World War the people of Mawnan decided that a hall should be built as a memorial to the men who had served and those who had fallen, rather than erecting the more usual war memorial cross, which was the focal point of many other communities.

Land was purchased on Sampy's Hill for £50 from Mr M.U. Tonkin of Penwarne. It was vested in five trustees – the Revd H. Leverton and Messrs A. Bray, J.G. Dunstan, P.H. Horton and R.N. Rogers. The deeds stipulated that 'a hall, club, institute, recreation or reading room, yard and outbuildings for entertainment or parties was to be built within five years. The building

Mawnan Memorial Hall.

would be for the use of parishioners and other people resident in Mawnan, within one mile of the boundary. Men and women above the age of 16 who were 'sober, industrious, and of good character' would be entitled to use the hall and to become subscribers, without regard to their political or religious opinions.

Mr Toy of Mabe agreed to build the hall. When no work had been started on the site by mid-1922, the President of the newly-formed Women's Institute, Lady Rendlesham, told the Chairman of the Hall Committee that the WI would take things in hand. As a result, several ladies joined the committee and within a month work had begun, with the foundation stone being laid on 8 November 1922.

The opening ceremony on 20 July 1923 was an impressive affair, and was attended by such prestigious names as the Bishop of Truro, Dr Guy Warman, the President of the Cornwall Federation of Women's Institutes, Lady Molesworth of St Aubyn and the Lord Lieutenant of the County, Mr J.C. Williams. Led by Mawnan Brass Band, the officials, members of the WI and the schoolchildren processed from the school (now Trevanion Court) to the hall, where Mr Williams unlocked the door. A concert by Falmouth Male Voice Choir in the evening filled the hall to overflowing.

Although the hall was in use, a debt of around £300 remained, so fund-raising continued. In August 1925, the WI organised a fête at Bosloe, where the stalls did a brisk trade in the

sunshine. This was followed by a dance in the hall. A few of the older residents did not approve of dancing in the hall; they were conscious of the fact that the building was erected in memory of those who had died in the war and as such were distressed by the idea of 'dancing on the dead'.

Three months after the opening ceremony, the first of many wedding receptions took place, when Mr and Mrs J. Gundry of Trebah Farm celebrated the marriage of their eldest son, Pearce. Pearce remembered this occasion by sending a donation to the hall committee some 50 years after the event.

By August 1924, the debt had finally been paid and the War Memorial Hall did, at last, belong to the village. The total cost of £2000, all raised locally, was a vast sum in those days. (Remember a cup of tea cost one penny, a pasty three pence and a concert admission one shilling!)

In 1928 a local builder, Mr H. Rashleigh, added a billiard room for the Men's Club at a cost of £450, whilst Lady Rendlesham presented the £50 billiard table. On the day that Mrs Black of The Crag at Maenporth opened the billiard room, Mrs Hodgkin of Treworgan opened the children's playing field (adjacent to the Bowling Club) and a village fair was held in Goldmartin Field.

Electricity was installed in the hall during 1933, which meant goodbye to lamps and the onerous task of lighting the copper (the furnace) to boil water.

The hall played its part in the Second World War. For quite a time it was, by day, the school for the evacuated Latymer children, whilst in the evenings there were plenty of morale-boosting social gatherings. The billiard room (later converted into the kitchen and Rendlesham Room) was used as a canteen for the soldiers who were billeted at Penwarne at the beginning of the war, while the pill-boxes and beach defences were erected. The kitchen (now the toilets beside the stage) was a hive of industry, as the band of loyal workers (including Lorna and Angela Croft and led by the first Lady Tuker) cooked chips, sausages, eggs and beans on two primus stoves at weekends.

When Mrs Joyce Dyer came to live in Mawnan after the war, she was instrumental in arranging for the regular celebration of Mass in the hall on Sunday mornings, until St Edward's Church was built at Nansidwell Corner.

In 1957 a proposed resolution that the hall be closed for a year, as not many people were prepared to serve on the management committee, resulted in a flurry of interest from concerned residents. As such, by 1961 the officers, Mr Ivor Rashleigh, Mrs B.O. Stephens and Mr Harry Pascoe, headed a thriving group once again. In 1969 the Chairman, Mr David Dyer, was astonished with the attendance at another Extraordinary General Meeting after the same problem had arisen; this time over 60 residents turned up to give their support.

More than 20 years later, Mrs Daphne Benham suggested that the premises be refurbished. The stage area was extended and the billiard/snooker room was moved to below the new stage. This allowed for the construction of a superb kitchen and committee room as well as modern toilet facilities, with financial assistance from the Parish Council, the County Council, Kerrier District Council and the Rendlesham Trust.

The 75th anniversary of the opening of the hall was marked by a poignant exhibition reminding everyone what the loss of the young men in the two world wars meant to their families, friends and neighbours. During the exhibition the Chairman of the hall committee, Mr Nigel McLusky, was on hand to point out the improvements that were being undertaken, which included an induction loop for the hard of hearing, a new sound system, new tarmac at the front of the building and on the side path, a refurbished committee room, plus a dishwasher and a new floor.

One unpopular but necessary task that falls to the management committee is the setting of rental charges for the use of the facility. They have been subsidised in recent years by profits received from the annual summer craft fairs. More financial assistance has come from legacies left by former residents and visitors in appreciation of the happy times they have spent in the hall.

Volunteers who have carried out most of the administrative, maintenance and repair work over the years, giving generously of their time and expertise, have served the community well since 1922 and have ensured that Mawnan has a superb up-to-date hall for use by future residents.

Ristorante Italiano

Giuseppe Di Maio came from the island of Ischia, Italy, to Cornwall in 1973. He eventually bought his own restaurant, which he called Giusseppe's Ristorante Italiano, in 1987 in the picturesque village square of Mawnan Smith.

Giuseppe's is a family-run business, which has established a fine reputation over the last 14 years or so. The staff pride themselves on the warm and friendly atmosphere and service they offer to every customer. The restaurant serves only the best in fresh local produce, cooked with Italian imagination and flair. It specialises in the finest seafood cuisine using locally-caught fresh fish, although it caters for many other tastes as well. A fully licensed bar and a full range of wines is also available.

The Square & Goldmartin Garage
by Phyll Stevens

Jim Stevens was born in Mawnan in 1920. On leaving Mawnan school, he was apprenticed to Mr Thomas, who had a garage in Porth Navas. During the Second World War, he was conscripted to work on aircraft; he worked for A.V. Rowe at various airfields. Two years' compulsory National Service followed, which meant that Jim didn't return home until 1948.

For a short time he helped Mr Phil Pascoe create and repair bowling greens, but cars were his first love, so Mr Pascoe cleared the garage behind what is now Berry's Estate Agent, so that Jim could open his own garage. This business was so successful that it became necessary to expand.

In the early 1950s Jim purchased a parcel of land opposite the Memorial Hall from Mr Matthews, constructed a workshop, and estab-

lished Goldmartin Garage. The twins, Gill and Jan, were born in 1953, so Jim built a bungalow behind the garage in 1956, where they lived until 1978. He spent a lot of time at motor trials, and boating on the Helford River.

In 1962 when Phil Pascoe put his General Stores, unique bowling green and petrol pumps on the market, Reg and Rita Tremayne acquired the shop and Jim purchased the rest of the Square. The original Miss Cochrane's shop (now Feathers) became 'Sou'wester', selling boating wear, sailing gear and fishing tackle, with a row of shops and flats built alongside.

When the main sewer pipes came through the village in the early 1970s, permission was granted for another row of flats and shops (which included Hammer 'n' Hoe) to be built on the bowling green.

Development of Goldmartin Garage in the early 1950s.

First stage in the development of the Square, by Jim Stevens, c.1962.

P.C. Pascoe's General Stores until 1962. (It is now Berrys Estate Agent.)

Chapter 11

A MISCELLANY OF MEMORIES

The Way Things Were

The village itself was, until relatively recently, comprised mostly of pretty little thatched cottages with thick walls and large, open chimneys – possibly prettier to look at than to live in, by our present standards. Many of these old cob houses still stand, although some have been faced and others have had the thatch replaced with slate or covered with iron sheeting.

Thatch caught fire all too easily, hence the reason for a slated 'Cocks Close', for that roof caught fire about 100 years ago. Men with the appropriate skills and the necessary materials for thatching became scarce and the undertaking was so expensive that few were able to keep their 'bee-hive bonnets', so slates were used instead. Very high-pitched roofs were a feature of the oldest cottages, made in this shape so that the rain (of which Cornwall has a large amount during the course of most winters) ran off without sinking in. Floors were of beaten earth, laster lime-ash sprinkled with yellow sand – this was originally brought round by the well-known figure of Samuel Davy from Penryn with his grey horse, and sold at 2d. per bucket. The oldest windows were sliding ones, seldom opened, and most doors were similar to those found on a stable.

Cob building, unless in a granite district (which Mawnan is not), was fairly commonplace until at least 1814. Cob was really only mud dug from clay ground, mixed with broken straw to bind it, and then beaten hard. The most solid cottages had stone for about two feet up and then cob on the top walls often to a thickness of about two feet.

Cooking was done on the open fires. This was called 'baking under' – a good fire of wood or turf was made (peat was seldom used in this district and no coal was used until later) and a flat iron baking sheet was placed on top to make bread or pasties. The bread was often made from barley. Over this an inverted iron basin, called a kettle or baker, was placed and the fire was built up around it.

About 120–130 years ago the large chimneys were mostly filled in and replaced with Cornish ranges (slabs). Unless sold to the incoming tenant, they were often taken away with the tenant vacating the property and installed in the new cottage. It is quite likely that one of the first things to be made on the range would have been a 'heavy cake' for the mason who had installed it! Rafters in the living room were often made into shelves and the bread kept there as there were no pantries for food. Bread was not usually eaten until it was a week old. Food was very plain. Girty milk (thickened milk) was usual for breakfast, as were 'sinkers' (lumps of heavy bread). Potatoes, fish and bread formed much of the staple diet, as meat was seldom eaten until much later when the standard of living began to improve and most cottages began to keep a pig. Even butter at 9d. per lb was considered too expensive. Tea was rarely bought, except for the mother and father of the household.

One old lady says that she can well remember being sent in from Bareppa to Falmouth for 'two penny worth of bits' from the butcher, and as a bribe to get her back quickly was promised 'a drink

Inset: *Mr J. Ould (Uncle Joe) in the doorway of his house 'Ivey Cottage'. He spent many hours on the bench in the Square talking to passers-by; hence the inscription, 'Uncle Joe's seat'. Mawnan's oldest resident, he died in 1956.*

of tea right out of the teapot'. This was a great treat that sent her scampering across the fields as quickly as she could manage. Once she returned and the pasties were cooked, she took one to her brother at school, then went on to Budock Vean to give one to her father. This would now be considered a very long walk for a small child to manage on her own.

'Uncle Joe' remembered when thrashing was done by hand. Around 300 sheaves represented a normal day's work, which earned payment of 1s.10d.

Carts were drawn by two oxen and although Uncle Joe could not remember oxen being used to plough in Mawnan, they were used in Manaccan. Oxen were shod on the outside half of their hind feet. There are two old granite stones with rings in the centre, near where the Post Office is, to which the oxen were tied when they were being shod. One of the blacksmith's shops was just across the road.

Women, recalled Uncle Joe, wore print-corded Suzbonnets with 'turn overs' while they were working in the fields, but had a shawl and bonnet for best wear. Smocks for men were worn until the 1870s. Women were paid about 6d. per day to pick stones from fields, or scare birds, which did great damage to crops, so much so that half a penny was given for each bird head or egg. Cock fighting and other baiting, he said, were only done on the quiet.

Stocks were in use until 1821 – this date is the last time they are mentioned in the church accounts. It is thought that they stood on the right-hand side of the churchyard, just as one went down the steps into the church. As the service was well attended every Sunday, the wrongdoers would be seen by lots of folk and were often given bits of bread by those passing.

Rush candles were made by dipping the pitch of rushes in tallow until the required thickness was obtained. Matches were made by dipping wood sticks into liquid limestone and pipe lighters were made out of a cow's horn, cut off level at the top so that it could be plugged with cork. It was then stuffed with old rag that would easily smoulder; steel and flint were then struck over it in the hope that a spark would drop down and so set the rag alight.

There were various small shops in the village. Additionally, the Red Lion seems to be as old as any other building in the village although its exact age is uncertain. There seem to have been several beerhouses; Mrs Moore at Bareppa ran one, and around 150 years or so ago there was the Pig and Whistle on Grove Hill. This was divided into two cottages, with a very heavily stoned granite passage leading right through one

of them – a very handy spot to catch the Anna Maria miners as they returned home, many with their donkey shay, which was a favourite form of transport for a miner. There was a skittle alley at the back of the Red Lion which later became stables for Mr William Houghton's horses.

There were also carpenter's shops, each with saw pits. One was where Miss Cochrane's shop was built after the First World War, and another where the present Post Office stands. The present sorting office was originally a small cobbler's shop; there seem to have been several of these about the village. Before the present Post Office was established, the village's postal work took place in 'Fairview' a cottage near the old reading room steps; 110–120 years ago a postman walked from Falmouth via Maenporth and delivered letters for all the big houses he passed, but the majority of villagers had to collect their own mail from the Post Office in the village. The Western Morning News could be seen in the old reading room and illustrated papers were sent by several of the big houses and served a very useful purpose 100 years ago. A Band of Hope meeting was also held there once a month.

Underneath (the reading room was up steps to the second floor) was housed a thrashing machine and tackle.

One of the very old villagers told how he started work at the age of eight. Being one of a large family (they mostly were in those days) his parents were glad for him to go into a house where someone was wanted to 'run up' to their distant farm, etc. He served as a kind of errand boy at this house for about three years and earned 'his meat' then he went and lived-in on a farm for 1s.0d. a week.

Another old villager remembers the treatment when one of her family had a sore chest. The brown greasy paper in which a bundle of rush candles was always wrapped, and which were stored over the mantelpiece, was put on the sick person's chest, in the same way that mustard plasters were used much later. She also recalled that having a farthing to spend on sweets was a real treat.

A poorhouse is known to have existed at Goldmartin between 1829 and 1860.

After the difficult days of the First World War, the village celebrated Armistice Day (11 November 1918). The sirens sounded, while steamers and ships hooted to proclaim the cease-fire order. The schoolchildren were given a holiday and quickly formed themselves into a tin-can band parade, carrying any flags they could find at such short notice, including an upside-down French Tricolor.

An old view of Mawnan looking towards Sampys Hill.

Mawnan School 1833 to 1972, now Trevanion Court.

An old view of Mawnan with the Old Schoolhouse on the left and the Red Lion in the background on the right.

Looking towards Sampys Hill with the Thatched Cottage in the backround.

Left: *Herbert and Emma Willmet, who lived in Thatched Cottage in Mawnan, together with Emma's brother and sister, with the new charabanc, 1950.*

Below: *Enjoying 'Uncle Joe's seat' in 1992. Left to right: Percy Randlesome, Tom King, George Benney, Joe Hojak, Clifton Williams.*

Mawnan Smith, 1958. Mrs Mober (pushing her bicycle) and Mrs Hope walking towards the camera; Irene Minter and Phyllis Stevens running towards them.

Mawnan Smith, 1959.

Mrs Moore at Mount Pleasant, Bareppa

In September 1927 at Constantine, Emmie Reynolds married James Edwin Moore, son of the former Mawnan policeman. They moved into a cottage at Mount Pleasant, Bareppa. Edwin worked a few yards away at Bareppa House, where he was gardener to Mr Sherman and Mrs Holdsworth. He exhibited successfully in Mawnan Cottage Garden Society's shows and a

month before the wedding won a keenly-contested men's swimming race in Port Navas Regatta.

Four months later, Edwin died after a brief illness. His daughter, Edwina, was born shortly afterwards. Emmie spent many years at Mount Pleasant. Subsequently she had a son, Leslie, and married a neighbour, widower Mr Harry Rowe.

Transport

Mawnan Smith was on the route of the Richards' horse bus. This was usually called the horse ferry because the horse and wagonettes were brought across the river on a ferry. It was run by two generations; Fred and Tom. It started from Manaccan, went down to Helford and is shown in the photograph on page 40 just landing on the beach at the Ferry Boat Inn. From here, it went via the village and Penwarne and into Falmouth every Tuesday and Saturday. It also acted as a carrier, bringing bags of maize and barrels of beer, etc. Goods, it seems, were considered before passengers and sometimes the latter had to perch themselves on whatever they could – sometimes people sat on a barrel all the way to Falmouth. It left the Passage at 11am and returned through the village about 5pm or 6pm according to the condition of the driver after being in town! The return fare was 1s.0d. The village also had wagonettes, jingles and Jersey cars which could be hired out privately from Mr John Houghton who had stables opposite the back entrance to St Michael's Church. He drove an open carriage into Falmouth two or three times

a week, but always on a Saturday as that was market day. He also took excursions before the First World War. Around 2s.6d. hired a jingle for half a day, with extra cost if a driver was provided.

In around 1917, Mr Banfil started running an enclosed bus, which must have been a great improvement to the ferry. The bus journeyed three times a week and stopped at the old Kings Hotel (now 'Superdrug'). It had the largest stable yard in the town. In around 1921 the motor bus called 'Armeria' started to run via Maenporth. This was run by Mr Phil Pascoe and driven by his son. Another motor bus soon followed. 'Blue Bell' was run by Mr Ward of the Ferry Boat Inn and driven by Mr Cocking. By this time Mr Banfil had got a motor, 'Selene', so for a time all three were running. In around 1923/4 buses began running out of Falmouth, terminating at Trebah. These, journeyed via Maenporth, while Selene Two went via Penjerrick and Budock. The original 'Selene' ran until about 1947 when the new 'Selene' took her place. When Mr Banfil retired, Mr Barrington took over.

Village Expansion

Much expansion and improvement took place between the world wars, and many buildings were erected. Budock Vean Estate and Maenporth Hill were developed, 12 council houses were built, new homes were built in the village, mostly up Sampy's Hill and at Carlidnack.

Taps were installed, by the church steps, near Lloyds Bank and behind the telephone kiosk. Up to 1923/4 there had been no piped water; all drinking water had to be fetched from various wells including the one up Grove Hill, just above Carwinion Vean, another by the path near Cock Close, leading to Penpoll and others at Carlidnack and Bareppa. It was a great thing to have water piped to within or near the people's homes, although unfortunately it was not taken to the top of Sampy's Hill. It was only taken as far as the

Memorial Hall, and not down to Bareppa.

Lloyds built a small receiving bank in about 1935 for the convenience of their clients. It opened once a week but closed during the war, owing to a shortage of staff. During this period it was lent to the Home Guard.

In 1928 a bowling green and tennis courts were laid down, with a windmill to pump water for sprinkling the lawns. There is still a bowling green, although the location has moved, but unfortunately the tennis club lapsed. A football and cricket club use the playing field opposite Carwinion.

There are church and chapel activities, as well as a wide range of sporting associations as detailed in Chapter Ten. A Nursing Association was formed by Lady Rendlesham early in 1930; she had the nurse's bungalow built and gave it as a home for nurses 'for all time', also financing the Association until it became self-supporting. Later it was affiliated to the County Nursing Association. Prior to this Mary Ann Rapson and Nurse Houghton had been the village midwives. Later when the National Health Service took over, the County Council wanted to take possession of the bungalow, but the Parish Council insisted it was retained by them as it was not the property of the County Council. Eventually the bungalow was sold for £19,000 and the money was put into The Rendlesham Trust (originally for the 'sick and needy'). Over the years circumstances have changed and the money in the trust fund has been used for other purposes, such as various improvements to the Memorial Hall.

The Memorial Hall opened in 1923/4 as a memorial to the men who fell in the First World War. The WI helped to raise the funds and Lady Rendlesham donated the curtains and furniture. In 1928 Mrs Hodgkin gave the children's playing field in the hope that the children would keep off the roads and play in safety. At the opening ceremony Mrs Hodgkin drew attention to the inscription on the wall of the pebble-dashed shelter, which is no longer in existence. It read:

Little deeds of kindness,
Little words of love,
Make our earth an Eden,
Like the heavens above.

This verse was written on the stone chimney piece at Mrs Hodgkin's previous home in Northumberland.

Over the years the village has grown, and the number of properties has increased greatly. New homes have been built, such as those at Trevena Gardens, Carlidnack Close, Castle View Park, Goldmartin Close, Chapel Town Close, Greenfield Close and Shute Hill. Other buildings have been erected in Carlidnack Road, Sampy's Hill and Grove Hill. The Mawnan Community Centre has also been built.

Council properties have appeared, which comprise six flats on the site of the old school. In June 1951 the first four houses in Parc-An-Manns were completed and occupied. The tenants were Gordon and Betty Meneer, Cath and Cecil Eddy, Tom King and family, Mr and Mrs Arthur Wilkinson and their daughters. After 1953 the remainder of the properties were then completed, but by this time using the 'Cornish unit' type of building method. These properties have recently had to be renovated and re-enforced due to 'Mundic block' problems.

In 1975 planning permission was sought for an estate of houses to be built on a 5.7-acre site, formerly part of the Carwinion Estate, given to the National Trust in 1968 and later sold to ECC Ltd of St Austell. Planning applications had varied from between 16 and 68 houses. Eventually, after much opposition from the villagers and the Parish Council, permission was granted and 47 properties were built. The estate is now known as Shute Hill, suitably so, for there are various shutes (springs) on the hill.

In 1977 representation was made to the Local Government Boundary Commission in London, suggesting that Mawnan Council become responsible for Budock Vean, Durgan, Helford Passage and Trebah. After much opposition from Constantine Parish Council, who would be asked to relinquish the areas, the Local Government Boundary Commission granted permission for the Mawnan parish boundary to be altered to take in the previously mentioned areas.

Inset: *Nurse Lottie Hoskin (1884–1967). Nurse Hoskin was District Nurse at Mawnan between 1941 and 1948. She took over from Nurse Fulton. Before coming to Mawnan, Nurse Hoskin worked in North Cornwall. She moved to Trelilian (the nurses bungalow) with her husband Richard and daughter Joyce who later married Selborne Comballack. In 1946 Constantine became part of Nurse Hoskin's round.*

Left: *'Trelilian' built as the nurses bungalow in 1929, now a private residence. An extension on the left has since been built.*

Shopping

Going back about 100 years, when working men were not able to take time off to go shopping, they had to walk into Falmouth in the evening (shops stayed open until 10pm). They often carried all their purchases by hanging them on a stick, which rested over one's shoulder. If the night was particularly dark, a candle lantern was often used. Men would often place a white handkerchief over their shoulders, so that the wife could see to follow if they were walking along a narrow lane.

The Millennium

To celebrate the millennium a granite Celtic cross was made for the village and sited at the junction of Carlidnack Road and Sampy's Hill, opposite the Post Office. This is approximately in the middle of what was the old road. The cross, to which a plaque will be added later, was made by Mark Pellow of Trenoweth Quarry, Mabe, and took two and a half weeks to make. It weighs three quarters of a tonne and stands on a plinth weighing 2.7 tonnes.

The committee who worked so hard on the project were Eileen and Ian Newman, Margaret Lugg and Gillian and Ted Glover. Money was raised in many ways including selling mugs and thimbles with the cross design, coffee mornings, sponsored events, cream teas and treasure hunts. The committee also revived the village carnival tradition, which was staged at the end of a week of events in the village. A booklet was also produced that outlined village organisations. A service of dedication, conducted by the Bishop of Truro on the 31 December 2000 was followed by a buffet lunch in the Memorial Hall. The committee had some money left over and presented £500 to the Mawnan Christmas lights committee.

Mawnan's Oldest Resident

Early in the spring of 2001 Mawnan Smith's oldest resident, Gwen Morris, died at the age of 108 years. Miss Morris, who was a popular resident in the village, had lived opposite the Memorial Hall in Sampy's Hill, for almost 20 years and was a keen supporter of village activities. Although she was born in Wrexham, North Wales, she was very proud to be Mawnan's first centenarian. During her life, Miss Morris worked as a hairdresser and was a lady's companion until she went to live with her brother and his wife in Canada. She travelled extensively around the world. Following the death of her brother and his wife, she returned to England and set up home in Mawnan where she could be close to relatives. As the last remaining member of a family of four boys and five girls, she was often visited by her many nieces and nephews. Speaking on her 100th birthday, Miss Morris said the secret to a long life was to be happy.

At a meeting of Mawnan's Parish Council, members expressed their sadness at Miss Morris' death and sent a letter of condolence to her family. Following her funeral service a reception in the Memorial Hall was attended by about 100 local friends.

Miss Morris was always very alert and knew exactly what she wanted! She had many helpful neighbours, who would perform such tasks as changing her library books on the mobile van and accompanying VIP visitors to the Memorial Hall across to her house to meet her. At the Queen Mother's 100th birthday celebrations, Miss Morris attended two functions – one at Langholme Methodist Home in Falmouth, and the other at Guiseppe's Ristorante in Mawnan's Square.

Socio-Economic Statistics

In 1801 Mawnan Parish had 85 houses and a population of 427. In 1951 Mawnan Parish had 250 houses and a population of 713. Details from the latest figures available (1991) are as follows:

Permanent households: 608.
84.7 per cent are occupied by the owner.
7.6 per cent are privately rented.
0.5 per cent Housing Association.
7.2 per cent local authority.

The population of Mawnan parish in 1981 was 1475, in 1991 1535 and in 1998 1580. These figures reflect a growth of 7.1 per cent between 1981 and 1998. Between the years of 1991 and 1999, 12 houses were built in the parish. During 1999 there were a further 36 commitments to build. The 48 completions and commitments since 1991 amount to a total increase in housing within the Mawnan Parish of 8 per cent. In 1991 12.8 per cent of households had no access to a car.

Village carnival, 1996. Carnival Queen Jenna Harvey with her attendants Karenza Harvey (left) and Martha Paget.

An Easter Parade. Frank Welch (left) with Bill Rashleigh and Bill's grandchildren.

Silver Jubilee Teas in the Cricket Pavilion, 1977. Left to right: *Eileen Newman, Emily Bolger, Pat Dyer, Kath Dyer, Cheryl Bird, Vera Kaiser, Dora Budd, Frances Hodge, Mrs Newman, Mrs Kingsley, Olive Rowe;* front: *Priscilla Stephens.*

Frank Welch, ex-licencee of the Red Lion, leading a parade of nurses into the village square during a village carnival, 1980s.

Frank Welch, ex-licencee of the Red Lion, with a number of babies and attendant nurses on the village playing fields during a village carnival, 1980s.

SUBSCRIBERS

Bob and Stephanie Acton, Penpol, Devoran, Truro, Cornwall

Alanco Motor Services Ltd, Mawnan Smith, Cornwall

Monica Allan, Little Findings, Mawnan, Cornwall

Pauline and Rod Allday, Mawnan, Cornwall

Michael and Susan Allen, Brooke, Rutland

Christine Allen (née Musto), Falmouth, Cornwall

Gillian Astle and Ivan Long, Mawnan Smith

Audrey Baker, Mawnan, Cornwall

Mrs Stella Baker

Stella Baker, Cowfold, West Sussex

Brian and Lorraine Bannister, Mawnan, Cornwall

S.E. and Patti Barden, Maenporth Road

Bob and Yvonne Bates, Mawnan, Cornwall

Lt Cdr J.W. Beck R.N., Meudon Farm House, Mawnan, Cornwall

Edward and Ann Benney, Mawnan, Cornwall

Phyllis Benney, Mawnan, Cornwall

Helen Benney, Newmarket, Suffolk

Mr P.J. Berridge, Mawnan Smith, Cornwall

Mr P.H. Berridge, Mawnan Smith, Cornwall

Mrs P. Berridge, Mawnan Smith, Cornwall

P. Berridge, Mawnan Smith, Cornwall

Peter Berry

John G. Bews, Helford Passage, Cornwall

Margaret Bird, Mawnan Smith, Cornwall

Anne and Peter Blake, Budock Vean

Mark and Polly Bodmer, Helford Passage

Susan, Peter and Christian Boulton, Mawnan Smith, Cornwall

Prue Bradley (née Randlesome), Truro, Cornwall

Marjorie Briars, Mawnan, Cornwall

Mae H. Brown, Mawnan, Cornwall

K.J. Burrow, Bucks Cross, Devon

Ernest Byrne, Alsager, Stoke-on-Trent

Mrs Eva M. Capon, Mawnan, Cornwall

Mrs Jacqueline Chaplin (née Allday), Truro, Cornwall

Nicholas E. Chinn, Milton Keynes, Buckinghamshire

Timothy J. Chinn, Farnham, Surrey

Philip and Christine Chinn, Mawnan Smith, Cornwall

Andrew, Catherine, Hollie and Rosie Chinn, Brill, Constantine, Cornwall

Matthew C. Chinn, York, Western Australia

Alexandra Christophers, Haxby, York

Grenville Christophers, Falmouth, Cornwall

Jim Christophers, Tavistock, Devon

Ray Christophers, Camborne, Cornwall

Katharina Christophers, Haxby, York

Sr. Ann Connolly, St Clare's Convent, Newry, Co. Down

Brian and Janet Coombes, Bodmin, Cornwall

Cornwall Archaeological Unit, Historic Environment, Cornwall

Geoffrey C. Courage

Stephen C.F. Courage, Flushing, Cornwall

Beryl Craze (née Musto), Falmouth, Cornwall

Mr and Mrs Brian G. Cuff, Mawnan Smith, Cornwall

Mrs P. Cullen, Wanganui, New Zealand

Brenda J. Curnow, Nailsea, North Somerset

Rosemary, Bill, Joanne, Stephanie, Emily & Olivia Curtis, Mawnan, Cornwall

Hugh and Thilly Davies, Helford Passage, Falmouth, Cornwall

Hugh Davies, Helford Passage

Mrs J.M.G. Davies, Mawnan Smith, Cornwall

Anthony Charles Day, Mawnan, Cornwall

Malcolm and Pam Dearnley, Mawnan, Cornwall

Christine Delbridge, Helston, Cornwall

Giuseppe and Dinah Di Maio, Mawnan, Cornwall

Mrs Nicola Dugdale (née Pilgrim), Mawnan Smith, Cornwall

Edwina Dugmore, West Bromwich

Desmond P. Dyer, Gweal Mellin, Constantine, Cornwall

Pat and David Eccleshall, Mabe, Cornwall

Margaret Jean Eddy, Mawnan Smith, Cornwall

Ken England, Castle View Park, Mawnan Smith, Cornwall

Mr and Mrs P. Eva, Tregarrick Farm, Helston, Cornwall

Mrs Robin Evans, Flushing, Cornwall

Paul M. Farmer, Mawnan Smith, Cornwall

Mrs Ella Farrington, Constantine, Cornwall

J. Vickers Fearnley, Mawnan Smith, Cornwall

Jette and Robert Fletcher, Budock Vean, Cornwall

Philip H. Fox

Bill and Jane Francke, Irvine, California, USA

John and Suzy Game, New Mills, Ladock, Cornwall

Denis and Louise Gartside, Mawnan Smith, Cornwall

Lina, John and Margaret Gaunt, Mawnan, Cornwall

Desmond Stuart Gendall

Nigel and Carrie Gilmore, Mawnan, Cornwall

Mrs M.D. Gilson, Constantine, Cornwall

The Glover Family, Mawnan Smith, Cornwall

Rod and Jean Good, Mawnan, Cornwall

Mr and Mrs John Green, Calamansac, Port Navas, Cornwall

G. Rodney Greenhalgh and Anne (née Bagot), Rochdale, Lancashire

The Grey Family, Mawnan Smith, Cornwall

Allan and Christine Grint, Mawnan Smith, Cornwall

Mervyn Hale, Nailsea, Bristol

Mrs Jillian I. Harrison (née Hodge), Penryn, Cornwall

Sylvia Harvey, Mawnan, Cornwall

Mr and Mrs Tim Harvey, Mawnan, Cornwall

Mr and Mrs Raymond Hatton, Mawnan Smith, Cornwall

Eleanor and John Hawes, Ponjeravah, Constantine, Cornwall

Michael and Cecilia Hayes, Mawnan Smith, Cornwall

Peter Hearn, Bradford on Avon, Wiltshire

Nancy Heppel, Mawnan, Cornwall

Miss Sandra Hinson, Enfield, Middlesex

Denise and Michael Hopkins, Milverton, Somerset

Mrs Catherine Horton (née Allday), Falmouth, Cornwall

Brian and Lizzie Hoskins, Mawnan Smith, Cornwall

Ethna Howard, Mawnan, Cornwall

Joan Imber (née Salisbury), Gloucester

Mrs Bertha May James, Camborne, Cornwall

Deborah and John Jessup

Grant S. Joffe, Caracas, Venezuela

Fay and Julian Joffe, Mawnan Smith, Cornwall

J.L. Keast, Field Place, Mawnan Smith, Cornwall

Martin Kemp, Mawnan, Cornwall

Jean Kerr, London, Latymer Evacuee

Alan R.W. Kerr, Mylor Bridge, Latymer Evacuee

SUBSCRIBERS

Kindness (Matzen Family), Macduff/Stonehaven, Scotland

Jeremy Kirk, Bristol

W.A. Knowles, Constantine, Cornwall

Miss Sally Jane Lawry, Lower Tregarne, Mawnan, Cornwall

Miss Susannah Emma Lawry, Lower Tregarne, Mawnan, Cornwall

Mr and Mrs R. Legge, Mawnan Smith, Cornwall

David and Jean Luckett, Mawnan, Cornwall

Christine and Eric MacDonald, Lovedean, Hampshire

Mrs Mary Mann, Lamanva

The Mann Family, Penwarne Barton, Mawnan, Cornwall

Mrs Zelonie Moyle Martin, Penryn, Cornwall

Ted Maylam, ex 'Rosewarren', Mawnan, Cornwall

Malcolm McCarthy, Padstow, Cornwall

Rosie and Nigel McLusky, Mawnan, Cornwall

Janette and Michael Mellor, Helford Passage, Cornwall

Matthew Minter, Mawnan Smith

Simon Minter, Mawnan Smith, Cornwall

Antony and Denise Minter, Mawnan Smith, Cornwall

Oliver Minter, Mawnan Smith, Cornwall

Mary Mitchell (née Hobro), Budock Water, Cornwall

Caroline Mitchell (née Jones), Brampton, Canada

Steve and Elizabeth Moore (née Mann), Constantine, Cornwall

John Moyle, Mawnan Smith, Cornwall

Phillip Moyle, Chairman Mawnan Smith Parish Council 2000–2002

Margaret Moyle,

John and Adella Mudge, Gweek, Helston, Cornwall

Mrs Margaret Mulady, Mawnan, Cornwall

Peggy Netcott, Sandford, North Somerset

Mrs A.C. North and Mrs V. Alexander, Palm Beach, Australia

Barry J. Northcott, North Beer, Launceston, Cornwall

Sue Oakes, Penjerrick, Cornwall

Philippa and David Oliver, Budock Vean

June Ould, Mawnan, Cornwall

Christine M. Overy, Mawnan Smith, Cornwall

Kent M. Paget, Colchester, Essex

Fred, Beatrice, Lewis and Martha Paget, Mawnan Smith, Cornwall

Mrs Judy M. Pascoe (née Hodge), Mawnan Smith, Falmouth, Cornwall

Miss Rachel I. Penhaligon, Mawnan Smith, Cornwall

Catherine Fay Penhaligon, Mawnan Smith, Cornwall

The Revd Canon Dr Anthony Phillips, Flushing, Cornwall

Harry Pilgrim, Meudon Hotel, Mawnan, Cornwall

Kathleen Portsmouth, Mawnan Smith, Cornwall

Derek and Sheila Portsmouth, Maenporth, Cornwall

Mrs Inge Powell, Mawnan, Cornwall

Claire and Mike Prosser, Mawnan Smith, Cornwall

Adrian Randlesome

Christine D. Randlesome, Mabe, Cornwall

Pam and John Reeds, Penwarne, Nr Mawnan, Cornwall

Naomi Richards, Mawnan, Cornwall

Shirley Richards, Porkellis

John and Anne Richardson, Truro, Cornwall

Mrs L.M. Rickard, Mawnan Smith, Cornwall

Ann Roberts, Falmouth, Cornwall

Mrs Dorothy Roberts, Mawnan Smith, Cornwall

Shirley Robinson (née Dale), Helston, Cornwall

N. and M. Rowe, Cirencester, Gloucestershire

P. Rowe, Bodmin, Cornwall

E.P. and D.L. Rowe, Mawnan, Cornwall

A. Rowe, Mawnan, Cornwall

Leonard H. Salisbury, Stoke Gabriel, Devon

David and Diana Sanderson, Mawnan Smith, Cornwall

James E. Sanderson, Mawnan Smith, Cornwall

Andrew C. Sanderson, Mawnan Smith, Cornwall

Anne and Bill Scott, Budock Vean, Mawnan Smith, Cornwall

Mr J. and Mrs M.P. Shiell, member of History Group, Mawnan Smith

Christopher and Pauline Smith, Port Navas, Cornwall

Marcia Smith (née Spike), Mawnan Smith, Cornwall

Richard and Patricia Spread, Rosewarne, Mawnan, Cornwall

Lucy M. Stamp, New England, USA

David and Rosemary Stamp, Bareppa

C.H. Stark, Australia

Victor Stevens, Mawnan, Cornwall

Janet Stevens, Richmond

Allen and Trudy Stevens

H.G. and M. Stone

Mary Stone (née Harvey), Beacon, Camborne, Cornwall

Miss Hilary Summerhayes Shaw, Port Navas, Cornwall

Colin Sweet (Milkman)

Jonathan and Katie Sykes, Mawnan, Cornwall

Sally Thomas, Port Navas, Cornwall

Jan Thomas, Port Navas, Cornwall

Robert and Rachel Thompson, Mawnan, Cornwall

Mrs Angela M.W. Thorne, Alstonville, New South Wales, Australia

Stella E. Thorne (née Mann)

Mrs Marjorie Tremaine, Mawnan, Cornwall

John Tremaine, Mawnan, Cornwall

Martin and Angela Tremayne

Philip C. Tresise, Lancaster (formerly of Bareppa)

Michael J. Tresise, Romsey

Nancy Tresise, Falmouth, Cornwall

G. and M. Trethowan, Constantine, Cornwall

Bridget Trout (née Stevens), Mawnan Smith, Cornwall

Mrs Muriel Vague, Goldsithney, Cornwall

Simon and Tina Walker, Helford Passage

Grant Walker, Penjerrick, Cornwall

John F.W. Walling, Newton Abbot, Devon

Ken and Lyn Watson, Constantine, Cornwall

Alice Webber (née Tresise), Falmouth, Cornwall

Reg Wheatley, formerly of Mawnan Smith (Evacuee)

C.N. Wiblin, Shrewton, Wiltshire

Lorraine M. Wickens, Mawnan, Cornwall

Gerald J. Wicks, Mawnan Smith, Cornwall

Granville C. Williams, Mawgan, Cornwall

Queenie, George, Nigel and Diane Wills,

Keith and Jan Wing, Falmouth, Cornwall

Mary Woodgate, Budock Water, Cornwall

Mr and Mrs D.E. Wooldridge, Port Navas, Cornwall

John O.C. Wright, Mawnan Smith, Cornwall

Roy Yardley, Mawnan Smith, Cornwall

Kim Young (née Courage), Farms Common, Porkellis, Helston

TITLES FROM THE SERIES

FORTHCOMING

For details of any of the above titles or if you are
interested in writing your own history, please contact:
Commissioning Editor Community Histories, Halsgrove
House, Lower Moor Way, Tiverton Business Park,
Tiverton, Devon EX16 6SS, England;
email: naomic@halsgrove.com

In order to include as many historic photographs as
possible in this volume, a printed index is not included.
However, the Community History Series is indexed by
Genuki. For further information and indexes to
volumes in the series, please visit:
http://www.cs.ncl.uk/genuki/DEV/indexingproject.html